ROBERT LOUIS STEVENSON
IN SAMOA

Also by Joseph Farrell

Leonardo Sciascia
Harlequins of the Revolution: Dario Fo and France Rame
Sicily: A Cultural History
Dario Fo and Franca Rame: Passion Unspent
Non è tempo di nostalgia (with Franca Rame)
La mia vita, le mie battaglie (with Dacia Maraini)

JOSEPH FARRELL is Emeritus Professor at the University of Strathclyde. His books include a cultural history of Sicily and biographies of Dario Fo and Leonardo Sciascia. He is also a renowned translator from the Italian, whose translations include works by Leonardo Sciascia, Vincenzo Consolo, Dario Fo and Valerio Varesi.

Joseph Farrell

ROBERT LOUIS STEVENSON IN SAMOA

MACLEHOSE PRESS
QUERCUS · LONDON

First published in Great Britain in 2017 by

MacLehose Press
An imprint of Quercus Publishing Ltd
Carmelite House
50 Victoria Embankment
London EC4Y 0DZ

An Hachette UK company

A CIP catalogue record for this book is available
from the British Library

ISBN (HB) 978 0 85705 995 6
ISBN (TPB) 978 0 85705 761 7
ISBN (Ebook) 978 1 84866 882 9

2 4 6 8 10 9 7 5 3 1

Designed and typeset in Haarlemmer by Libanus Press
Printed and bound in Great Britain by Clays Ltd, St Ives plc

To David Johnston and Graham Tulloch,
two much cherished friends on different continents

CONTENTS

Foreword   13
Introduction: The Romance and the Dominion   19

PART I: IN THE SOUTH SEAS
CHAPTER 1: Another Sky   33
CHAPTER 2: A Most Unlikely Couple   46
CHAPTER 3: A Wise Folly   59
CHAPTER 4: Distant Glimpses of Samoa   76

PART II: SAMOA
CHAPTER 5: The Sailing Gods   91
CHAPTER 6: Missionaries and Traders   109
CHAPTER 7: In the Margins of *A Footnote to History*   125
CHAPTER 8: Civil and Uncivil Life in Samoa   148
CHAPTER 9: A Deeply Interesting Time   163
CHAPTER 10: Outbreak of War   184

PART III: HOME AT VAILIMA
CHAPTER 11: A Real Domestic Man   197
CHAPTER 12: Residents and Visitors   218
CHAPTER 13: A Home for Angels   238
CHAPTER 14: Fanny: The Horror of Madness   260

PART IV: HOME AT VAILIMA
CHAPTER 15: The Sense of Kinship: Scottish and   273
    Pacific Ballads
CHAPTER 16: A Lot Accomplished   291
CHAPTER 17: A Far Cry from Samoa to Scotland?   312

PART V: FINAL DAYS
CHAPTER 18: Home is the Sailor   327

A Visit to Robert Louis Stevenson: A Letter by   338
    S.R. Lynaght

Index   344

LIST OF ILLUSTRATIONS

1 Robert Louis Stevenson with Chief Tui Malealiifano
2 Samoan girls making *kava*
3 Mata'afa Iosefo with attendants
4 A *taupou*, or village maiden
5 The Vailima house with Vaea Mountain in the background
6 A feast on the verandah at Vailima
7 Family and household staff gather on the verandah at Vailima
8 Stevenson in the Great Hall
9 A whimsical engraving in an Australian newspaper
10 Chief Tamasese and other Samoan war-chiefs
11 Stevenson, Joe Strong and Lloyd Osbourne
12 Stevenson sitting up in bed
13 Mourners gathered round Stevenson's grave
14 Stevenson's tomb

FOREWORD

The impulse to write this book was given by the remarkable welcome we received on our arrival in Apia. I was visiting professor in the University of Melbourne, and my wife and I took advantage of the Easter break to visit Samoa. We had to overcome unexpected resistance to this idea. The travel agent regarded our plans as incomprehensibly eccentric and tried to persuade us to change destination in favour of Fiji. When we said we wanted to visit the island where Robert Louis Stevenson had spent his last four years and where he was buried, she looked bemused, but being a thoroughly modern young lady, she tapped the name into her computer, and looked up in delight. "Oh, he was the author of *Treasure Island*!" That fact gave us authorisation to proceed.

Growing up in Scotland for my generation meant growing up with Robert Louis Stevenson. It was not that we were all avid readers, although many of us were, but the B.B.C. did adaptations of his fiction on radio and T.V., and a series of "classic comics" circulated and were keenly read and swopped. *Treasure Island* and *Kidnapped* were part of our lives, in the same way, I suppose, as social media is for today's younger generation. At least that was the case for boys. I was surprised when working on this book to be told by female friends that he was regarded as a boys' writer, not someone for them.

Later I read the South Seas stories, so the opportunity to visit Vailima was not one to be missed. The airport is at the opposite end of the island of Upolu from Apia, and the driver of the minibus for the hotels asked all his passengers where they were from. There was a German couple, a young man from Australia, a vivacious but intoxicated woman from California, and the rest were Samoans. When we told the driver we were from Scotland, the bus broke into a cheer. This might have been taken as confirmation of the deepest of all Scottish illusions, that all over the world everyone loves the Scots. Alas! banal experience does not confirm this fond fantasy. The bulk of the population have no idea of where Scotland is, what it is or why they should care, so they don't. But Samoa is different, precisely because of the years R.L.S. spent in the country, and the self-lessness with which he employed his talent and expended his energy in defence of Samoan interests in the high noon of piratical imperialism. His memory is still honoured. During an interview with the Minister for Culture, I saw him strike his breast over his heart as a sign of his deeply felt reverence for Stevenson's memory. The story of Stevenson and Samoa deserved detailed treatment, as did the story of Samoa itself. Samoa changed Stevenson. In a distinction the Greeks would have recognised, Samoa forced him to dedicate himself to the active as well as to the creative or contemplative life.

Samoa is a place to be wondered at. It is a captivating archipelago, and Upolu an island of a beauty particular to herself, magnificently and repeatedly described by an awe-struck Stevenson. Today, the sea is as blue, the mountains as haunt-ingly green and the palms still as omnipresent and as comically shaped or misshaped as ever. Among the people, the pull of the *aiga* (clan) is still as strong, they still live in the *fale,* the open-sided houses clustered round the *fono* (meeting place) or church, and the men and women are still tattooed although contemporary dress codes are more discreet than those of earlier times. Some 80 per cent of the population live in the villages scattered around the island, largely immune to globalised ways.

However, Apia is no longer the town Stevenson rode to from his home in Vailima on his horse, Jack. Some of the colonial buildings, such as the courthouse, still stand, but it is now deserted and dilapidated. There are few traces of the residences of the white men of another age, and why should there be? The visitor, a copy of *A Footnote to History* in his hand, will struggle to locate the Apia R.L.S. described, divided at the bridge over the Mulivai, with an area on one side where "Germans are supreme", and where "beyond, with a few exceptions, all is Anglo-Saxon". The Catholic cathedral still dominates the street facing the sea, and now contains the tomb of Samoa's first cardinal. Perhaps the status given to Cardinal Pio Taofinu'u can be taken as symbolic.

Today's tourist will no longer have to pose the question Stevenson invited his imaginary Victorian visitor to consider: where do the native Samoans whom he will have encountered on the "beach" in Apia actually dwell? Why are their houses hidden from view, in "the backyards of European establishments"? Stevenson's observations are sharp and his judgments acute. "At the boundary of the *Eleele Sa,* the 'Forbidden Soil', Europe ends, Samoa begins. Here is a singular state of things: all the money, luxury, and business of the kingdom centred in one place: that place excepted from the native government and governed by the whites, for the whites."

They have changed all that. Samoan institutions and ministries now stand where the symbols of white power once stood,
and the Samoan police salute the national flag every morning on
a green in the centre of the capital. Very few traces of the white
men's stores and clubs remain, in part because the building
material was wood, not stone, but largely because history has
moved on. Samoans rule their own land. The "one condition"
which Stevenson judged would allow them to "enjoy themselves
far beyond the average of man" has now been met. The one
condition was that "they should be let alone", something he
viewed as "no longer possible" in his day. It has now been
achieved, although whether it can be accompanied by happiness
beyond the average is a question I leave to philosophers. In the
darkest of days, R.L.S. coaxed the indigenous people to maintain faith in the *faa Samoa*, the Samoan way, and that way is
now dominant.

I am grateful to many people around the world for their help
and encouragement. In Australia to professors Roslyn Jolly and
Graham Tulloch, both experts on Stevenson in the South Seas
(and beyond); in New Zealand, to Professor Liam McIlvanney
in Dunedin and to the staff of the Auckland War Memorial
Museum; in Samoa to Mauliu Magele, the Minister for Culture,
to the brilliant historian, Malama Meleisea, to Margaret Silva,
keeper of Vailima, to the ever-obliging Iulai Lesa of the Samoan
Tourism Authority, and to the staff of the Nelson Memorial
Library; and then to the staff in the National Library of Scotland;
to John Fowler, Jenni Calder, Paul Selfa, Vincenzo Barbarotta,
Jim McCearney (himself author of an excellent study of R.L.S.
in French). I could not have found a better publisher, and am

deeply obliged to Christopher MacLehose and Paul Engles for their patience and encouragement, and to the editor Rukun Advani, whose acute comments improved the book greatly. I cannot quantify my debt to my wife, Maureen.

The Romance and the Dominion

In his memoir, *A Pattern of Islands*, universally described as charming and engrossing, Sir Arthur Grimble describes how, having successfully applied in 1913 for the post of colonial officer in the Gilbert and Ellice Islands, he had an attack of scruples and doubts. The doubts were of a lofty order, similar to those experienced in the late Victorian age by vicars in the Church of England after the certainties of the creed had been undermined by Darwin and Spencer. Grimble's concerns were not theological, but ethical and political. It is a cliché now to say the British Empire was managed by a clique of benighted military men, administrators, and clerks whose efforts were underwritten by flocks of missionaries providing ecclesiastical cover for the exploitative activities of ruthless commercial interests. Grimble was not of that stamp, but neither was the worldview he represented typical of his time, class, and culture. He was imbued with high-minded notions on the mission of Empire and the onerous moral and political responsibilities he believed he would be called on to discharge. He held noble ideals, such as belief in the civilising drive of the British Empire, but this spiritual idealism meant that after his appointment he was easy prey to a niggling uncertainty over whether he had the requisite qualities of mind and soul to meet those demanding ethical standards. He had no ambition to extend frontiers and was happy to see himself as a servant of the crown, but worried that he lacked the fibre and leadership attributes needed for the post.

Accordingly, in the same spirit that an afflicted Anglican clergyman might seek an audience with his bishop, Grimble requested an interview with the Chief Clerk at the Colonial Office responsible for Fiji and the Western Pacific High Commission. The meeting did not go according to plan. Never did Joseph Conrad's phrase in *Heart of Darkness* about the imperial mission consisting of filling "the blank spaces of the earth" have more literal application than in the case of the man Grimble viewed as his superior. As became clear in the course of the interview, the Gilbert and Ellice Islands were very much a blank space for this civil servant, who did not know where they actually were. Being open-minded and willing to admit his ignorance, he consulted an atlas. The two men located the islands in the South Pacific.

Once their location had been clarified, the discussion widened out into questions of ethics, psychology, and character. The Chief Clerk turned out to be neither a jingoist nor a closed-minded civil servant, but a man endowed with a sub-philosophical, quasi-poetical turn of mind, who laced his discussion with quotes from Kipling. If Kipling has come to seem to posterity the provider of grand phrases to embellish and mystify the imperial project, this forgotten official was equipped with the imagination and critical faculties that would have made him the ideal protagonist of novels by such writers as Conrad. He put the question of the qualifications required of a British colonial official in his own idiosyncratic, high-minded terms. "Do we stake our lives on Stevenson, *not*

Kipling? Do we insist on the dominion of romance, *not* the romance of dominion?" Grimble was flummoxed but also relieved at being offered a choice of how to interpret his new duties, or perhaps of how to lighten his conscience. Anyone reading his memoir would not detect in him an overt willingness to embrace the dominion of romance, but an underlying, perhaps self-deceiving taste for the romance of dominion. In the presence of the cultured Chief Clerk he "joyfully accepted Stevenson, ruled Kipling out", and set off for a career in the South Seas.

The antithesis "Kipling–Stevenson" in the context of imperial rule is intriguing, but not altogether straightforward. R.L.S. was an admirer of Kipling, had his books sent to him in Samoa, and later corresponded with him. He once wrote, with a certain embarrassment, that on his emergence as a writer Kipling had made a bigger stir in literary circles than anyone since . . . Stevenson himself. Kipling made a half-promise to come to Samoa, and R.L.S. even went down to meet an incoming passenger ship in the belief that Kipling was on board. It was mistaken information. Latterly, critics have taken to undermining the traditional view of Kipling as the outright advocate of imperial dominion over "lesser breeds without the law", and R.L.S. was not altogether the unblemished anti-imperialist that his admirers now, or his opponents then, liked to depict. That said, there does remain a contrast between the attitudes of the two men. R.L.S. very quickly developed reservations over colonialism and the imposition of foreign ways on peoples who wished to be left to themselves. "I am of the opinion that they (white officials) have been a meddling nuisance to the natives," he is reported as telling one Archie Gilfillan, who had been purser on the steamer that took Stevenson to the leper colony on Molokai.[1] He used stronger expressions on other occasions.

In 1889, R.L.S. himself visited the Gilbert Islands (now Kiribati) on his cruise around the South Seas on the *Equator*, a schooner he and his wife chartered in Hawaii and the second of the crafts they used in their voyages around the Pacific. Grimble later made the acquaintance of several people whom R.L.S. had met, including an unfortunate fellow Scotsman, George Murdoch, whom R.L.S. had treated dismissively under the mistaken belief that Murdoch had not taken the trouble to marry the woman with whom he was cohabiting. As Joe Strong and Lloyd Osbourne, two members of his family in Vailima, would discover, R.L.S. never jettisoned rigorously Presbyterian standards of sexual conduct. He also came to admire a particular kind of missionary and colonial servant, and Grimble might well have been included in that category had R.L.S. lived long enough to see him in action. Grimble developed into a well-established type distrusted back home, those who "went native", as the cant phrase then was. Such people studied the beliefs and rites of the subject peoples, learned their language, and in some cases came not only to admire their culture but to write perceptive and sympathetic treatises which have remained of value. Grimble learned the Gilbertese language and, in addition to *A Pattern of Islands*, he wrote what have remained standard works on the folklore and traditions of the islanders.

R.L.S. had died a couple of decades before Grimble's encounter in the ministry took place. Many people then and

1 Arthur Johnstone, *Robert Louis Stevenson and the Pacific*, London, Chatto & Windus, 1905, p. 91.

later, both in the Pacific and in Britain, "joyfully accepted Stevenson" even when they were bewildered by what he was getting up to in exile in Samoa. Oscar Wilde ignored the dominion, but focused sardonically on the romance. "I see that romantic surroundings are the worst possible for a romantic writer. In Gower Street, Stevenson could have written a new *Trois Mousquetaires*. In Samoa he wrote letters to *The Times* about Germans."[2] It was little more than a snigger and not one of Wilde's more memorable or perspicacious *bons mots*, but it draws attention to the fact that R.L.S. did emerge as a champion of the Samoans among whom he settled, and a nuisance not only to Germans but also to Americans and the British. An aura of romance clustered around the figure of the writer in the South Seas. Towards the end of his life, the Argentinian writer J.L. Borges said that one of the books to which he returned with greatest pleasure was the *Memoirs* of Robert Louis Stevenson. It is an enchanting thought, but a curious one, for R.L.S. never wrote any *Memoirs*. Perhaps Borges had in mind R.L.S.' voluminous *Correspondence* with its own distinctive interweaving of incisive commentary, vivid reporting, wry reflectiveness, and amused whimsy, or perhaps he regretted the absence of a genuine autobiography. G.K. Chesterton, in a review of the authorised biography by Graham Balfour, wondered if the only genuine account of the life of a writer like R.L.S. would be autobiography.[3]

The central fact is that in the last four years of his life, spent

2 Merlin Holland and Rupert Hart-Davis (editors), *The Complete Letters of Oscar Wilde*, London, Fourth Estate, 1962, p. 789.
3 Graham Balfour, *The Life of Robert Louis Stevenson*, London, Methuen, 1901.

on Samoa, the term "works" applies not only to R.L.S.' literary output but to the active work he undertook on behalf of a people he adopted, whose interests he defended, and whom he regarded as having been wronged. He came to abominate the "horrid white mismanagement", and even proposed himself for consulship of Samoa, while at the same time being threatened with deportation by Sir John Thurston, High Commissioner of the Western Pacific.[4] He was spared the ignominy at least in part because the Foreign Secretary, Lord Rosebery, was an admirer of Stevenson and once even wrote to him to request his autograph. R.L.S. was perhaps more productive and certainly more politically active in these years than at any other point of his life. He was still writing fiction, but not only romance. The letters about Germans that amused Oscar Wilde were concerned with dominion and its impact.

His residence in Samoa fascinated people in Britain and America. Edmund Gosse, better disposed towards R.L.S. than Wilde, made a different comparison, this time with Byron. In a letter in late 1893, when his friends were reconciled to the fact that he would never return home, Gosse told R.L.S., "since Byron was in Greece, nothing has appealed to the ordinary literary man as so picturesque as that you should be in the South Seas. And I partly agree."[5] All the same, Gosse continued to deplore the fact that R.L.S. chose to live so far from the only society he regarded as civilised, the society of London men of

4 *The Letters of Robert Louis Stevenson,* 8 volumes, edited by Bradford A. Booth and Ernest Mehew, New Haven and London, Yale University Press, 1994–5. All subsequent quotations are given in the body of the text by volume and letter number, thus: VIII, 2744 and VII, 2258.

5 Evan Charteris, *The Life and Letters of Sir Edmund Gosse,* London, Harper & Brothers, 1932, p. 249.

letters. The parallels and contrasts with Byron could be pushed further than Gosse wished. Byron was fêted in Victorian Britain as a fighter for a romantic cause, Greek independence from the oppressive Turk. Stevenson was similarly identified with the cause of the Polynesians, but since they were conventionally viewed as backward savages who required the guiding hand of superior European powers, his stance was considered eccentric, bizarre, unaccountable, and potentially dangerous. While Byron's views were formed initially from a distance, Stevenson's opinions on the rights of Samoans developed as he gathered information on the spot. His defence of Samoa led to his being viewed in the corridors of power as an interfering, ill-informed busybody who should have stuck to writing adventure stories for boys. "The unfortunate state of affairs in Samoa, which occupied so much of his time, has cheated literature of much that all are loath to lose", wrote one *bien pensant* critic at the time.[6]

He was already famous as the author of such books as *Treasure Island* (1883) and *The Strange Case of Dr Jekyll and Mr Hyde* (1886) when he became the chronicler of events in a small archipelago, of which it could be truly said, as Neville Chamberlain said of Czechoslovakia, that it was a land of which British people knew little, and – he might have added – cared even less. The resident traders, consuls, missionaries, and administrators, as well as officials in the ministries and chancelleries in Western capitals, cursed the events that brought there an observer of such literary talent and unbending humanist vision. The East India Company, Cecil Rhodes, anonymous

6 Arthur Johnstone, *Stevenson*, op. cit., p. 50.

traders in East Africa, and slave owners in the Caribbean were never subjected to such scrutiny. Their activities were occasionally recorded by a few contemporary journalists, and later, when they were long dead, by historians working in archives. On the other hand, the mischief and misdeeds of the company with the unwieldy title of Deutsche Handels-und Plantagen-Gesellschaft der Südsee-Inseln zu Hamburg; the miscalculations and mischief of minor figures like British Consul Thomas Berry Cusack-Smith, Chief Justice Otto Conrad Waldemar Cedercrantz, and President Baron Senff von Pilsach; and the poisonous rivalries between Laupepa, Mata'afa, and Tamasese – names that would otherwise have long since disappeared from all but the most specialised of history books – were subjected to pitiless scrutiny by a pen and a mind guaranteed to command an international audience. The political insouciance of Western establishments which sanctioned the systematic depredation and exploitation endured by the islanders was recorded in their lifetime by a writer of genius who set aside his own interests to defend those of a harmless folk whose peace and well-being were threatened and destroyed by outside powers whose behaviour was itself often nothing short of piratical.

It was a common view among his many friends in London that by writing letters to *The Times* on the South Seas and by authoring pamphlets and books on the same subject, R.L.S. was squandering his talents. What was the sense of taking up the cause of a primitive people routinely compared, sometimes by R.L.S. himself, to schoolchildren, whose future development would be aided by the benevolent intervention and occasional firm treatment meted out by well-intentioned Western powers? Stevenson arrived in the Pacific in the heyday of imperialism, when brute power was justified by revered religious bodies, when Western financial expansionism by whatever means was not questioned, and when a cultural-religious sense of the innate superiority of the white man was taken for granted. He came to Samoa at a crucial turning point in its history and is remembered with gratitude both there and in other islands in the Pacific for his disparaging views of empire, and for his sympathetic understanding and presentation of the native civilisation which many white contemporaries defined unthinkingly as barbarism. Recent criticism from a school of critics labelled "post-colonial" has made some of the views advanced by R.L.S. seem more ambiguous, but no post-factum judgement should be allowed to detract from the courageous stance he adopted at a time when, the rush for Africa being completed, the attention of the Western powers, European and North American, turned to the Pacific. He detected no romance in dominion or in the brutality of empire. He sided with the people of Samoa and other Pacific islands whose way of life, identity, culture, and future prospects he saw as being threatened by the indifference, callousness, self-interest, exploitation, and unsympathetic or uncomprehending attitudes of traders, missionaries, and officials appointed by distant ministries. The future of Samoa was indeed a matter of anxious concern in the political establishments of Western powers, but only as lands to be controlled, brought to heel and pacified, and thus rendered amenable for commerce and international trade.

Stevenson's attitudes and outlook are clear from his private correspondence, his letters to *The Times* and other London publications, as well as from what is perhaps the least read of all his works, *A Footnote to History*, which first appeared in 1892.

Footnote is a work of history or investigative journalism, with an unassuming and enigmatic title which implies that the matters discussed in the work are of little import, while Stevenson's own belief was quite the reverse. The subtitle, *Eight Years of Trouble in Samoa*, clarifies his topic. The initial plan for his cruise of the Pacific saw him land, supposedly briefly, in Samoa to gather material on the recent war as part of a projected book on the South Seas. He changed his mind, and chose to settle in Samoa. As he learnt of conditions in the country and identified more and more with Samoan people, he became convinced of the need to bring the contemporary condition of his adopted homeland to the attention of a worldwide audience. He generously devoted his talents and resources, mental and financial, to that cause.

For purely pragmatic reasons, he was unsure of the wisdom of undertaking the writing and publication of *Footnote*, but such doubts did not arise from his awareness that he was challenging the nostrums of the age. He was doubtful, with good reason, whether his work would be noticed and have any impact. Yet R.L.S. did not abandon literature or, for that matter, romance, and certainly was never able to renounce a Scottish frame of mind. *The Master of Ballantrae* was completed and *Catriona* and *Weir of Hermiston* written in the South Seas, and his knowledge of Scottish, especially Highland, history provided a touchstone against which he judged much that he witnessed in Samoa. At the same time, he prided himself on being, with works like "The Beach of Falesá", the first writer to provide a realistic, unromantic view of life in the South Seas. The distinction between his Scottish and Samoan writing is real, but the same concerns are evident in both. Questions of the rule of law and of basic jurisprudence recur in the novels written in those years, whether set in Scotland or in the South Seas.[7]

The questions which will be considered in this book concern both what R.L.S. brought to Samoa and what he found there, how he responded to the politics of empire, and how what he observed changed him as a man and as a writer. Samoa was not merely the background of his writing. My aim is to provide a study of Robert Louis Stevenson *and* Samoa, not only of Stevenson in Samoa. In short, how both the romance of dominion and the dominion of romance played out in his mind and imagination in his new home.

7 Roslyn Jolly, *Robert Louis Stevenson in the Pacific*, Farnham, Ashgate, 2009.

PART I

In the South Seas

CHAPTER I

Another Sky

The journey from Heriot Row in Edinburgh to the island of Upolu was an improbable one, as was the road from *Kidnapped* to "The Beach of Falesá". The two trails were parallel. Stevenson's reasons for travelling to the South Seas and settling in Samoa were personal, based largely on his lifelong health problems, but it is not fanciful to detect at the same time a surrender to the appeal strongly present in the contemporary European imagination of those elusive and imprecise factors termed exoticism, charm, mystique, glamour, all treasured qualities believed to be located in the Pacific Islands. There was something in Stevenson of what was later defined as the nomadic Scot, a person with a vision rooted in his homeland but keen to move towards ever more distant, dream-like horizons.[8] In *A Child's Garden of Verses*, he expressed in delicate lines a longing he never disclaimed:

> I should like to rise and go
> Where the golden apples grow;
> Where below another sky
> Parrot islands anchored lie . . .

8 Kenneth White, *The Wanderer and His Charts*, Edinburgh, Polygon Books, 2004.

In a striking judgment, Chesterton pointed out that R.L.S. went where he did "partly because he was an adventurer and partly because he was an invalid". These twin aspects of Stevenson's life should always be kept in balance. He had the imagination of an adventurer but the body of an invalid, and the combination made him the man and writer he was. His library was stocked with biographies of generals and histories of military campaigns, and his preferred career would have been, according to his wife, a soldier's.[9] Chesterton added that he found "a curious aptness in the quaint simplicity of his childish rhyme that ran 'my bed is like a little boat'. Through all his varied experience, his bed was a boat and his boat was a bed. Panoramas of tropic palm and Californian orange-grove passed over that moving couch like the long nightmare of the nursery walls."[10] The urge to roam found repeated expression in his prose and poetry, explicitly so in *Songs of Travel and Other Verses*, published while he was in Samoa, but the compulsion to travel arose, as he wrote, from the "needs and hitches of (my) life". In the late 1880s, his health required that he find a climate which allowed him to live life more fully, but the search for that climate, combined with his own inscape, became a process of awakening and discovery.

Stevenson's earliest published works were travel books – *An Inland Voyage, Travels with a Donkey, The Amateur Emigrant* –

9 Introduction by Mrs R.L. Stevenson to *St. Ives,* London, Heinemann, 1924, Tusitala Edition, volume XV, p. xv. All subsequent quotations from Stevenson's work are to this edition, and given by volume number and page in the text itself. "Tusitala", meaning "writer of tales", was R.L.S.' Samoan title.

10 G.K. Chesterton, *Robert Louis Stevenson,* London, Hodder & Stoughton, 1928, p. 18.

while journeys by land and sea are intrinsic to the plot of such novels as *Treasure Island*, *Kidnapped*, *The Master of Ballantrae*, and *St. Ives*. He was by instinct and longing a traveller, a writer concerned with landscapes, but also one with an interest in the unveiling of what Gerard Manley Hopkins at about the same time was calling "inscape", the structure of the inner psyche. He cared about the distinctiveness of the people who inhabited the lands he moved in, and revelled in the freedom that travelling gave him to unshackle himself from ingrained habits of mind, manners, and mores. In *Travels with a Donkey*, he recalled a conversation with the Father Abbot in the monastery of Our Lady of the Snows in the Cévennes which enabled him, or so he believed, to shake off the Calvinist instincts which he had acquired from his father and from his nanny, Cummy, although these instincts were more deeply rooted than he then believed. "What went ye out for to see?" he asked himself as he stood before a board in Cheylard, and the question could be taken as underlying the quest he undertook in all his walking trips and his tramps behind a donkey as well as his rowing, sailing, and cruising. He gave a partial answer as he proceeded between Cheylard and Luc, dismissing that terrain as "one of the most beggarly countries in the world," but concluding that he travelled "not to go anywhere, but to go. I travel for travel's sake. The great affair is to move; to feel the needs and hitches of our life more nearly; to come down off this feather-bed of civilisation, and find the globe of granite underfoot and strewn with cutting flints" (Tusitala, XVII, 117–18). R.L.S.' principal test of the "feather-bed of civilisation" which had formed him came in the Pacific, and in that horizon he found the feather-bed wanting.

There are many kinds of maps, of which the geographical is

only one, to be set alongside cultural, historical, and even fantasy maps. For generations, the Pacific Ocean lay not just between a certain longitude and latitude, but somewhere between fable and reality, almost as much as Homer's Medi-terranean. Several writers and travellers were responsible for the creation of that myth. Rousseau's introduction of the concept of the noble savage into the Western collective imagination caused unexplored areas of northern America, of unvisited China, or even of the Highlands of Scotland to be viewed in the salons of Paris and London as realms of gold where a purer life was lived by peoples uncontaminated by the debased standards of European civilisation, or even by that unworthy standard which was civilisation as such. The pseudo-idyllic life could be re-created by Marie Antoinette and her ladies in artificial paradises in the gardens of the Petit Trianon, but this was a poor substitute for a magical dimension elsewhere. By the nineteenth century, the Pacific islands were firmly established as a site for dreams and dreamers. The three voyages of Captain Cook between 1768 and 1779 and the subsequent publication of his Journals were significant steps in the elaboration, particularly in Anglophone countries, of an imaginary utopia. The captain's original intentions were strictly scientific, to record the transit of Venus across the sun, but, while he fulfilled that goal, his writings spread knowledge of an alien culture and way of life. In so doing, they also made them the subject of imprecise hankerings and longings in Europe for a freer, richer life, where social mores were less restrictive, where an imagined alternative to personal or social inadequacies was available.

The French admiral Louis-Antoine de Bougainville, with a crew including the celebrated botanist Philibert Commerçon, who named the bougainvillea plant after the admiral, set out for the South Seas in 1766. Once again, the stated purpose of the voyage was sternly scientific, but when in 1771 Bougainville published his account of his voyages under the title *Le voyage autour du monde, par la frégate* La Boudeuse, *et la flûte* L'Étoile, it became an instant and international success. More than any other individual work, this was responsible for the legend of Tahiti as the earthly paradise. The following year, Denis Diderot wrote his *Supplement to Bougainville's Voyage* in which he portrayed an imaginary Tahiti free of what were for the philosopher the main curses of civilisation: tyranny and an undue attachment to property. It was not the only blessing of that marvellous place, at least to male eyes. Women, it was alleged, were free of the obligations of pre-conjugal celibacy and post-conjugal fidelity, and were uninhibited in sharing their favours. The supposed sexual permissiveness and the availability of alluring women were common themes in the extravagant fantasies on Pacific life which began to circulate in the West.

In the nineteenth century, writers such as Herman Melville, Pierre Loti, and Jack London enhanced the myth in different ways, but none of these reached as wide an audience as did Charles Warren Stoddard, author of the then well-known and much admired *South-Sea Idylls* (1873), a series of letters on his travels in the Pacific. His *Summer Cruising in the South Seas* (1874) attracted a wide audience, and R.L.S. sought him out in San Francisco in 1879, while he was in California waiting for Fanny to make up her mind about divorcing Sam Osbourne and committing herself to him. It was seemingly Stoddard who introduced Stevenson to the work of Melville, but Stoddard himself had wider circulation at the time. His books are filled with bright, entrancing sketches of the landscape and the habits of life of the islanders. Stevenson regarded him with respect.

A place apart has to be reserved for the paintings of Stevenson's contemporary, Paul Gauguin. There is no reason to believe he was known to R.L.S. or vice versa, but he was in Tahiti when Stevenson was in Samoa. Those who make history with the "what might have been" can construct a pleasing fantasy featuring a meeting between the artist and the writer. Gauguin left behind European landscapes in 1891 specifically to escape all that was conventional, artificial, or false. He wrote travel diaries during his travels in the Pacific, which appeared posthumously as a book entitled *Noa Noa*, supposedly autobiographical in character, though sterner critics have dismissed it as a fantasy and near hoax. "Your civilisation is your disease, my barbarism is my restoration to health," the artist allegedly said as he departed Paris for the Marquesas and later Tahiti, both places visited by R.L.S. Whether or not he actually spoke that line, Gauguin gave definitive expression to the prevailing mythic view of life under the palms, conjuring up an idyllic, exotic vision of Tahitian life – as artificial as the supposedly inauthentic European life he was leaving behind. For the more discerning, some of his canvases also raised philosophical dilemmas on the nature of civilisation. The celebrated painting with the title "D'où venons-nous? Que sommes-nous? Où allons-nous?" is a wistful meditation on life and death. Do the three seemingly unrelated scenes within it present an Eden or an Inferno?

This question of the line dividing civilisation from barbarism, of the costs exacted by the one and the desirability of the other, became central to any consideration – political, moral, literary, religious, sexual, and even sartorial – of the life of the Polynesians. R.L.S. certainly pondered this question after his first impact with islanders in the Marquesas, and while it is not possible to present his thoughts on this issue as developing in one straightforward, unswerving direction, or as being free of contradictions, he does deserve credit as a pioneer determined to debunk legends and fantasies, to question the notion of primitivism, and to present positively life in the Pacific as he found it. R.L.S. was not swayed by myths of noble savages and nothing in his writing expands or strengthens that fantasy image. He is known and celebrated in the islands, particularly in Samoa, both for having defended the rights of the people in face of the imperialist advance of Western powers, and for describing sympathetically and objectively their everyday life and beliefs.

However, R.L.S. had not always been immune to the pull of the fantasy. In his youth, he had been introduced to the appeal of the South Seas, and specifically of Samoa, by a man who knew the islands well. Swanston Cottage in the Pentland Hills had been a Stevenson family holiday home since 1867, and was even introduced into *St. Ives* as the home of Flora, with whom St Ives fell in love. R.L.S. spent a great deal of his free time there reading and writing. In a letter to Frances Sitwell written in 1875 from the cottage he tells her of an interesting encounter:

> Awfully nice man here tonight. Public servant – New Zealand. Telling us about the South Sea Islands till I was sick with desire to go there; beautiful places, green forever; perfect climate, perfect shapes of men and women, with red flowers in their hair; nothing to do but to study oratory and etiquette, sit in the sun, and pick up the fruits as they fall. Navigator's Island [*sic*] is the place; absolute balm for the weary. (II, 397)

Navigator Islands was the name by which Samoa was first known to European cartographers, and the visitor was William Seed, a civil servant in New Zealand who had visited Samoa in the course of his duties in 1875.[11] He was also a relative by marriage of the Stevensons. Since it appears the entire family had gathered to meet him, one must assume that his account of the "perfect shapes" of the islanders was restrained, but his description was obviously lush and fulsome, and fired R.L.S.' imagination. For all his personal knowledge of the social conditions of the islands and of the impact on them of the first traders and beachcombers, Seed's description is a retelling of the golden myth and can be viewed as the verbal equivalent of a Gauguin canvas.

Experience is often formed by expectation, and R.L.S. had now certain fully formed images and expectations of the Samoan archipelago. The conversation with Seed must have lingered in his mind, for fully fourteen years later he recalled it in a letter from Honolulu to his American publisher, Edward L. Burlingame. The letter was primarily intended to accompany the completed text of *The Master of Ballantrae*, but went on:

> Work, I clearly discern, does not agree with me; being at sea and scooting about islands does; but who will pay me for that? I should have been a beachcomber. I should have gone fifteen years ago to Samoa, as I truly designed to do, under the spur of Mr Seed's advice. I should then have had the life that suited me. But we know not our good . . .
> (VI, 2170)

11 Booth and Mehew, *Letters of Stevenson*, op. cit., volume II, p. 145n.

There is no evidence that the two men met again, but plainly Seed's colourful and hypnotic description of Samoa had enchanted R.L.S. He was to make one further appearance in R.L.S.' correspondence, still in reference to that evening in the cottage. In Sydney in 1890, R.L.S. wrote to Elizabeth Fairchild, mainly to apologise for some rudeness of which he had been guilty. The main interest of the letter for biographers and critics lies in the regret he expresses for having been misled by his zeal to defend Father Damien into using unduly severe and contemptuous language towards Dr Hyde, the clergyman whose calumnies on the Belgian priest had occasioned Stevenson's pamphlet, *Father Damien* (1890), written in Damien's defence.[12] Once these matters had been cleared up, the tone of the letter changes to one of exuberant joyousness. He presses Fairchild to come and visit him in Samoa, when she will see "a healthy and happy people", and he takes up, not altogether seriously, the refrain of the inadequacy of life in the supposedly civilised state:

> You are quite right; our civilisation is a hollow fraud, all the fun of life is lost by it, all that it gains is that a larger number of persons can continue to be contemporaneously unhappy on the surface of the globe. O, unhappy! There is a big word and a false – continue to be not nearly – by about seventy per cent – so happy as they might be; that would be nearer the mark.

12 The Dr Hyde referred to here has no connection with Stevenson's Mr Hyde in *The Strange Case of Dr Jekyll and Mr Hyde*. One biographer refers to Dr Hyde as "the uncannily named Dr Hyde": William Gray, *Robert Louis Stevenson: A Literary Life*, London, Palgrave Macmillan, 2004, p. 128.

He goes on to reflect that he might possibly have found his happiness sooner had he taken Seed's advice:

> Let me tell you this: in '74 or 5, there came to stay with my father and mother, a certain Mr Seed, a prime minister or something of New Zealand. He spotted what my complaint was; told me I had no business to stay in Europe; that I should find all I cared for, and all that was good for me in the Navigator Islands; sat up until four in the morning, persuading me, demolishing my scruples. And I resisted; I refused to go so far, from my father and mother. O, it was virtuous, and O, wasn't it silly! But my father, who was always my dearest, got to his grave without that pang; and now in 1890, I (or what is left of me) go at last to the Navigator Islands. God go with us. It is but a Pisgah sight when all is said; I go there only to die; but when you come you will see it is a fair place for the purpose. (VI, 2249)

R.L.S. repeated on other occasions in those years that he viewed himself as being in the outer chamber of death, so the reference to Pisgah – the mountain in Sinai which Jehovah ordered Moses to climb to glimpse the Promised Land which he himself would never see – is a telling one, although R.L.S. did succeed in reaching his own promised land. Seed had obviously been a captivating conversationalist, but there are in the life of sensitive human beings chance encounters with paintings or chapters in books which have an effect quite disproportionate to the words spoken or the image offered. The other members of the Stevenson family continued their lives undisturbed, but it is undeniable that a vision of some exotic land where he would find all that was good for him had been planted in the mind of R.L.S. by that meeting, and had germinated. That is not to say that he travelled to Samoa primarily in fulfilment of some long-suppressed youthful longing, but an awareness of the fantasy image was there in him. In May 1888, on the eve of embarking on the schooner *Casco*, he wrote to Lady Taylor, an acquaintance from Bournemouth days: "you can conceive what a state of excitement we are in: Lloyd perhaps first; but this is an old dream of mine which actually seems to be coming true" (VI, 2084).

Samoa makes a further appearance as the pined-for destination of the youthful, pampered wastrels in *The Hair Trunk or The Ideal Commonwealth: An Extravaganza*, a "comic novel" written in the period 1877–9, when Stevenson was embarking tentatively on fiction, but only published in 2014.[13] The novel was left unfinished, as were many of his works. Reading it is like stumbling across a rediscovered, early scherzo by Mozart, causing the finder not only to evaluate the work in itself but to seek out links with compositions and themes which will recur in the major work. At the time he was writing *The Hair Trunk*, Stevenson was a self-conscious bohemian, a dissident from the bourgeois world and a crusader for the ways of the youthful idler. All his days, he would present life as a disputed field between the bourgeois and the bohemian, where he identified with the latter and viewed himself, perhaps self-deceptively, as the independent thinker unharnessed by convention and liberated from the dogmas of church and society. R.L.S.' bohemian

---

13 *The Hair Trunk or The Ideal Commonwealth: An Extravaganza*, by Robert Louis Stevenson, edited by Roger G. Swearingen, Kilkerran, Humming Earth, 2014.

beliefs and behaviour should not be overstated, and the conflict was to remain abstract and unresolved.

In the novel, a group of high-spirited Cambridge students, who have sauntered through university days enjoying a series of japes and pranks, now find themselves facing an uncertain future with poor degrees, no resources, and no identifiable skills. An outsider named Blackburn is introduced into their company and he outlines a wildly visionary scheme to set sail for no less a place than the Navigator Islands, and there establish for themselves a utopia where life can be enjoyed in ease without the need for anything as vulgar as money. Blackburn discourses with lush rhetoric on the delights of this mythic place:

> A young man is simply Not Sane, who stays to dry-rot here in beggarly England, when he has only to step aboard the first ship, and find happiness ready-made in Navigator Islands . . . The word is out! The South Sea is the true home of mankind . . . Gold, vines, tobacco, eternal summer and a handsome race . . . An easy rudimentary civilisation already afoot . . . people with no clothes, and flowers in their hair! Scenery and sunsets for those who like them . . . and the first comer, who feels the want of them and has nothing else to do, free to fill a whole Island with children, mossy waterwheels and drawing-masters' cottages!

The passage is the perfect expression of the longing for a mythic El Dorado situated over the horizon, described by early travellers but retold with that necessary touch of late Victorian restraint. Sexual desire and the prospect of libertinism can be hinted at in terms like "a handsome race", an echo of Seed's "perfect shapes of men and women", but not yet too openly expressed. "People with no clothes, and flowers in their hair" would shortly afterwards appear in Gauguin's paintings. Meantime, the more material dilemma for the adventurers is that money is needed to establish a commonwealth free of the nuisance of money. They have to become burglars, like Villon, the medieval French poet who was one of R.L.S.' heroes then and later. Their quest takes them to a Scottish island where treasure is known to be available within a hairy trunk inside a ghastly, pseudo-baronial, private villa. Here, frustratingly, the tale runs out.

The discovery not of the wonderland loosely called Samoa, but of the reality of the historical Samoa, was still in the future. However, the voyage in the Pacific does represent, among many other things, the fulfilment of an old dream. It did not endure. As Lloyd Osbourne writes in his introduction to *The Wrecker* (1892), R.L.S. was progressively disabused of his illusions about life there, and completely abandoned them after witnessing on the *Equator*, the second vessel they hired, "the seamy side" of life in the Pacific.[14] The side thus exposed to him included "the tricks, the false scales, the bamboozling and the chicanery that were customary in dealing with the natives, who were themselves irritatingly dishonest" (Tusitala, XII, xi). But the myths did not entirely lose their allure.

14 Lloyd Osbourne was R.L.S.' stepson and co-author of *The Wrecker*.

CHAPTER 2

A Most Unlikely Couple

Samoa was the terminus of a long quest for a suitable climate which began in 1888 on a schooner that sailed out of San Francisco. In a wider perspective, the origins of the journey can be traced to the marriage in May 1880 of R.L.S. and Fanny, and to the death of R.L.S.' father in 1887. On hearing that Thomas Stevenson was dying, R.L.S. rushed back to Edinburgh from Bournemouth, where he and Fanny were residing, but arrived too late for any communication with him. It was the last time he set foot in Scotland. Under the terms of his father's will, he came into an inheritance which gave him financial independence and the option of spending his resources as he wished. At the same time, he received medical advice, highly convenient but from unimpeachable sources, that he should move away from Britain to a drier climate, Colorado being the first suggestion.

Perhaps the search for a place where Stevenson's health would improve really began with his wedding, when Fanny took responsibility for his well-being. The couple moved from country to country in the search, settling temporarily in Davos in Switzerland, Hyères in the south of France, in Bournemouth at a house he named Skerryvore, and then in Saranac of New York State. He was glad to get out of Bournemouth, which he increasingly found stifling and tedious. Visits from friends, especially Henry James, could not compensate for a provincial atmosphere which was too similar to the one he had grown to detest in Edinburgh years previously.

Since the lives of the two were intertwined on the voyage in the Pacific and during the years of residence on Samoa, it is necessary to bring to prominence the story of Fanny Van de Grift Osbourne Stevenson. She added the name Osbourne after her first marriage, later changed it to Stevenson, and used various combinations of these names during her life. Her maiden name sometimes appears as Van de Grift, almost as though the plurality of names reflects her own seemingly divergent masks or personalities, or the sheer multiplicity of responses she has aroused.

Born in Indianapolis, Frances Matilda Van de Grift was a woman who has intrigued, mystified, and occasionally enraged contemporaries and later commentators. Undoubtedly gifted with enormous resourcefulness, resilience, and ingenuity, she evinced a strange mixture of on the one hand vulnerability and instability of character, and on the other physical and mental strength. She also suffered from health problems of her own. Familiarity with her achievements will compel contemporary readers to dispel cosy clichés about the restricted lives, horizons, and opportunities afforded Victorian women. When she and R.L.S. first met, she was still the wife of Sam Osbourne, whom she had married in 1857 when she was seventeen and he twenty. The couple had three children. She called on all her native strength of will and independence of mind when, at the age of twenty-one, and with a baby girl in tow, she set off on her own from Indiana to California to join her husband, who had settled there as a gold miner on his return from the American

Civil War. San Francisco was still a frontier town when she arrived, and from there she proceeded to the mining camp of Austin in the Toiyabe Range. The Indian wars were not over and life was not comfortable.

Sam Osbourne was away prospecting with, as the phrase was, one Samuel Orr as his "pardner", a relationship John Wayne would have recognised. For a time he was lost in the mountains and word got back he had died. He had already a well-earned fame as a womaniser, and it would be interesting to know Fanny's reaction to word of his demise, but she dutifully donned widow's weeds and demonstrated her enterprise and spirit by finding work as a dressmaker to support her family. The news turned out to be false, and Sam returned, not hale but certainly hearty. By 1875 Fanny had had enough of his philandering ways and left him to go to Europe to try to develop her artistic talents. How real these talents were is a matter for debate, but all her life she had ambitions to express herself in the arts, first in painting and later in literature. Her younger son, Hervey, took ill and died in Paris in April 1876. The other two children, Isabel (Belle) and Lloyd, were to become part of Stevenson's life.

She and R.L.S. met in September 1876 at an artists' colony in Grez-sur-Loing, near Paris, though Fanny was initially more attracted to his vivacious cousin Bob Stevenson. Her relationship with R.L.S. deepened over the following two years, but when he informed his parents of his love for Fanny, they made no secret of their dismay at his affair with a married woman. Unexpectedly, in August 1878 Fanny made the decision to return to her husband in America. Her motives have intrigued biographers ever since. She and R.L.S. remained in contact, although he was driven to spasms of anxiety and jealousy by her long silences. Mystery surrounds a telegram she allegedly sent him in summer 1879, which has vanished, and which may never have existed, but at any rate it spurred R.L.S. to set off for California. Perhaps he had decided to force the issue and establish where he stood with the woman whom he was now sure he wanted to marry. The epic journey across the Atlantic and over the continent by rail is chronicled in *The Amateur Emigrant* (1895). The travels took their toll and when he arrived in California, sickly and weak, little more than skin and bones, he did not receive from Fanny the enthusiastic, loving welcome he had anticipated. Whatever the state of her relations with Sam, she was disconcerted by the arrival of this invalid who was only a shadow of the man she had known in Europe.

In spite of this unpromising start, their relationship revived and they decided to marry, but delays in securing a divorce were caused by Fanny's hesitations as much as by Sam's stalling tactics. Being left to kick his heels in California, R.L.S. settled happily in Monterey, where there is still a museum to mark his residence. Finally, on December 12, 1879, Fanny's divorce was granted. In April the following year, R.L.S.' parents, who had watched aghast as the situation developed, changed their minds and wrote to him promising him an allowance of £250 a year. In May the couple were married in San Francisco. They spent their honeymoon in a shack on Mount Saint Helena in the Napa Valley, as R.L.S. recounts in *The Silverado Squatters* (1883). In August 1880 they took a ship from New York to Liverpool, where his parents came to meet the couple. Against all expectations, his staunchly Presbyterian parents took to Fanny and relations between Stevenson's mother and wife remained generally harmonious for the rest of their lives.

Fanny has remained an enigma. Discussion of her and R.L.S. is fraught with risks of the sort St Ives faced when he broached the question of the Scottish Sabbath with his Edinburgh land-lady, Mrs McRankine: "'there are knots and contortions', he declared, meaning that any observer 'walks among explosives'." Few people have ever been the subject of such divergent judge-ments. Germaine Greer once lamented that "anyone steeped in Western literary culture must wonder why any woman of spirit would want to be a wife".[15] She was referring to Shakespeare's spouse, but the comment could apply to any number of women who married celebrated artists. The principle of selective sympathy routinely applies, whereby faults in the artist-hero are analysed and explained, but deficiencies in his partner are subject to absolute censure. This approach has the advantage of confirming what readers wish to believe.

In dealing with the relationship between two strong-minded individuals where love and resentment, cooperation and com-petitiveness intermingle inconsistently and intermittently, there is no insight of much value above the level of pseudo-psychology. Assessments are often guesses, a process at work in discussions of such other couples as Leo and Sonya Tolstoy, Thomas and Jane Carlyle, Scott and Zelda Fitzgerald, Ted Hughes and Sylvia Plath, and many others. The famous opening lines of *Anna Karenina* do not quite meet these cases, and certainly not that of the Stevensons. It may well be that all happy marriages are happy in the same way while unhappy marriages are unhappy

15 Germaine Greer, *Shakespeare's Wife*, London, Bloomsbury, 2007, p. 1.

in a wholly distinctive way, but most marriages are neither totally unhappy nor totally happy. The emotional expectations, the level of attained union, and the general condition of couples are confusingly diverse and ambivalent. Maybe both R.L.S. and Fanny were, as would now be said, damaged by their past. Chesterton made the acute judgement that "it is no disrespect to either to say that in both, psychologically, there was an element of patching up as well as of binding together".[16]

J.C. Furnas noted that "most biographies of Louis blur Fanny over as vaguely but gleamingly perfect or else slander her on inadequate evidence".[17] In fact there is an overabundance of evidence, but none that leads to one agreed verdict. Fanny was undoubtedly a woman of spirit and strength of will, but also displayed on occasion remarkable meanness of mind. In some cases, she has been presented as a modern Lady Macbeth, if not as one of the witches on the blasted heath. While alive, she had her worshippers, and latterly she has gained a new generation of defenders who, motivated by modern feminism, see her only as a plucky, enterprising woman, focused on her own needs, heedless of the conventions of the age, at odds with the oppressive, perhaps misogynistic, culture of her time. In this perspective, the treatment she receives from hostile critics is portrayed as typical of that afforded a woman unwilling to slip into the subordinate role of helpmate, bed-warmer, and undemanding guardian angel.

A further misfortune awaiting the wives of writers is that of necessity they move among highly articulate onlookers, prompt

16 G.K. Chesterton, *Stevenson*, op. cit., p. 20.
17 J.C. Furnas, *Voyage to Windward*, London, Faber and Faber, 1953, p. 224.

at delivering judgements and skilled in forging memorable prose. Perhaps, however paradoxical it may sound, we simply know too much about the marriage to be able to arrive at a balanced view. Those moments of anger, quarrelsomeness, or downright aversion which occur in every relationship between men and women are in their case pitilessly chronicled, providing a sea of sludge from which every critic can choose the unwholesome slick on which to base a case. On her introduction to literary life in London, Fanny was viewed by his friends as an exotic creature. "One of the strangest people who have lived in our time, a sort of savage in some ways, but very loveable – extraordinarily passionate and unlike everyone else in her violent feelings and unrestrained ways of expressing them," opined Edmund Gosse, who never shied clear of hyperbole. During the time of his collaboration with R.L.S. in the production of lacklustre plays, W.E. Henley referred to her as the "Bedlamite Fanny", although he did add the rider "I love her."[18] The love, never sincere, did not endure, and Fanny and Henley were soon at daggers drawn. For Henry James, the gentlest of men and in general well disposed towards Fanny, she was a "poor, barbarous and merely *instinctive* lady".[19] She was fond of James and would have been wounded by the epithet "*instinctive*", with its deliberate underlining and its enhancement by the adverb "merely", since she viewed herself as having that elusive quality, the artistic temperament. Her frustration over the lack of recognition wounded her deeply. Alice James was no

18 Both the quotes are from Margaret Mackay, *The Violent Friend*, London, J. M. Dent, 1969, pp. 92 and 100.
19 Janet Adam Smith, *Henry James and Robert Louis Stevenson*, London, Rupert Hart-Davis, 1948, p. 22.

less forthright. She had heard reports that Fanny possessed "great wifely virtues", but her own comments were damning: "such egoism and so naked! giving me the strangest feeling of being in the presence of an unclothed being".[20] To the art historian Sidney Colvin she certainly seemed clothed, but in hostile garb. He reported that she had the "build and character that somehow suggested Napoleon".

They were a most unlikely couple, and their relationship and married life made a witch's brew of conflict and mutual support, of neurotic dependence, profound need, mutual love, periods of antagonism, episodes of rivalry, and unequal public success. Roslyn Jolly set out a series of antitheses, ending with the principal one: "She was a wonderful emotional and professional support; she was a terrible emotional and financial drain."[21] Adelaide Boodle, who knew them in Bournemouth, recalls sometimes turning away from their house when she heard the two bawling at each other.[22] There is no doubt that they were linked by the deepest of love, and those who have felt it necessary to show partisan feelings towards one or the other are ipso facto constrained to disregard the enduring intensity of feeling between them. R.L.S. always viewed her as beautiful, even if she demurred. Her looks were of an unconventional sort, and it did not help that she was dark skinned at a time when conventional ideas of beauty required a pale complexion. He said of his marriage that it was "the most successful in

20 *The Diary of Alice James*, London, Rupert Hart-Davis, 1964, p. 93.
21 Roslyn Jolly, "Introduction", in Fanny Stevenson, *The Cruise of the "Janet Nichol"*, Sydney, University of New South Wales Press, 2004, p. 22.
22 Adelaide A. Boodle, *R.L.S. and his Sine Qua Non*, London, John Murray, 1926.

the world", although at other times he was less certain. In a somewhat ungallant letter to his Edinburgh friend Philip Gilbert Hammerton, he wrote, "It was not my bliss that I was interested in when I was married; it was a sort of marriage *in extremis*; and if I am where I am, it is thanks to the care of that lady, who married me when I was a mere complication of cough and bones, much fitter for an emblem of mortality than a bridegroom" (III, 821). Being nurse to R.L.S. was no easy task, as Fanny explained to his mother. "Taking care of Louis is, as you must know, very like angling a shy trout; one must understand when to play out the line, and exercise the greatest caution in drawing him in. I am becoming most expert, though it is an anxious business" (III, 709).

Fanny does not fit any of the neat conventional categories into which women are now fitted, or perhaps she fits all of them in part. Some biographers, Frank McLynn being the most conspicuous example, plumb depths of dislike which seem to have a pathological basis.[23] He displays unusual ingenuity in twisting every episode of life to Fanny's disadvantage, seeing in her every move some sign of wicked stepmother self-interest, detecting an overall pattern of callous exploitation of the innocent R.L.S. to her own advantage and that of her children, Belle and Lloyd.

The underlying question remains – did R.L.S. profit or suffer as a writer from Fanny's attentions? Would he have been better off without her? She was domineering, argumentative, unwilling to compromise, indifferent to his concerns over money, demanding in her requests for expenditure not just for

23 Frank McLynn, *Robert Louis Stevenson,* London, Hutchison, 1993.

their own needs and fancies but for her offspring. At the same time, she was his nurse, even the angel of the hearth. She rushed to his side in Hawaii when he had gone there on his own and was struck down by illness. She managed his recovery. If she aroused hostility, she was also the recipient of love and respect. Thomas Stevenson had the highest regard for Fanny's literary judgement and made his son promise never to publish anything without her approval.

Only the most purblind can deny that, at least most of the time, she fulfilled the role of carer with dedication and self-abnegation. She did not brook opposition when it came to Stevenson's interests and alienated several of his friends during their time in Bournemouth. There can be no doubt that she kept him alive longer than would have been the case if this chronic invalid had been without her care: this was certainly his own view. His problems with his health conditioned their life together. Bournemouth was chosen because its climate was considered beneficial for a sickly man, but their period of residence there was not one of uninterrupted bliss. Fanny grew sulky and irritated when visitors, including writers and men of letters who were Stevenson's close friends, outstayed what she considered to be the due period of welcome. She claimed to be concerned that the exertion of conviviality was a strain on his health.

Both R.L.S. and Fanny suffered bouts of ill health, so they decided to move on. In August 1887, they took up residence at Saranac Lake in upstate New York, since the air was reputedly good for people suffering from pulmonary diseases and the village had a sanatorium run by a doctor who had developed innovative treatments. R.L.S.' widowed mother left Edinburgh to join them in North America. The winters were severe, and photographs show the party cowering on the verandah of their wooden cottage, wrapped in bearskins, wearing woolly hats over their ears and putting on a brave show. R.L.S.' health held up and he made a start on *The Master of Ballantrae*, but Fanny encountered medical problems and found it harder to cope. She moved temporarily to New York, but they agreed they could not continue that way and decided to charter a yacht for a cruise.

R.L.S. was still considering various options for the future, one of which was making Madeira his permanent home. It was only at a late stage that he plumped for the Pacific rather than the Mediterranean or the Indian Ocean, which had been other possibilities. History, as we are told by grave practitioners of the trade, is not written by the "what ifs" of human choice, so it is undoubtedly idle, but irresistible, to speculate what would have become of R.L.S. and what he would have produced had they chosen to sail in a different sea. With his deep classical education, how would he have reacted to the Mediterranean and its islands? Or had the choice fallen on the Indian Ocean, would his keen mind and moral sensibilities have been appalled by the Raj? He became critical of colonialism in the Pacific, and was once moved to wonder if Britain's policies there were really different from those it was following in India. What would he have made of the Indian Empire observed at first hand? All worthless speculation. The choice fell on the Pacific, but there was no intention to take up final residence there.

Fanny was dispatched from New York to California to explore the possibilities of finding some suitable vessel. She cabled from San Francisco to say that she could secure a schooner-yacht, the *Casco*, "with most comfortable accommodation for six aft and six forward". She needed an immediate reply, which she received from her husband, who wrote back, "Blessed girl, take the yacht and expect us in ten days."

The yacht was big enough to accommodate R.L.S., Fanny, his mother (thereafter known as Aunt Maggie), Fanny's son Lloyd, and the Swiss maid Valentine. R.L.S. had always been fond of Lloyd, and in one version, later disputed, it was Lloyd who, by sketching out a map for a deserted island while they were in a cottage in Braemar, gave R.L.S. the inspiration for *Treasure Island*. The two co-authored three novels, and Lloyd remained with R.L.S. until his death.

Aunt Maggie, to whom R.L.S. was always close, was another member of the party. While all the others who were with him in the South Seas have been discussed in biographies, little attention has been paid to the remarkable woman who was Margaret Stevenson. Was there ever such a change, such a fracturing of bonds, as in her case? In Edinburgh's New Town, she had been a staid, dutiful, Presbyterian, Victorian bourgeois wife to her engineer husband, but on being widowed she showed her true mettle and demonstrated a wholly unpredicted independence of attitude. She had been as outraged as her husband at R.L.S.' youthful apostasy and at his later relationship with a married woman, but overcame her reservations. After being widowed, she refused to settle into a quietly domestic life, leaving her home to join R.L.S. and his wife in America and then to accompany them in the Pacific. In spite of her routine declarations of devotion to the memory of her late husband, she gives every appearance of revelling in the freedom from the restrictions imposed on women in Victorian society.

In the South Seas, she blossomed in a way which would have left the good wives of Edinburgh perplexed and perhaps shocked. Her letters and journals, published after her death, show an independent and enquiring mind, as well as devotion to her son.[24]

24 M.I. Stevenson, *From Saranac to the Marquesas and Beyond*, edited by Marie Clothilde Balfour, London, Methuen, 1903; idem, *Letters from Samoa*, London, Methuen, 1906.

CHAPTER 3

A Wise Folly

In May 1888, R.L.S. left New York to join his wife and take possession of the vessel she had found. If he was not by any means wealthy, R.L.S. now had a healthy bank account with the money left by his father. Further financial backing for the enterprise was provided by Sam McClure, who worked for a publishing firm in New York. McClure had earlier offered R.L.S. an "irresistible sum" to churn out articles and essays for his journal, but initially R.L.S. opted for a different contract with another firm. Later, when McClure heard of the interest of the family group in going to sea, he offered a new contract with generous fees for articles on any subject of R.L.S.' choosing. McClure would also syndicate the articles in Britain. The contract was signed but the venture ended unhappily. The two men had different expectations of the kind of article R.L.S. would file.

It took longer than the promised ten days to make the yacht fully seaworthy. At the first meeting, the owner, Dr Merritt, was upset at Stevenson's unconventional dress and viewed him as an unreliable bohemian who might kick over the traces in God knows what unspeakable ways, and wreak all manner of outrage upon his yacht's fine furnishing and upholstery. He was eventually talked round, but it took longer to convince the captain,

Albert H. Otis, a hardened matelot who was initially hostile to any project which involved taking non-mariners on a pleasure trip. The fact that there were three women among the travellers increased his dismay. Fanny Stevenson once asked him what he would do if Mrs Stevenson were to fall overboard. "Put it in the log" was the no-nonsense answer. His reservations about those he was taking on board deepened when he was made aware of the physical condition of the principal traveller. He resolved his doubts about R.L.S.' chances of survival in his own way by including tackle for burial at sea among the tackle taken on board. By the time the cruise ended in Hawaii, Stevenson and Otis were firm friends. He impressed R.L.S., but offended his mother, by admitting that while he had enjoyed *Treasure Island*, Stevenson's other books were not for him.

In San Francisco, while the boat was being made ready, R.L.S. immersed himself in the literature on the Pacific. After negotiation with the owner, the terms of the hire of the yacht were agreed, and if the price was high, it was because the vessel was luxurious, ninety-four feet long and seventy-four register tons, as R.L.S. described it. There was no intention to follow a Spartan lifestyle while at sea. Cases of champagne were included among the supplies deemed necessary for subsistence. The cosmopolitan crew comprised the captain and five men of different nationalities, including the cook, who proved unsatisfactory and was later dismissed. R.L.S. loved the time at sea, although Fanny suffered dreadfully from seasickness. Maggie enthused about the sunsets, "the great spectacle of the day". She kept a journal in which she gave a detailed description of the yacht, the layout of the rooms, the furnishing on board, and the sleeping and dining arrangements. R.L.S. had the stateroom to himself, with both a bed and a sofa. Lloyd too had a bedroom and the three women slept in quarters which doubled as the drawing room during the day. The routine had to vary with conditions at sea, but most evenings the company played two rubbers of whist. Lloyd brought along a typewriter to take dictation as well as two cameras to provide illustrations for the planned book, although one was lost overboard at the first stop. The route was set, as R.L.S. explained in a letter to Henry James:

> This, dear James, is a valedictory. On June 15th the schooner yacht *Casco* will (weather and a jealous providence permitting) steam through the Golden Gate for Honolulu, Tahiti, the Galapagos, Guayaquil, and – I hope not the bottom of the Pacific. It will contain your obedient 'umble servant and party. It seems too good to be true, and is a very good way of getting through the greensickness of maturity which, with all its accompanying ills, is now declaring itself on my mind and life. (VI, 2098)

It was June 28 before the *Casco* finally left port. The intention was to cruise around the Pacific, see the sights, delve into unfamiliar ways, write articles which might become a book, perhaps find new material for fiction, and then make their way back to Bournemouth, London and the Savile Club, maybe even Edinburgh. In the event, there was to be no return. The route was altered as they proceeded, so while R.L.S. told Lady Taylor that "from Skerryvore to Galapagos is a far cry", they did not in the end reach the Galapagos (VI, 2084). In Honolulu in October 1889, he was able to announce about the voyage: "in health, spirits, renewed interest in life, and (I do believe) refreshed capacity for work, the cruise has proved a Wise Folly" (VI, 2132).

In the years 1888–9, there were in fact three cruises on three different vessels. The *Casco* zigzagged across the Pacific, taking in the Marquesas, the Paumotus islands (now Tuamotus), Tahiti, and Hawaii, from where the yacht was sent back to California in January 1889. In June, a slightly changed group continued on their way on the trading schooner *Equator*, no luxury vessel but a transport ship whose main business was inter-island trade. Valentine was expelled from the group for obscure reasons, not made any clearer by R.L.S.' enigmatic remark that it was done to "mutual glee", and that it was "the usual tale of the maid on board the yacht" (VI, 2133). The maid had previously been much appreciated, so there is no knowing how the supposedly usual tale played out, although some indication may be given by Fanny's statement that "Valentine is madly in love with every Chinaman she sees." She even "threatened" to marry Cousina, the Chinese cook hired for the cruise but fired by the captain for his impertinence and drunkenness. Maggie did not embark on the *Equator* but returned to Scotland, while Joe Strong, Belle's husband, who had been resident in Hawaii, joined the party on the *Equator*, as did a new cook, Ah Fu. Both Joe and Belle had annoyed Stevenson and Fanny during the residence at Hawaii, and initially both were told they were not welcome on board. Joe pleaded with R.L.S., who took a liking to him in spite of his unreliability, and gave way. There was no such reprieve for Belle, who was dispatched to Sydney with her son, Austin, and told to wait there until the ship arrived. The voyage ended in December 1889, when they arrived at the Samoan island of Upolu, where they decided to make their permanent home. The journeying was not done, and in February 1890, while their house was being built on Samoa, the Stevensons left for Sydney, from where, after a stay of some months, they continued their travels.

The agreement with the owners was different on each occasion. With the *Casco*, they negotiated a hire and were in charge, although there were some fraught discussions with Captain Otis over their stops. With the *Equator*, the party was carried on the understanding that while they were free to request stops on islands that attracted them, they would generally be taken where the ship was chartered to go on its commercial business in Micronesia. The captain was a Scotsman, Dennis Reid, and while on board R.L.S. had one of his fantasy notions of setting up a company in partnership with Lloyd and Reid to trade in copra. The idea came to nothing. The weather was unexpectedly stormy, so the cruise lasted six months instead of the planned four. The high point was a visit to the Gilbert Islands, where they spent six weeks in the capital, Apemama, then ruled by King Tembinoka, a despot known as the Napoleon of the Pacific and feared throughout the seas.[25] Few whites dared to land on his domain, so that, as Fanny noted, all the books written about him were based on hearsay. The Stevensons made a favourable impression on him and he on them. The king not only allowed them to stay but had a special compound built on his island for them. Tears were shed on both sides when it came time to leave.

The *Equator* reached Apia, the capital of Samoa, on December 7, 1889. The intention was to make a brief stop to gather material on a recent war for a chapter in the book on the South Seas R.L.S. was preparing, but once landed their plans changed radically. They made the acquaintance of Harry J.

25 "Abemama", "Tembinok", and "Tem Binoka" are alternative spellings often used.

Moors, an American trader resident on the island, and decided that although this was not the most beautiful of the islands in the ocean, it was where they would make their home. With the aid of Moors, they bought a stretch of land inland from Apia. Moors undertook to oversee the construction of a house there while R.L.S. and Fanny continued on their excursions. Some of Stevenson's friends in Britain blamed Fanny for keeping him from them and from London, which they considered the natural residence of a man of letters, but the decision was not hers and the couple's overall plans were still in flux. They intended to return home at least temporarily to see friends and family and sell off Skerryvore.

This was still the plan when in February 1890 they travelled on to Sydney, where R.L.S. suffered yet another of his recurrent lung haemorrhages. Having seen how well her husband had been when on the seas, Fanny took to scouring the harbour area in Sydney to find a suitable craft to take them away from the city. The problem was that a shipping strike had been called, but she managed to persuade the captain of the *Janet Nicoll* to take the group, now reduced to R.L.S., Fanny, and Lloyd, on board as paying passengers. They left Sydney on April 11. Once again, they were on a trading vessel and had no say in where they were bound. The first ports of call were Auckland, followed by Samoa, where they used the time to renew acquaintance with Moors and see how work was progressing on their house. They were happy to re-embark when the ship was ready to sail. It rambled around the Pacific on a voyage which took them to over thirty islands, including the Marshall Islands and New Caledonia. There is no account of this voyage in Stevenson's *In the South Seas*, but Fanny kept a journal. Since the decision had now been made to remain in Samoa, Lloyd was dispatched to England to oversee the sale of Skerryvore. After further cruising, R.L.S. and Fanny were back in Samoa by mid September 1890.

These vessels carried a formidably literate group of passengers, so the travels are probably as well documented as any maritime journey since Dr Johnson and James Boswell's tour of the Hebrides. The passengers were not continuously on the seas, but spent extended periods on land, giving the party the opportunity to observe the ways of life of, and make friends among, the islanders, very often with their rulers. R.L.S. planned to write a book which would be based on the articles he sent back. He also continued with his correspondence, as did Fanny and Maggie. They kept diaries, Maggie of life on the *Casco* and Fanny of the *Janet Nicoll* (which she curiously misspelt "*Nichol*").[26] Travel can often narrow the mind and reinforce innate prejudices, but R.L.S. was among the few of his background and age whose horizons were genuinely widened. His journey from Skerryvore to Samoa was intellectual, moral, political, and psychological as well as physical. His vision of himself as a writer underwent a sea change, in every sense of the word, involving a change of sensibility, a widening of discernment, and a deepening of sympathy.

The choice of literature on the first voyage, Gibbon's *Decline and Fall*, is intriguing. Aunt Maggie read aloud for the company, since "reading in the open air was too much for Louis". Gibbon was not selected at random, nor was this merely an effort to catch up on a worthy classic which R.L.S. felt he really should

26 M.I. Stevenson, *From Saranac to the Marquesas and Beyond*, op. cit.; Fanny Stevenson, *The Cruise of the "Janet Nichol"*, op. cit.

have got round to long before. Like many in Victorian times, he had a deep knowledge of classical history and literature, and while in the South Seas was reinforced in his view that Rome was the basis of Western civilisation, and that the Roman Empire marked its enduring boundaries. It was to Roman law and Roman civilisation in general that he made reference when discussing the distinctions between the culture in which he had grown up and that which he was encountering. Sailing in the South Seas, he was not merely embarking on an adventure, but was undertaking an enterprise akin to that of Dante's Ulysses when he went beyond the Pillars of Hercules. R.L.S. was travelling outwith the Roman area in which he was cultur- ally at home, trespassing on territory in which he was a cultural stranger. As he put it:

> To cross the channel is, for a boy of twelve, to change heavens; to cross the Atlantic, for a man of twenty-four, is hardly to modify his diet. But I was now escaped out of the shadows of the Roman Empire, under whose toppling monuments we were all cradled, whose laws and letters are on every hand of us, containing and preventing. I was now to see what men might be whose fathers had never studied Virgil, had never been conquered by Caesar, and never been ruled by the wisdom of Gaius and Papinian. (Tusitala, XX, 4 and 8)

Time and again, as he landed on the Marquesas, Tahiti, or the Gilberts, he reminded himself that he was now moving among men and women whose notions of law were not founded on Justinian, whose ethical and cultural parameters were not grounded in Cicero, and whose ways were thus alien, foreign, and strange. Crucially, and here he was atypical, he did not regard the new customs and habits of mind as inferior, and went out of his way to orientate himself in the beliefs of the people he met.

In reading Gibbon, he was reminding himself of his own moorings while also preparing with openness of mind and goodwill for the challenge of confronting other ways of life. The first encounter came when they made landfall on the Marquesas. His initial response is lyrical. "The first experience can never be repeated. The first love, the first sunrise, the first South Sea island are memories apart and touched by a virginity of sense." However, before the anchor had been cast, the first canoe emerged from the village on the shore, followed by others, and "stalwart, six-foot men in every stage of undress" swarmed on board the *Casco*. To his dismay, "there was no word of welcome, no show of civility". That evening, as he sat writing up his journal, he found himself surrounded by "three brown-skinned generations", and admits to a kind of impotent rage that they were "beyond the reach of articulate communication". The problem was not only the lack of a common language, but of shared standards of thought and conduct.

He was now out of "that comfortable zone of kindred languages", though not altogether bereft of parameters of observation and judgement. He had read writers like Melville, and had some familiarity with the works of the early anthro-pologists, notably Edward Burnett Tylor, author of the seminal work *Primitive Culture*.[27] This knowledge assisted him in avoid-ing the trap of the facile savagery/civilisation dialectic which

27 Roslyn Jolly, *Stevenson in the Pacific*, op. cit., pp. 39–40.

imprisoned the mind of many colonials and even missionaries.

While at sea, Stevenson was rejuvenated physically and mentally, as he delightedly told his correspondents at home. He actively enjoyed being on board a vessel and drew Otis' admiration for his fearlessness in the face of storms. In September, he wrote from the French colony of Fakarava, an atoll in the Tuamoto group:

> My health has stood me splendidly: I am up for hours wading over the knees in shells. I have been five hours on horseback . . . Withal I still have colds: I have one now, and feel pretty sick too; but not as at home: instead of being in bed for instance I am at this moment sitting snuffling and writing in an undershirt and trousers: and as for colour, hands, arms, feet, legs and face, I am browner than the berry . . . (VI, 2109)

The optimism was not wholly justified, for he had a relapse shortly afterwards on Tahiti, and was looked after with great gentleness by Princess Moe, a member of the local aristocracy who prepared special food for him and found accommodation for the party. She also spoke English and initiated R.L.S. into Polynesian folklore.

The first and most obvious characteristic of his response to the environment in which he found himself is its sheer sybaritism, evident in his unalloyed delight at finding himself in a place of such beauty, among a people he found so open-hearted, whose attractiveness he found beguiling, whose ways he found so winning, and all this in a climate which agreed with his health. Plainly inebriated with *joie de vivre* over being in Polynesia, he wrote to Charles Baxter, seemingly to apologise for having unwittingly given him offence, but in reality to express his exuberance:

> I have just been away a week alone on the lee coast of Hawaii, the only white creature in many miles, riding 5½ miles one day, living with a native, seeing poor lepers shipped off to Molokai, hearing native causes and giving my opinion as *amicus curiae* as to the interpretation of a statute in English: a lovely week among God's best – or at least God's sweetest works – Polynesians. It bettered me greatly. If I could only stay there the time that remains, I could get my work done and be happy; but the care of a large, costly, and no preceesely forrit-gaun family keep me in vile Honolulu where I am almost out of sorts . . . after so long a dose of whites, it was a blessing to get among Polynesians again, even for a week. (VI, 2165)

A spontaneous sensuality underwrites every intellectual judgement, but, however insightful, nothing is more arresting in the letters written from the South Seas than the sense of a reawakening to life, an outburst of renewed energy, a dawning of wonder, and restlessness of mind and imagination. R.L.S. says he "did not dream there were such places or such races". He became engrossed in fable and history, while contemporary politics increasingly commanded his attention and caused ever more frequent and passionate outbursts of indignation. The first expression of his new state of mind was a split with the unfortunate McClure. He had already written such books as *Travels with a Donkey* (1879), but the production of another work in that style no longer seemed to him adequate. His desire to convey the acuteness of impression required him to write what he described only as a "big book", one which contained reflections occasioned by his observations and experiences and which would touch on culture, history, and anthropology.

The nature of the projected book caused a rift between him and Fanny. He had begun taking notes and sending articles back ever since landing on the Marquesas, but these were not in line with those McClure believed he had commissioned. R.L.S.' thought was acquiring a sharper edge, and he rejected the temptation of assuming that the chronology of development in the West was universally applicable, and that Victorian standards of what constituted civilisation were the only valid ones. He was increasingly critical of the impact of the white man, an attitude which hardened as he travelled and which found full expression on Samoa.

The "big book" was never published in his lifetime, although a version, big or little, was eventually edited by Sidney Colvin and published with the title *In the South Seas* (1896). It is an excellent travelogue, lively and colourful, but also full of insights which historians today still find valuable. His style throughout has a relaxing warmth and flows gently. The book opens on a note of resignation; he says he "was come to the afterpiece of life, and had only the nurse and the undertaker to expect". To his surprise he has attained a state of contentment for he has discovered a place where "life [is] most pleasant and man most interesting". He began serious work on his intended book between 1889 and 1891, while on the *Janet Nicoll*, and continued in Samoa, but between his own dissatisfaction and Fanny's objections it ended as one of his many unfinished projects. While writing it, he complained to Henry James about the labour of a long book, but he was evidently excited, at least initially, by the rethinking involved. "My book is now practically modelled; if I can execute what is designed, there are few better books extant on the globe; bar the epics, and the big tragedies, and histories, and the choice lyric poetics, and a novel or two – none. But it is not executed yet ..." (VI, 2191).

Ironic hyperbole conceals his real aspirations. R.L.S. gives the impression of entering an unknown cosmos, an area of man's estate to be chronicled with an elation of spirit similar to that expressed in the closing lines of *The Great Gatsby*, where Scott Fitzgerald writes that in discovering the Americas Western explorers experienced for the last time in history something equal to their own capacity for wonder. R.L.S. felt a comparable state of awe as the vessels moored in island after island. He was enthralled, and unsure of how to convey the sheer vastness and novelty of what he saw. Authors like Melville and Stoddard had helped him form preliminary images, but he became convinced of the need for a different approach. Known as a writer of romances, he was willing to dedicate time and energy to producing a big book of some seriousness, even of scholarly gravitas, basically an anthropological work on the islands he was visiting, the sort of work which was in his own day described as "scientific" and which would now be labelled "academic".

Kenneth White, an analyst of intellectual nomadism in various writers, was intrigued by the manifestation of this new concept in R.L.S. The big book, he believed, belonged in a totally different category from the novels and was much more ambitious both in conception and intent. "It would try to penetrate into that 'strange place', the Pacific. It would show humanity at its limits. It would move through time and space.

It would consist of one kaleidoscopic scene after the other."[28] Fanny would not have agreed. She wanted an undemanding, relaxed, and relaxing read, packed with local colour and vivid anecdotes, one which would not make excessive demands on his time and energy and would, perhaps crucially, sell and make money. She had in mind a Pacific equivalent of *Travels with a Donkey*, with the celebrated author presenting vividly, in the first person, the sights, the adventures, the picturesque strangeness of the life he saw there; whereas he planned a work penned by an objective, invisible writer, combining the approach of the emerging social sciences of anthropology, sociology, and history, one which would constitute a study of mores and morals, similar to *The Golden Bough* which Sir James Frazer was writing at about the same time. Fanny sought allies in her efforts to dissuade R.L.S. She wrote in May 1889 to Sidney Colvin, a man R.L.S. held in the highest esteem, and who was one of his closest friends and most frequent correspondents. Fanny writes in the exasperated tones of a governess at the end of her tether with an unruly, wilful pupil committed to her charge but unwilling to do her bidding:

> I am very much exercised by one thing. Louis has the most enchanting material that anyone ever had in the whole world for his book, and I am afraid he is going to spoil it all. He has taken it into his Scotch Stevenson head that a stern duty lies before him, and that his book must be a sort of scientific and historical impersonal thing comparing the different languages (of which he knows

28 Kenneth White, *The Wanderer*, op. cit., p. 93.

nothing really) and the different peoples, the object being to settle the question of whether they are of common Malay origin or not. Also to compare the Protestant and Catholic missions etc. In fact to bring to the surface all the prejudices, and all the mistakes and all the ignorance concerning the subject that he can get together . . . Louis says it is a stern sense of duty that is at the bottom of it all, which is more alarming than anything else. (VI, 2173)

For all her spluttering tone, Fanny provides an accurate manifesto of what R.L.S. sought to accomplish, and an insight into his altered outlook. Stories based on myth and misapprehension had been circulating freely in Europe, and he was out to correct them. Even granted that he was motivated by an overall aim which Fanny did not share, it is hard to understand her "alarm". She was always his sternest critic, and held to her views with a tenacity which was at least the equal of the Scotch Stevenson head. On this occasion she found him unmoveable. The knowledge that her husband could be stubborn in adhering to his convictions, that he was prone to adhering to a stern, Calvinistic sense of duty, and when driven could develop a quasi-vocational urge to state certain truths, however unpalatable, could not have come as a surprise to her, but she still found his stance unsettling. R.L.S. was finding the vision and voice with which he would speak in Samoa.

The editor McClure, like Fanny, was looking for bright, light, glossy pieces, for tales of native ways, descriptions of vibrant scenes under palms, and sketches of extravagant personalities which would entertain tired businessmen and suburban housewives. He was perturbed by the evidence that

R.L.S. was turning increasingly serious as the voyage continued. Some articles were rejected, and when the cooperation
between the two men broke down and the contract was torn
up, McClure wrote a tetchy but shrewd memo suggesting that
there were two souls in Stevenson, "the romantic adventurer"
and "the Scotch covenanter". He knew which one he believed
he had engaged and was dismayed by the one who was coming
forward. "Contrary to our expectation, it was the moralist and
not the romancer which his observations in the South Seas
awoke in him and the public found the moralist less interesting
than the romancer."[29] McClure was no fool. The swing between
the moraliser and the romancer marks out twin aspects of the
writer's mind in Samoa. The vision of the moralist underlay
his abhorrence of the treatment meted out to the islanders in
the South Seas, but there was also in that vision a recurring
search for some higher truth and high seriousness which are,
as Matthew Arnold had been telling his readers, the essential
foundation of ethics and poetics.[30] The nature of evil had
always intrigued him, as was clear in *Jekyll and Hyde*, and he
probed that question more deeply and explicitly in his work in
the South Seas.

The temptation of the romancer was to veer in an opposing
direction, where the desire to tell a tale and to use experience
and character purely as elements in story-telling predominated.
Fanny and McClure both had a shrewd idea of this as the real
market, but R.L.S. held fast to the outlook of the moralist and
resisted their blandishments. He wrote tales in the South Seas

29 Sam McClure, *My Autobiography,* London, John Murray, 1914, p. 192.
30 A point of view most famously outlined in Arnold's essay of 1880, "The
Study of Poetry".

built of his observation of men and events, but they were not romances. He did also write romances, like *St. Ives*, but that was a separate enterprise, and he knew it. There were also picturesque notes of his travels, but they were entertainments and distinct from what he now regarded as his serious work. On this voyage, R.L.S. developed as a writer in ways neither Fanny, Colvin, nor McClure anticipated, or relished.

Colvin was as worried as Fanny about the content of the book R.L.S. had outlined, and about its likely reception, but his deeper concern was that R.L.S. was squandering his talent in writing about obscure matters in a far-off land of which good British citizens knew little and cared less. This concern about spoiled genius became a recurrent theme in Colvin's letters, and led eventually to his expostulating about R.L.S.' obsession with his "beloved blacks – or chocolates – confound them" (VIII, 2726), rather than getting on with producing the great works of literature of which Colvin and his other London friends believed him capable.

R.L.S. took the trouble to set out the proposed structure of *The South Seas* ("a rather large title", but the one he preferred) in a letter of his own. The book would consist of seven parts: General, the Marquesas, the Dangerous Archipelago, Tahiti, the Eight Islands, the Gilberts, and Samoa. Each part would be subdivided into further chapters, but for Samoa he added only the parenthesis "which I have not yet reached". Samoa had no privileged position, since, as he explained, "I am minded to stay not very long in Samoa and confine my studies there (as far as anyone can forecast) to the history of the late war" (VI, 2191).

CHAPTER 4

Distant Glimpses of Samoa

In the South Seas, the title given to the book by Sidney Colvin when he edited it after the death of R.L.S., does in fact enchant, as Fanny wished, but it is also a quest for a sensitive understanding of a different culture, and of the impact of Western ways on the lives of the peoples in the Pacific Islands. Some of the wild stories and incredible scenes which Fanny wanted did appear in the posthumous work but they were accompanied by chronicles of the way of life of the Polynesians and warnings of the dangers threatening them. Even before reaching Samoa, R.L.S. saw for himself the disastrous effects of the prevailing, presumptuous view that the native peoples were basically cultural blanks which could be casually overwritten by incomers in possession of higher truths. Figures as diverse as Cecil Rhodes, Lord Randolph Churchill, and John Ruskin supported the supposedly civilising mission of British expansionism as represented by traders and missionaries. The evidence R.L.S. accumulated gave him grounds for challenging the image of the Polynesians as primitive savages, and to question received notions of the clear separation between (Western) civilisation and (African or Asian) barbarism.

He was captivated by the vigour and charm of habits of mind unfamiliar to Western readers, and determined to alter perceptions in Western society. While there are descriptive

passages of idyllic loveliness and character sketches of idiosyncratic personalities in his writings of this period, R.L.S. is
above all anxious to convey and analyse the distinctive tenor of
life "outside the shadow of the Roman empire". He had never
had much truck with the values of the eminent Victorians, and
this may have made it easier for him to question the binary
barbarism/civilisation split. The youthful bohemianism, the
style of thought and behaviour of "Velvet Jacket" – as he had
been known in his student days in Edinburgh – were acts of
rebellion not only against his family but against the whole
Calvinist-bourgeois background of his native city.

His disdain for conventional notions of society was strength-
ened during his 1879 voyage across the Atlantic to meet Fanny.
Travelling steerage, he was in daily contact with impoverished
emigrants, and was appalled by the snobbery displayed towards
them by the wealthy and privileged who regarded themselves,
and whom R.L.S. might previously have regarded, as the pillars
of society. At that stage in his life, the political was purely personal. He remained formally conservative all his life, yet objected
to conduct and states of mind which justified discrimination
against other human beings. There was a significant foretaste
of this outlook in his reaction to an incident he witnessed
at a railway station as he continued his journey westward across
the North American continent. He watched a mob jeer at a
"noble red man of old story, he over whose hereditary continent
we had been streaming all these days". Stevenson contrasted the
traces of pride and independence in the old man and his family
with the behaviour of his white fellow passengers, "disgracefully
dressed out in the sweepings of civilisation". The dignity of the
one side was a rebuke to the other. "The silent stoicism of their

conduct, and the pathetic degradation of their appearance would have touched any thinking creature, but my fellow passengers danced and jested around them with truly Cockney baseness. I was ashamed for the thing we call civilisation."

It is an instructive passage, and he would find equal dignity of bearing in many of the Samoan chiefs, especially Mata'afa, as they faced the depredations and provocations of white power. In the South Seas, R.L.S. came to question even more strongly the idea of civilisation taken as dogma in the columns of *The Times* or in the clubs of Pall Mall. From the earliest days in the Marquesas, the philosophy, concepts, and standards which he would employ when defending Samoa from intellectual condescension and commercial exploitation began to take shape in his mind. In his first letter to Sidney Colvin, he wrote: "It is all a swindle; I chose these isles as having the most beastly population, and they are far better and far more civilised than we" (VI, 2016). The style is playful, but the underlying sentiment is not. He sided from the outset with a people he saw as misunderstood, maltreated, and exploited.

For the book on the South Seas he aspired to write, R.L.S. showed interest in the scientific approach and regretted his ignorance of the field. Writing to Sir Walter Simpson, a friend since student days in Edinburgh and son of the doctor who discovered chloroform, he returned to the theme of the uninhabited desolation of the islands he had visited, attributing the blame to the introduction of opium by Westerners, a question he would take up shortly after his arrival in Samoa. We should "stick to our ancestral stimulants; it seems good in science; a new deal in vices, like a new environment, will discover any imperfection in our organism," he suggested, and continued:

... this cruise is deeply interesting: questions of race and civilisation at every step; I wish you had been here to discuss as we went. In some ways, our civilisation shows in very bright colours; in others of course it looks black enough; but on the whole civilisation has it ... I should have come here years ago and studied these islands properly; 'tis pitiful, to come here an ignorant, elderly ass and glance at them at them a quarter of an hour out of a ship. (VI, 2114)

If his grasp of the scientific method was, by his own admission, lacking, he was more hopeful about an alternative approach to understanding, the identification of parallels with Scotland. He was insatiably curious about the oral traditions of the places he visited and always anxious to engage in conversation. The complaints he heard in the Pacific reminded him of voices he had read about "in the days of Lovat and Struan". However, whatever each people had endured, he noted that "hospitality, tact, natural fine manners and a touchy punctilio" are to be found in both. An air he heard the Marquesans singing reminded him of Allan Ramsay's lament, "Lochaber No More", the song David Balfour heard being sung by emigrants on board the ship carrying them from Skye to the Americas. A stronger and deeper resemblance was with the experiences of Highland clans after the failure of the Jacobite Rising in 1745. Like the Highlanders, the Marquesans and later the Samoans faced the occupation of their country and the suppression of their ways, by the military in the one case, by traders and missionaries on the other. His own romantic Jacobitism stood R.L.S. in good stead as he coaxed chieftains and their orators, or "talking men", to recount legends and tales which he planned to reproduce in his book, and he in return told them stories about the people who lived in the glens and by the side of the lochs of Scotland. Being able to tell such tales enhanced his status in the Marquesas, as he recounted in a chapter entitled "Making Friends".

> I had enjoyed in my youth some knowledge of our Scots folk of the Highlands and Islands. Not much beyond a century has passed since these were in the same convulsive and transitory state as the Marquesans of today. In both cases an alien authority enforced, the clans disarmed, the chiefs deposed, new customs introduced, and chiefly that habit of regarding money as the means and object of existence. The commercial age, in each, succeeding at a bound to an age of war abroad and patriarchal communism at home. (Tusitala, XX, 12)

This was the first time he had employed the word "communism", later identified as a central aspect of Samoan social life. There was no deeper analysis, since at this stage he was mainly intrigued by the similarities of custom and practice.

Other parallels were more quixotic. He noted that the two peoples had lost their chief luxury foods, beef in the one case and "long-pig", i.e. human flesh, in the other. He was also struck by the fact that the idiom employed in both countries involved the dropping of medial consonants. He even expatiated on the habit common to both idioms of the "catch", or glottal stop, found, he informs his readers, in the Scots pronunciation of "water, better or bottle as *wa'er, be'er or bo'le*". Regrettably he did not record how this linguistic oddity aided mutual comprehension.

His most significant conviction was that the civilisation of the Polynesians really *was* a civilisation and not a state of primitive barbarism awaiting improvement, or a childlike condition likely to benefit from the intervention of more mature peoples. The devastation wreaked by the white man appalled him, and his conclusions were blunt. "Where there have been fewest changes, important or unimportant, salutary or hurtful, there the race survives. Each change, however small, augments the sum of new conditions to which a race has to become inured." This question of the balance of advantages between the "primitive" and the "civilised" life was plainly a subject of conversation in the family, so we find his mother ill at ease in Tahiti, "which seemed a sort of halfway house between the savage life and civilisation, with all the drawbacks of both and the advantages of neither".[31] R.L.S. may have been prone to undue romanticism, as in a letter to the American painter, Will H. Low, but his affection and admiration were genuine:

O Low, I love the Polynesian: this civilisation of ours is a dingy, ungentlemanly business; it drops out too much of man, and too much of that the very beauty of the poor beast: who has his beauties in spite of Zola and Co . . . But if you could live, the only white folk, in a Polynesian village: and drink that warm, light *vin du pays* of human affection and enjoy the simple dignity all around you – I will not gush for I am now in my fortieth year, which seems highly unjust but there it is, Mr Low. (VI, 2172)

31 Letter to Jane Whyte Balfour, 26 September, 1888, in *From Saranac to the Marquesas and Beyond*, op. cit.

Their travels took them to Honolulu, where they met up with Fanny's daughter Belle and her husband, the artist Joe Strong, together with their eight-year-old son, Austin. R.L.S. was not impressed by what he found in Hawaii, which he regarded as too "civilised", and specifically as partaking of that American dream towards which he had always nurtured deep reservations. He never managed to convince himself that the island group was the better for the American domination which followed an American-backed *coup d'état*, and never developed any warm feelings for the city of Honolulu. The sight of tram cars and telephones – a modern innovation he abhorred – the general bustle and busyness of the life upset and displeased him, now that he had acquired a taste for the supposedly more primitive, and certainly more relaxed, ways of the Polynesian islands.

It may then seem paradoxical that within the five months in Hawaii in 1889 he had what can be termed an epiphany of sorts, which took the form of a gradual reshaping of the lumber of his mind rather than of a blazing *coup de foudre*. He had until then been a voyager in a far-off land which left him dazzled but bewildered, like Shelley's traveller before the statue of Ozymandias. His conversations and observations with people resident in Honolulu, both native-born and incomers, convinced him finally of the need to make a commitment. Fanny remained a tourist while he was becoming a committed traveller-activist, although both were still of the view that their travels were an interlude in their lives.

In Honolulu he began to immerse himself more deeply in the politics and culture, and began taking the side of the island-ers against the forces which were prowling around them, avariciously eying their homeland and their resources. R.L.S.' mind and imagination began to take up residence in an imprecise area on no known map, where Scotland adjoins Polynesia. Through Joe and Belle, he came into contact with Kalakaua, King of Hawaii, in the grand Iolani Palace he had had built for himself. As a man and ruler, King Kalakaua divided opinion in life, and still does after his death. For some, he was a tragic figure who did his best in the face of overwhelming odds to protect his people and preserve their culture, while for others he was a buffoon or a wastrel known under a mocking nickname, the Merry Monarch. A convinced royalist, R.L.S. took the king's side. The two men exchanged tales, and at the first reception organised for the king on the yacht *Casco*, he recited "Ticonderoga", his narrative poem set in the Highlands. He gathered material for similar works which would feature along with "Ticonderoga" in the volume *Ballads*, published after his arrival in Samoa.

The king, for all his faults, had ascended the throne at a delicate and dangerous period in the history of his country, and indeed of the South Seas. Missionaries had arrived and some members of the royal family had been converted, but Kalakaua made valiant efforts to hold back the tide of westernisation and keep alive Hawaiian traditions and folklore. By the time of Stevenson's arrival, Kalakaua had been stripped of much of his royal power under a settlement, popularly known as the Bayonet Constitution, imposed by American force. The king retained his palace and the trappings of monarchy, but power was transferred away. This constitution was a veil which concealed a power-grab by a new white, mainly American, cabal that made no effort to disguise its financial and commercial desire to exploit Hawaiian land and resources. American companies developed the fruit plantations and a sugar-growing industry for which the archipelago's climate was ideal. It was a pattern R.L.S. would see repeated, and against which he would protest, in Samoa.

Conversations with the king and other members of what Stevenson later termed "the royal crowd" awakened his interest in the plight of the Pacific islands in general and of Samoa in particular. Kalakaua cultivated a vision of a pan-Polynesian empire, or perhaps confederation, with himself as its head. To achieve this aim, in 1886 he dispatched an embassy, or naval task force, to Samoa, with Joe Strong as official artist. Joe's presence would have important consequences for R.L.S., since he made the acquaintance of Harry J. Moors, the American trader and long-time resident in Samoa who would be instrumental in persuading R.L.S. to settle there.

The underlying mission of this armada was never precisely defined, but in its most coherent form the plan was to persuade or coerce Samoa to join a union sprawling across the ocean, with Hawaii as central force. Was this a far-sighted defensive move at a time of encroaching imperial powers, or proof of blundering megalomania by an unhinged monarch? Stevenson changed his mind several times, but initially he was bewitched by the idea and outraged at the reception the Hawaiians received when they called at Upolu. The situation in Samoa was more complex than the Hawaiians had expected, although they would not be the last to be baffled by internal Samoan politics. The enterprise descended into farce, and the impoverished fleet, whose captain was a drunkard and whose crew consisted of boys press-ganged from a reformatory, had to borrow money to make their way home. The German consul in Samoa interpreted the mission as a hostile act designed to foment a rising against them and seized the opportunity to declare national honour offended, and to expel some American and British citizens.

R.L.S. was given a partial account of this affair, and his reaction, however intemperate, marks his first direct intervention in the affairs of Samoa. He fired off on February 10, 1889 an indignant letter to *The Times* (VI, 2136), the first of a series to the British press which would bring the affairs of Samoa to public attention in Britain. Some of the subsequent comments in editorials were bemused and perplexed, but Samoa received, and would continue to receive, the sort of attention its geopolitical importance as seen from London would not have otherwise merited at that moment. The information contained in the letter was all second hand. R.L.S. later believed he had been duped, but the tone of the letter was wrathful, indicating a man worked up to a fine state of outrage over a wrong done to a friend. The main target of his ire was Germany, specifically the German community and consular officials. The Samoan archipelago was at the time the unwilling object of the expansionist aims of three imperial powers, Britain, Germany, and the U.S.A. In Britain, anti-German sentiment, expressed in bellicose pamphlets and works of fiction, was on the increase, and R.L.S. was not immune to that feeling.

In the opening lines, Stevenson conceded that knowledge of Samoan affairs was not likely to be widespread in Britain. News had been distributed "piecemeal", so he begged permission to recapitulate on the past before launching into his philippic on the present, but it is hard to imagine that many readers of *The Times* would have put the paper down with a clearer mind. He conceded that the islands had been largely opened up by German enterprise, and that the port of Apia was the creation of the Godeffroy Company of Hamburg, but omitted to explain anything about the company which went under that name. Authority in Apia, but not elsewhere in the islands, was exercised by an unofficial tripartite body made up of German, British, and American consular representatives. R.L.S. lamented the fact that while the Germans and Americans had each used their position to build harbours for trading purposes, Britain had failed to act. There is here some confusion of purpose, since he wished overtly to defend Samoa from foreign intrusion, yet simultaneously complains that Britain was not following other countries in claiming profitable pieces of land and sea. To complicate matters further, he expresses dismay that a request from the King of Samoa, the Malietoa, asking for his domain to be taken under the protection of the British Empire, had been rejected. In spite of this, R.L.S. continued, the prestige of Britain was untainted.

The tenor of the letter is anti-German, and his complaint is that the events he exposed had been brought about by a "sudden change in the attitude of Germany". The Malietoa had been made a prisoner by the Germans and was then in exile in the Marshall Islands, while on Samoa itself a "reign of terror has been brought about". Previous agreements were disregarded, the flags of Britain and America disrespected, and the Hawaiian embassy "dismissed with threats and insults", even as the German consul had arrogated to himself ultimate power and threatened punishments, including the death penalty, on those who stood in his way. "Who is Dr. Knappe," asked Stevenson, and readers in London might have posed the same question. In fact he was the German consul.

> Who is Dr Knappe, thus to make peace and war, deal in life and death, and close with a buffet the mouth of English consuls? By what process known to diplomacy has he risen from his one-sixth part of municipal authority to be the Bismarck of a Polynesian island? And what spell has been cast on the Cabinets of Washington and St. James's that Mr. Blacklock should have been left so long unsupported, and that Colonel de Coetlogon must bow his head under a public buffet? (VI, 2136)

Blacklock was the American acting consul, and de Coetlogon the British consul in Samoa whom R.L.S. would later meet. R.L.S. would treat Samoan politics in greater detail and with greater authority in later letters and in his *Footnote to History*, but, for all its inadequacies and misinformation, the letter was the first shot in what would be a long war conducted on behalf of the Samoans. Already for Stevenson they were not naïve, untutored, uncivilised, and uncultured bystanders who should be required to look on while superior white men, gifted with the advantages which flow from civilisation and Christianity, not to mention the Gatling gun, fought over their land and seized its resources. R.L.S. aligned himself with them, but, because of the image they had in the European mind, he was dubious about his ability to arouse the active sympathy and solidarity of British people. "I despair, in so short a space, to interest English readers in their wrongs; with the mass of people at home they will pass for some sort of cannibal islanders; with whom faith were superfluous, upon whom kindness might be partly thrown away."

He made it his purpose to demolish the image of "cannibal islanders", but had not yet completely clarified his own thinking. His basic protest against Western intrusion into Samoan affairs implied that the Germans were uniquely responsible. He appeared to accept the basically good intentions of the Americans and British, if only they could be aroused from their apathy. He railed against their supine response to German aggression, whether towards the Samoan people or towards their own citizens when threatened by agents of the German consul. He provided two instances, one involving an American journalist, who was accidentally caught up in hostilities but was then confined to the American consulate until he could make his escape on an American warship, and the other concerning an English artist who had been seen in the camp of the side opposed to German interests and who then suffered the indignity of being seized while actually on board a British vessel. "Is it what the English people understand by the sover-eignty of the seas?" he concluded with a rhetorical flourish. Over the following years, he would redirect his fire so that British people too became his target.

PART II

Samoa

CHAPTER 5

The Sailing Gods

In December 1889, the Rev. W.E. Clarke, who had been dispatched to Samoa by the London Missionary Society, was taking what we can presume to have been his customary stroll along the shoreline in Apia, when he saw a singular sight. He recorded the experience in sharp and vivid prose years later in a book of reminiscences, one of many such works produced after the death of R.L.S.:

Making my way along the "Beach" – the sandy track with its long straggling line of "stores" and drink saloons – I met a little group of three European strangers – two men and a woman. The latter wore a print gown, large gold crescent earrings, a Gilbert-Island hat of plaited straw, encircled by a wreath of small shells, a scarlet silk scarf round her neck, and a brilliant plaid shawl across her shoulders; her bare feet were encased in white canvas shoes, and across her back was strung a guitar. The younger of her two companions was dressed in a striped pyjama suit – the undress costume of most Europeans in these seas – a slouch straw hat of native make, dark blue sun-spectacles, and over his shoulders a banjo. The other man was dressed in a shabby suit of white flannels that had seen many better days, a white drill yachting cap with a prominent peak, a cigarette in his mouth, a photographic camera in his hand. Both the men were bare-footed. They had evidently just landed from the little schooner now lying placidly at anchor, and my first thought was that, probably, they were wandering players en route to New Zealand, compelled by their poverty to take the cheap conveyance of a trading vessel.[32]

There are alternative versions of his reception on Upolu. Harry J. Moors, who became a close friend and who later wrote a chatty account of R.L.S.' time there, said that he went on board the craft to introduce himself to the writer, having been informed of his arrival by Joe Strong, whose acquaintance he had made during the abortive Hawaiian expedition to Samoa.

The three curiously attired individuals were of course R.L.S., Fanny, and Lloyd Osbourne. Though not mentioned, Joe Strong must have been part of the company; perhaps he had remained on the *Equator*, or possibly Clarke excised all reference to him because of his later misdemeanours. Later that day, Clarke met the group in the Tivoli, one of the town's more reputable hostelries, where the conversation took a freakish turn. He must have divined that his new companion was a man of literary interests, for he turned the conversation onto a question which has intrigued theorists and critics since Aristotle: why do sad and tragic, or shocking and alarming, tales produce pleasure? These thoughts were occasioned for him by his reading of Edgar Allan Poe. Stevenson concurred on the enjoyment he too had

32 W.E. Clarke, *Reminiscences of Robert Louis Stevenson,* L.M.S. pamphlet, 1908, no page numbers.

found in reading Poe's tales, and this allowed Clarke to widen the talk and report how much he had admired a book entitled *Jekyll and Hyde*, coincidentally written by a namesake of the man who had just landed in Samoa. Had he, Clarke wondered, read the novel? "Not only have I read it, I wrote it and before that I dreamt it," came the reply. Misunderstandings having been resolved, Clarke and Stevenson took to each other, became friends, and met frequently thereafter. Clarke may be the model for the missionary, Tarleton, in "The Beach of Falesá".

The opening lines of that novella express the wonder of the trader Wiltshire on first drawing near an unnamed island.

> I saw the island when it was neither night nor morning. The moon was to the west, setting, but still broad and bright. To the east, and right amidships of the dawn, which was all pink, the daystar sparkled like a diamond. The land breeze blew in our faces, and smelt of wild lime and vanilla . . . the look of these woods and mountains, and the rare smell of them, renewed my blood. (Tusitala, XIII, 1)

Nothing can give us back the appearance or atmosphere of Apia, then and now the capital of Samoa, with its distinctive menace and cosmopolitan feel produced by the varied people who had settled there in the second half of the nineteenth century. The self-sufficient culture and the isolation in which Samoans had lived for centuries had been disrupted by the arrival of the white men who had imposed their rule on the islanders. Samoa had gained a reputation as the "hell hole of the Pacific", not because of the supposed violence of the native Samoans, but because of the assorted drifters and beachcombers who had made it their home and lived apart from the respectable Western residents. It was they who frequented the "drink saloons" the Rev. Clarke referred to, and who had introduced alcohol to the natives.

Apia was a conglomerate of eight or nine separate native villages, all within a few yards of each other, but contemporary photographs show it as one long street, the "Beach", flanked by palm trees.[33] In the opening section of *Footnote*, R.L.S. took visitors on an imaginary stroll through the town and offered a disenchanted view.[34] "Apia, the port and the mart, is the seat of the political sickness of Samoa," he wrote. On this walk, he pointed out churches, offices, and trading stores; the German, British, and American consulates; various missions; and the houses, some little more than lean-tos, but others grander structures where the Westerners lived. The Samoans themselves lived out of sight in the pell-mell of "the back yards of European establishments", for the reality was that the "handful of whites have everything; the natives walk in a foreign town" (Tusitala, XXI, 83). The town itself was quite without any hint of loveliness, but it looked out over an enclosed stretch of enticing and tranquil sea to an encircling boundary of coral reefs, whose beauty would be of no interest to the captains of the trading vessels or warships huddled uncomfortably together in its natural harbour. More than one writer compared the bay to the Gulf of Naples. The men-o'-war were there as an assertive gesture to defend their co-nationals in the prevailing climate

33 *The Cyclopedia of Samoa*, Sydney, McCarron, Stewart and Co., 1907, p. 4. Reprinted, Apia, 1984.
34 *A Footnote to History*, in Tusitala XXI, p. 81. Subsequent references are given within brackets in the text.

of instability and rivalry. Behind the town, the land sloped upwards through thick foliage and woodland, across fields and hillsides as green as those of Scotland. For a tropical island, Samoa was generously supplied with freshwater streams and rivers, "of about the bigness of our waters in the Lothians" (VI, 2194). The temperature was even all year, with the only valid meteorological division being between the wet and the dry season. The Christian churches, whose spires stood out against the skyline, and the commercial offices of the various nations were engaged in intense competition for dollars or souls. Samoa was already the arena for rivalries of differing types and intensity, between the Western nationalities, between Samoan factions, and between the Samoan community as a whole and incoming whites.

On their first meeting, Clarke was not unduly dismayed by the appearance of the threesome, nor would they have stood out. The "Beach", wrapped in embarrassed inverted commas by the clergyman, was not only a geographical area but the generic term used to denote the community and subculture of beachcombers, that disparate group of drifters, misfits, freaks, fugitives, and renegades who clustered in Samoa on the fringes of an already marginal society. If the Beach consisted of the most varied types, this trio was unusually eye-catching, singled out by dress and baggage. They seemed to have decided not to risk leaving their musical instruments on board for fear of theft, or of the tendency among Samoans, who had little concept of private property, to take casual possession of any goods which attracted their attention. Their nonchalant style of dress underlines how far they had come, mentally as well as sartorially, from Heriot Row in Edinburgh.

At this stage, R.L.S. had no plans to settle in Samoa, which was to be simply one more stop on the cruise. When they were frustratingly becalmed off Samoa waiting for the wind to change, he wrote to Sidney Colvin to set out his immediate plans. "I am minded to stay not very long in Samoa and confine my studies there (so far as anyone can forecast) to the history of the war. My book is now practically modelled . . . But it is not executed" (VI, 2191). His interest had been aroused by the information given him by royal circles in Hawaii, and after landing he explained his plans more fully to Charles Baxter.

> I must not leave here till I have finished my recollections on the war: a very interesting bit of history, the truth often very hard to come at, and the search (for me) much complicated by the German tongue from the use of which I have desisted (I suppose) these fifteen years. The last two days I have been mugging with a dictionary from five to six hours a day; besides this, I have to call upon, keep sweet and judiciously interview all sorts of persons, English, American, German and Samoan. It makes a hard life. (VI, 2194)

He was to find over the coming years just how hard it was to establish truth in Samoa. Only half-humorously he wrote, "Should Apia ever choose to have a coat of arms, I have a motto ready: 'Enter Rumour painted full of tongues.'" He was no dilettante historian given to turning out potboilers when his fictional inspiration failed him. In Samoa he clearly took seriously his need for research into what he referred to as "the Samoan Trouble". He told Baxter that while Fanny and Lloyd were "in a house in the bush with Ah Fu," their cook, he himself was living "in Apia for history's sake with Moors, an American trader".

The history and politics of Samoa in all their complexity absorbed a large part of his energies over the following years. *Footnote*, his most important work about the island, has the subtitle *Eight Years of Trouble in Samoa*. The first two chapters are both entitled "Elements of Discord", but with significantly different subtitles: "Native" for the first and "Foreign" for the second. Both elements required analysis and both contributed to the current turmoil. R.L.S. was insistent on the impact of the past on the present and saw troubles in any country, and certainly in Scotland, in a historical context. In his view, the problems in the Samoan archipelago in the late nineteenth century were in part a continuation of age-old internecine struggles, exacerbated and aggravated by the intrusion of the white man. At the time of his arrival, such white intruders probably numbered no more than two hundred, but they had taken over.

In Samoan tradition, the rim of the world was the point on the horizon where the sky and the sea met, so when the first white men arrived it was easy to believe that they had burst through from some mysterious "beyond", perhaps by raising the sky. They were known as the *papalagi* (pronounced *palanghi*), a word which can be translated as "sailing gods", but conveys the more sinister image of people crashing through the junction of sky and sea to disrupt harmony and peace. George Turner, a missionary and author of several instructive books on Samoan mores and creeds, records an equivocal prayer recited to the old gods: "Drive away from us the sailing gods, lest they come and cause disease and death."[35] Diseases such as smallpox, influenza, and measles were unpleasant for Europeans but deadly for Polynesians, who had no acquired immunity.

Although he did not flinch from outlining the occasional brutality of Samoan history, R.L.S. remained convinced of the admirable qualities of the people, even in times of war. "The religious sentiment of the people is indeed for peace at any price," he wrote. The recurrent warfare among Samoans puzzled even the most benevolently disposed observers. They had no need to go to war to secure command of land or sea trade routes or to take possessions of resources, as Europeans did, and yet, as R.L.S. wrote, "the land is full of war and rumours of war. Scarce a year goes by but what some province is in arms, or sits sulky and menacing, holding parliaments, disregarding the kings' proclamations and planting food in the bush, the first step of military preparations" (Tusitala, XXI, 75). What caused people, he wondered, to go to war when they inhabited such a temperate land where the necessities of life were readily available? Even when myths of the noble savage had been set aside, it still seemed that nature presented itself to the inhabitants of the islands in its most alluring guise, offering the temperate, benevolent, life-enhancing conditions needed to create the El Dorado of human yearnings. The coconut palm, for instance, grows wild and is known in Samoa as the "tree of life", since every part of it is pressed for human use in some form. Medicinal substances are extracted from its roots, the trunk and bark are used for the construction of habitations

35 George Turner, *Samoa,* London, Macmillan, 1884, p. ix.

and canoes, the leaves are employed as serving dishes and as thatch for roofing, while the coconut itself provides food and drink. Its inner fruit could also be used to provide an oil which men and women spread over their skin on ceremonial occasions, and when dried it was transformed into copra, the resource which attracted European businesses.

In his memoirs, William B. Churchward, British consul in Samoa from 1881 to 1885, agreed that the Samoan people may have been "the happiest, that is, before the arrival of the whites", although as a good Victorian Christian he also worried that they must seem from a foreign perspective "the laziest people on earth". Sloth is a deadly sin, and the availability of the good things of life ran counter to St Paul's injunction that those who do not work cannot, should not, eat. On Samoa, however, the necessities of life could be produced without intense labour, and without the labour that Puritanism considered indispensable. Churchward outlined the benevolence of nature:

> They have a fine climate, abundance of native food requiring no cultivation whatsoever, such as cocoa-nuts and bread fruit to be had simply for the gathering, the former not even asking for the exertion of cooking. The sea produces fish in abundance, and the reefs afford many other edible animals, and the capture of which is merely classed amongst their national sports, whilst the cultivation of the taro and yam require [*sic*] the minimum of labour ... their clothing is made either from leaves plucked in the bush, or from the bark of a paper [*sic*] mulberry-tree.[36]

36 William B. Churchward, *My Consulate in Samoa*, London, Richard Bentley and Son, 1887, p. 318.

Churchward was only one of several newcomers who wrote sympathetic scholarly works which are an invaluable repository of Samoan history and mythology. The Samoans themselves were happy to agree that they had been the special beneficiaries of providence. Since in the course of the nineteenth century Samoa became, as it remains, an overwhelmingly Christian country, some Samoans have been attracted by the notion that they might be the elusive lost tribe of Israel.[37] Another view expressed in the mythology of the islands is that the Samoans were specially created for the privilege of inhabiting islands which were so evidently favoured by God and nature. The missionary George Turner provided a scrupulously objective account of a mythology which is as rich as that of Greece and Rome, basing his findings on his "archaeological researches for upwards of forty years". In his account of the original creation myth, Salevao, the god of the rocks, married the earth and made her pregnant with a child who was named Moa. The god then produced water to wash the newborn, and declared it sacred, or *sa*, to Moa.[38]

Free of any notion of gods and heroes, the more sober historians, archaeologists, and palaeontologists suggest tentatively that the earliest settlers arrived around 1500 B.C. The Samoan archipelago is situated in a central position in the Pacific and consists of thirteen main islands, all part of the one cultural and political unit at the time of R.L.S.' arrival. The two main

37 According to the 2014 census, some 99 per cent of the population identifies itself as belonging to one of the many Christian denominations present on the islands.
38 George Turner, *An Hundred Years Ago and Long Before*, first edition 1884, reprinted London, Echo Library, 2006, p. 10.

islands are Upolu, on which Apia is sited, near where R.L.S. took up residence, and Savaii, which covers a greater land expanse but has a lower population. It is difficult to reconstruct early history, and Samoan historians bridle, justifiably, at the suggestion that there was no history before the arrival of the white man. But for our purposes it will be convenient to skip forward to 1722 when the arrival of the Dutch explorer Jacob Roggeveen marked the dawning of European interest in the South Pacific. He was followed in 1768 by the French Admiral Louis de Bougainville, who had problems with the navigation of the waters and who gave Samoa the name Navigator Islands, used by Stevenson in *The Hair Trunk*. Captain Lapérouse and his flotilla of French ships came in 1787 on a voyage of scientific exploration, but were responsible for a change of perspective. The captain initially formed a favourable opinion of life there, writing admiringly of the "elegant shapes of their houses", and noting that Samoans "spend their days in idleness or engaged in tasks that have no other purpose than their clothing and their luxury". However, when he sent a detachment ashore to bring fresh water on board, it provoked a fatal skirmish. Accounts of what actually occurred vary. Perhaps some of the French sailors molested some of the local women, perhaps the Samoans viewed the crew's arrival as a hostile act, but at some stage the French boats were surrounded by groups of armed men and a battle ensued, resulting in the death of eleven or twelve French sailors and perhaps as many as thirty Samoans. Lapérouse's account of the events contributed to establishing the reputation of the Samoans as a violent people, unlike others in the Pacific.

Western trade relations with other islands in the South

Pacific were tentatively established by the late 1790s, but Samoa's image meant that most ships avoided it until accounts by a Russian navigator, Otto von Kotzebue, who arrived in the years following the cessation of the Napoleonic wars, reversed the way Samoans were viewed. Although he repeated that they were ferocious, he admitted that his men had not been attacked. Other visitors announced more clearly that the Samoans did not deserve the reputation for treachery and violence they had acquired. It might have been better for them had their ill fame been reinforced and outsiders kept at bay, but from the early nineteenth century contact with Western nations became more frequent. France planted the tricolour elsewhere in the South Seas and the three nations who vied for primacy in Samoa were Germany, Britain, and the U.S.A. Companies from Europe and America discovered in the South Seas natural resources which could be utilised by developing industries at home.

By the 1820s, the Pacific was on the physical and mental maps of the Great Powers on both sides of the Atlantic, and Samoa and other islands became pawns in the imperial game. Western governments put their presence on an official footing by appointing consuls who sought to exercise influence beyond what is normally regarded as the realm of the diplomat. As the reach and ambitions of Victorian businessmen, statesmen, military officers, diplomats, and missionaries widened, the destiny of Samoa was increasingly determined by geopolitical imperatives, or by political, economic, and commercial decisions made in London, Berlin, and Washington. Other African or Asian states were ravaged more cruelly, but like them the Samoans found themselves subjected to the systematic or casual incursions of foreign companies. As Western trade with the region expanded, so did the desire for domination. Samoa was still in international law a sovereign state, a status officially confirmed as late as 1889 by the Treaty of Berlin, but the actual provisions of that treaty undermined the fiction, and de facto since at least 1860 its affairs were governed by the American, British, and German consuls on the spot. The local chieftains could not, however, be entirely ignored.

Most historical work on nineteenth-century imperial expansion has focused on the "scramble for Africa", but a similar scramble for the Pacific islands soon got under way. The French acquired the Society Islands and the Marquesas in 1842 and took over New Caledonia in 1853. Fiji became a British colony in 1874, while ten years later Germany annexed New Britain, New Ireland, and part of New Guinea. American firms and companies from individual German cities established in many islands a presence which became stronger and more visible as the countries turned outwards after the end of the Civil War in the U.S.A. and after German Unification.

The need for guaranteed access to ports on the trade routes heightened competition. The establishment of British colonies in Australia and New Zealand, including the penal settlement in New South Wales and its offshoot on Norfolk Island, meant that Britain was anxious to ensure the safety of passenger and trade routes across the Pacific. France, America, and some German cities vied with each other for access to ports, for the exploitation of prime materials, for the establishment of plantations, and for monopoly control of the commercial potential of the area. Both Germany and the U.S.A. signed treaties with the Samoan authorities to grant them the use and management of a harbour, the Americans in Pago Pago under an agreement signed in 1853, and the Germans in Apia. Britain made no such moves, something R.L.S. regretted in the previously mentioned letter to *The Times*. As a byproduct of this naval traffic, some white families began to set up home in Samoa and elsewhere in the Pacific.

The majority, but by no means the totality, of traders and businessmen in Samoa were Germans, while the missionaries were mainly British, with some French. The Americans, anxious to maintain a stable balance of power in the Pacific and to ensure safe passage for their commercial fleets, took a deep interest in Samoan affairs. There were some American companies but they did not employ Samoans in any numbers, and their missionaries, excepting the Mormons who first arrived in 1888, acted as subsidiaries to British ministers of the same faith. All the Christian denominations, the established Churches of England and Scotland, the non-conformist Methodist or Baptist churches, as well as the Catholic Church, dispatched missionaries.

In the main, the nineteenth-century colonial powers had a number of different, perhaps contradictory, aims, even if the contradiction was not obvious to them. By extending their area of domination, they primarily secured benefits for themselves, but were also persuaded that they were motivated by moral imperatives to spread what they called civilisation. Rarely did they entertain any doubt that their efforts – ruthless and exploitative though they appear in retrospect – would be of benefit, material as well as moral, to the subject people in Africa and Asia. In the words of the anthropologist Lucy Mair, "they also believed that there were certain absolute standards of good government which it was their duty to impose on peoples who had not worked these out for themselves."[39]

All doubt had been swept aside by a sense of inevitability, an unformulated, inchoate, but firm belief in the idea of progress, where "progress" meant movement towards the social and moral order prevailing in the West. A writer-anthropologist who signs himself E.B.T. (the initials would suggest Edward Burnett Tylor) contributed an introduction to Turner's book and puts the matter from a standard Western point of view. "For good or evil the old order had to change, till now the South Sea Islanders are people dressed in Manchester print and Bradford cloth, receiving European ideas from the pulpit, the school, and the newspaper, indoctrinated with white men's virtues and, alas!, often more deeply imbued with white men's vices."

The surface, sorrowful tone should not deflect attention from the deeper belief that the arrival of the white man was part of a preordained order, that it was the expression of a destiny which was as ineluctable as any in Greek tragedy. E.B.T.'s comments reflect articles of faith among Europeans and Americans. The dogma of progress required change in the global order, and the new order was introduced in a Western idiom, perhaps ordained by a Divinity who was equally Western. There was an invisible golden chain which led from primitive nakedness to Manchester print and Bradford cloth, to the donning of knickers or breeches, gingham blouses and the "Mother Hubbard" dresses in which women in Polynesia were clad by missionaries and their wives. R.L.S. responded to this spiritual and economic colonialism of the mind and body with dismay, sometimes with

39 Lucy Mair, *Primitive Government*, Harmondsworth, Penguin, 1962, p. 252.

outrage, but only sometimes. While he invariably championed the cause of the islanders, the expression of his sympathies was subject to shifts.

Whatever positions he adopted, they were sufficiently strongly articulated to draw the criticism of right-thinking contemporary commentators. Arthur Johnstone's may be taken as a typical voice:

> In the cause of the Polynesians he was no laggard, and, from the moment of his arrival until the end, he remained their steadfast champion. Wisely or unwisely, he was always up and active in their behalf, as his sympathies or his prejudices urged; and while one of his first traits was his love of fairness, yet there were times when neither his conclusions nor his actions were free from bias. This always came out sharply where native interests fell into competition, or came into conflict with the white man's vanguard. . . . he believed that under an ideal leadership and the fostering sympathy of the right kind of white men, the racial defects of the Polynesians could be reformed. His plan, if such it could be called, was noble and humane; but it was wholly theoretical and everywhere impractical: the forces already somewhat rudely at work in the Pacific entirely excluded a theory that demanded either their withdrawal or quiescence, thus permitting retrogression in a large part of the new empire civilisation was upbuilding in the western sea [sic].[40]

40 Arthur Johnstone, *Stevenson*, op. cit., p. 7.

R.L.S. was anything but convinced of the "racial defects" which allegedly made the Polynesians inferior to the white men. For Johnstone and other more significant thinkers, the construction of the new empire and new civilisation was a commercial boon justified as moral imperative. Social Darwinism provided one plank of the imperial ideology, and muscular Christianity another, but trade and the Western requirement for resources were the ultimate motor forces. The spreading of Western vices was, to be sure, regrettable, as both Turner and Johnstone agreed, but it was an unfortunate by-product of a generally benevolent and irresistible move towards betterment and progress. The essential, recurring cultural binary, repeated in varying forms in works of exploration, missionary endeavour, or domination in the Pacific, was steadfastly barbarism/civilisation.

For less sophisticated souls in high office, it was helpful to keep the subject people in their place by abasing them, as did the British High Commissioner for the Western Pacific, Sir John Thurston. He was the author of a report to the Foreign Office included in the Blue Book (1885–1889), written just before R.L.S.' first arrival in the islands. He demeaned the Samoans in bitter, slighting terms as "an excitable, voluble and credulous people, much given to lying and the circulation of false or extravagant rumours. In some degree they are thieves by instinct and in many cases they are so now by necessity."[41] Thurston would later attempt to have R.L.S. expelled from Samoa, supposedly for sedition, in reality for alerting public opinion at home to the consequences of imperial policy in Samoa. He was slapped down by the Colonial Office.

41 Quoted by C. Brunsdon Fletcher, *Stevenson's Germany*, New York, Charles Scribner's Sons, 1920, p. 150.

The ultimate basis of power is always force or the threat of force. However concealed in day-to-day dealings, the recourse to legal violence was viewed as necessary when the going got rough, as it frequently did in Samoa. In his satirical mock-epic, *The Modern Traveller*, Hilaire Belloc features two English adventurers named, with no great subtlety, Blood and Sin. Finding themselves in some troublesome, colonised land, Blood intones "we must be firm but kind", but when the result of this policy is mutiny, Blood outlines the necessary policy in a telling couplet: "Whatever happens we have got/ the Maxim gun, and they have not." To resolve disputes, the narrator goes on, "We shot and hanged a few and then/ the rest became devoted men."[42] R.L.S. had no objection in principle to hanging, but he fretted over the process which produced "devoted men" from a population which had once been free.

42 Hilaire Belloc, *The Modern Traveller,* London, Duckworth, 1972, pp. 41–2.

CHAPTER 6

Missionaries and Traders

The history of modern Samoa can be taken as dating from 1830, the year when the missionary John Williams landed at Sapapalii on the island of Savaii. It appears that there was not one European or American in permanent residence at the time. Williams came to love the islands and wrote a valuable book on his experiences.[43] Before deciding to follow a religious calling, he had been an ironmonger. His son John C. Williams, who had previously been invited to take on the role of American consul, was officially appointed British consul in Samoa in 1858. The two generations demonstrate the overlap between religion, trade, and authority which was a feature of colonialism.

It is difficult now to recapture and reconstruct the supremacist culture and mentality which underlay the Western imperialist project in the nineteenth century. One historian of empire suggests that there was an evolution in Britain's imperial methods and aims: "In the eighteenth century, the British Empire had been, at best, amoral . . . The Victorians had more elevated ambitions. They dreamt not just of ruling the world but of redeeming it." He goes on to underline the paradox that while eighteenth-century colonial administrators had often

43 John Williams, *A Narrative of Missionary Enterprises in the South Seas,* London, John Snow, 1837.

developed a respect bordering on love for the original cultures, the Victorian drive was to implement change by Christianising and civilising, where the latter term is synonymous with suppression of the pre-existing culture.[44] It was this objective, however disguised, which most offended R.L.S.

Missionary activity came to constitute a "problem" on which R.L.S. was ambivalent. He counted some individual missionaries as close and valued friends, but was dubious about missionary activity in the abstract. In a letter written in 1894 to Adelaide Boodle, a friend from Bournemouth days, he responds to her request for guidance on her wish to become a missionary. He stops short of attempting to dissuade her and agrees that "there is some good work to be done in the long run", and that it is "a useful and honourable career", but he has reservations: "Forget wholly and for ever all small pruderies and remember that *you cannot change ancestral feelings of right and wrong without what is practically soul-murder.* Remember that all you can do to is to civilise a man in the line of his own civilisation such as it is" (VIII, 2755).[45] The preservation of their "own civilisation" on Samoa was by that time R.L.S.' central goal.

Williams was a representative of the London Missionary Society, which had been founded in 1795 as a union of several Protestant denominations, and which was to be a major force in the affairs of Samoa and the rest of the Pacific. It moved with remarkable rapidity after foundation, and was able to dispatch its first missionaries the following year. It established a presence in Tonga, the Marquesas, and Tahiti, and from there spread

44 Niall Ferguson, *Empire: How Britain Made the Modern World*, London, Allen Lane, 2003, p. 116.
45 Emphasis in the original.

out. The missionaries encountered opposition in some islands, and several met violent deaths, in some cases falling victim to cannibalism, a custom never practised in Samoa. Williams and his party sailed on a vessel known as the *Messenger of Peace*, accompanied by eight Polynesians who had been previously converted to Christianity. Strangely, if Samoa had a strong and rich tradition of mythological belief, this was not associated with any cult which could be called religious. Unlike other Polynesian islands – Easter Island most notably – there are no temples or places of pilgrimage on the islands, no tradition of sacrifice or invocation of the gods. The enigmatic Pulemelei Pyramid stands in the centre of Savaii, as deserted and abandoned as the statue of Ozymandias, but all memory of what it represented has been lost beyond recall. It might even have been, according to one hypothesis, not a religious site at all but nothing more grand than a massive dovecote.

On the other hand, the forests of Samoa were filled with malign spirits, the *aitu*, which could if provoked even take up residence in the most diverse and unlikely places, in animals, human beings, or even objects. *Aitu* lingered on as devils into the Christian era, as endemic, as ubiquitous, and as powerful as before. Fanny's journal and R.L.S.' correspondence are filled with incidents recording the terror aroused in their staff by these spirits. Fanny noted that "there are devils everywhere in the bush, it is believed: creatures who take on the semblance of man and kill those with whom they converse; but our banana patch is exceptionally cursed with the presence of those demons."[46] Stevenson's story, "The Bottle Imp", was taken as

46 Fanny and Robert Louis Stevenson, *Our Samoan Adventure*, edited by Charles Neider, London, Weidenfeld and Nicolson, 1956, p. 57. The

a historical account and it was believed that the safe in Vailima was the prison of the *aitu* in the bottle.

If there was on Samoa no strong pre-existing religion, the ground had been prepared for Williams and Christianity in unexpected ways. Some idea of Christian teaching had been spread by castaways or beachcombers with such exotic names as "Dan the Convict" or "Jimmy the Sweet", who were hardly models of grace, but who were moved by a vocation to preach. Writing in 1874, the American A.B. Steinberger, who provides thumbnail sketches of these men, adds somewhat bathetically that "many interesting stories are related of these characters by the natives".[47] Dan, for instance, had hijacked a ship, killed the captain, and ordered the crew to make for Savaii, where he settled and made converts to the rudimentary form of Christianity he preached but failed to practise. Of greater moment is the fact that the swaggering disregard by the beach-combers for the power of the local *aitu*, and their apparent immunity from any consequences of their behaviour, under-mined traditional beliefs. In Samoa some beachcombers even went so far as to set up nominally Christian churches and convince hundreds of people to become followers of a cult of their devising, with considerable material and sexual advantage to themselves.

Another factor which facilitated the endeavours of the missionaries was a prophecy made by the war goddess, Nafanua,

book in its published form contains Fanny's diary, with passages by R.L.S. interspersed.
47 Albert Barnes Steinberger, *Report Upon Samoa*, presented to the U.S. Senate Foreign Affairs Committee, 1874, reprinted Memphis, General Books, 2006, p. 12.

that a new religion would be brought to Samoa by men of light skin from across the sea. The clinching, decisive proof of divine oversight in the eyes of many Samoans was the choice of Sapapalii as Williams' landing point, since this town was a seat of monarchy. The nature and basis of power in Samoa is complex, and will be discussed later, but if its chieftains did not necessarily exercise power over the whole archipelago, it was an absolute requirement that their family be rooted in, and that they themselves have a relationship with, some specific towns. Malie in Upolu was the principal town for the Malietoa, a title which can be loosely translated as king, and indeed the title derives from the town. Sapapalii in Savaii was another of the Malietoa's towns, and was at the time of Williams' arrival the residence of Vaiinu'upo, a claimant to the position of Malietoa. He was then engaged in a war of succession, from which he emerged as victor. He went on board Williams' vessel and accepted Williams' arrival as the fulfilment of the prophecy. He was converted and his example was followed very widely. By 1860, well before the arrival of R.L.S., Samoa was a Christian land.

Williams established the Congregationalist Church, which remains the strongest on the island, but he himself was butchered in 1839 on Eromanga island in Vanuatu (then the New Hebrides) by a tribe of cannibals. He is commemorated by a memorial column in Apia. Other missionaries arrived in his wake, and the L.M.S. and the Wesleyans agreed on a division of areas of influence. Further denominations, Baptists, Mormons, Seventh Day Adventists, Presbyterians, and various local breakaway sects, became part of the fabric of life. The fact that one village converted to one denomination often meant that its neighbours chose a different allegiance. Today, each village in Samoa has one or more imposing church, invariably in some style of European architecture, standing in the midst of the lower houses which are residences of the people. The Catholics came later, their progress having been impeded by a belief that they were the avant-garde of a French invasion, as well as by the anti-Catholic feeling still widespread among Protestant missionaries. A Catholic mission was finally established in Apia in 1845 with the purchase of land from John C. Williams, whose action drew the disapproval of the Protestant missions, but money talks. Samoa's leading contemporary historian, Malama Meleisea, says "it is an unfortunate fact that the religious rivalries of Europe came to be transferred to the Pacific islands in the nineteenth century. Disagreements over doctrine between Catholics and Protestants, and between Protestant sects, led to the establishment of competitive missions and missionary organisations."[48] The Marist brothers built on the land a grand cathedral modelled on Notre Dame in Paris. Catholics were known as "popeys", a term employed by Fanny. R.L.S. numbered the Bishop of Samoa among friends who were frequent guests at his table. Most of the servants in Vailima were Catholic.

If foreign missionaries introduced devout competition in religious matters, traders and consular officials were equally zealous in their own rivalries. Their first irritation was over the dispersal of power in Samoa. Samoan traditions of rule diverged sharply from Western expectations, and left for Westerners a vacuum where they thought the centre should be, with the result that incoming traders were unsure who to deal with and

48 Malama Meleisea, *Lagaga: A Short History of Western Samoa*, Apia, University of the South Pacific, 1987, pp. 53–4.

whether agreements they made would be recognised all over the islands. Once again, those with power based on force, in this case individual captains of ships, imposed their own idea of order. In 1838, a British captain with the unlikely name of Drinkwater Bethune drew up a code of commercial practice under which visiting vessels would make a payment for the use of the port of Apia and receive protection in return. This was the first official treaty between Samoa, represented by chiefs in the neighbourhood of Apia, and a foreign country. The following year, an American fleet consisting of six ships carrying botanists, reached a similar agreement, but these were ad hoc arrangements. The absence of one universally recognised authority was deemed intolerable, and the white men set out to impose their own idea of stability in the interests of commerce.

White power evolved gradually over the century. For the U.S.A., the Pacific was its own backyard. The United States Exploring Company set up shop in 1839 and appointed the Englishman John C. Williams as U.S. consul, a position never confirmed by Washington. In 1847 George Pritchard, also a former missionary, was appointed the first British consul, and two years later his son William opened the first store in Apia. In 1853 a U.S. commercial agent was appointed, and the following year the Foreign Residents Society was established in Apia.

Of greater importance was the setting up in 1855 of Godeffroy & Sohn, a Hamburg firm which traced its origins back to the expulsion of the Huguenots from France. This event marked the beginning of a process which would lead, after many mishaps and squabbles, to international rivalry and to German dominance in trade. On most occasions, the U.K. and the U.S.A. allied against the Germans, who were viewed with great suspicion, their alleged designs on the Australian and New Zealand colonies being another source of disquiet.[49] Within fifteen years, the Godeffroy company overreached itself in Europe, and finally went bankrupt in 1870, but its interests in Samoa were taken over by another German firm, which was fully operational when R.L.S. arrived in Samoa. The firm's name, but only its name, gave him some innocent fun: "[Godeffroy] is now run by a company rejoicing in the gargantuan name of the *Deutsche Handels und Plantagen Gesellschaft für Süd-See Inseln zu Hamburg.* This piece of literature is (in practice) shortened to D.H. and P.G., the Old Firm, the German Firm, the Firm and (among humourists [*sic*]) the Long Handle Firm" (Tusitala, XXI, 86).

The first manager of the company was August Unshelm, but his time in charge was brief since he drowned in 1860. His successor was a dynamic figure, Theodore Weber, who had arrived shortly before as consul for the city of Hamburg. Weber was only twenty-seven when he took over, but his skilful management ensured that the firm would play a decisive role in the history of nineteenth-century Samoa. After Bismarck's success in uniting Germany, Weber was made consul for the German Empire as a whole, but he retained his commercial position. He returned to Germany in 1887, before Stevenson's arrival, but his name was still revered, or feared, and crops up frequently in the writings of R.L.S. on Samoa. Weber was by no means the object of universal admiration, but the seemingly hostile description of his methods as "an admixture of Machiavelli and the caveman" cannot conceal a sense of respect, however

49 The subtitle of C. Brunsdon Fletcher, *Stevenson's Germany* (op. cit.) is *The Case Against Germany in the Pacific.*

reluctant.[50] Unscrupulous he undoubtedly was, but he also emerges as the very incarnation of those imaginative, inventive, plucky, strong-minded, bourgeois entrepreneurs whose skills in facing and overcoming obstacles to create societies and companies drew the admiration even of Karl Marx. R.L.S. gives a lively portrait of the man's character and achievements, making him resemble, in his aura and strength of character, the Master of Ballantrae:

> He was of an artful and remarkable character: in the smallest thing or the greatest without fear or scruple: equally able to affect, equally ready to adopt, the most engaging politeness or the most imperious airs of dominion. It was he who did most damage to rival traders; it was he who most harried the Samoans; and yet I never heard any one, white or native, who did not respect his memory. All felt that it was a gallant battle, and the man a great fighter; and now when he is dead, and the war seems to have gone against him, many can scarce remember, without a hint of regret, how much devotion and audacity have been spent in vain. His name still lives in the songs of Samoa ... one sings plaintively of how all things, land and food and property, pass progressively, as by a law of nature, into the hands of *Misi Ueba* (Mister Weber), and soon nothing will be left for Samoans. This is an epitaph the man would have enjoyed. (Tusitala, XXI, 89)

50   Robert Mackenzie Watson, *History of Samoa*, first edition, Wellington, Whitcombe and Tombs, 1918, p. 46.

Under his guidance, and with the expenditure of tireless energy, the company prospered. Large tracts of Samoa became private property from which outsiders were barred and on which, it was alleged, brutal punishment, including whipping, was meted out to recalcitrant workers. The company had its own prison in which offenders from all its plantations were detained.[51] Nothing was allowed to stand in Weber's way. The purchased land was planted with coconut palms, where the trees, once the tree of life for Samoans, became a money-making crop. Coconuts were the prime material for the production of the highly prized, and priced, copra. In 1861, Weber bought up thousands of acres of prime land, the exact figure still subject to dispute. The historian Mackenzie Watson puts the company's total landowning by 1888 at seventy-five thousand acres, but this figure is hard to confirm. In 1907, when Samoa was a German colony, the *Cyclopedia of Samoa*, in a rhapsodic entry on the company's benevolence and industry, put the figure at sixty thousand. It was all acquired through officially legal channels, but often in the most disreputable of circumstances, from chiefs whose right to sell was contested. By tradition and custom, which have the power of law in a primitive society, land was held in trust for future generations and was not the possession of any one man. The *matai* (chiefs) were, like clan chieftains in Scotland before the Clearances, leaders of an *aiga* (extended family), and their first duty was the protection of their families and the custody of the land for future generations. The years of feuding or of internecine warfare from around 1838 on had reduced many of these *aiga* to conditions

51 *The Cyclopedia of Samoa*, op. cit., p. 84.

of poverty and hunger, and some chiefs took advantage of the straitened situations to sell off communal land to European, mainly German, bidders. The land sales caused friction because Western-style ownership was an alien concept in Samoan society. Some of the *matai* were no doubt motivated by despair and by the need to find a means to provide for their charges in desperate conditions, but others were as grasping as had been the Scottish clan chiefs when similar opportunities presented themselves. R.L.S. became aware that some of the ceded lands had been abandoned only temporarily in the face of invading armies but seized by the Germans, while others had been sold off by the chieftains in blatant disregard of the rights of the rest of the family and the claims of future generations.[52]

In a letter to Charles Baxter, written shortly after his arrival, R.L.S. makes reference to Samoa's "gentle scene, gentle acclivities, tamer face of nature; and this much aided for the wanderer, by the great German plantations, with their countless avenues of palms". Closer familiarity with the island's history would lead him to use terms more bitter. The remnants of the plantations, long since abandoned, are still visible all over the island, immediately identifiable by the long, straight rows of coconut palms, perfectly spaced and perfectly lined, standing at a meticulously measured symmetrical distance one from the other, jarringly at odds with the unplanned surrounds where the trees bunch together or spread out anarchically, or poetically, over the landscape. "You shall walk for hours in the parks of palm-tree alleys, regular, like soldiers on parade" was how R.L.S. put it (Tusitala XXI, 86). Weber was no romantic and had no eye

52 Malama Meleisea, *Lagaga*, op. cit., p. 76.

for, or interest in, the traditional environment. Objections to the destruction of natural beauty would have produced from him the scoffing response given by like-minded men in *Bleak House*. For Weber, the coconut palm was a piece of productive machinery from which profit could be extracted, provided it was subjected to proper planning, exactly like a factory line. Ahead of time, he introduced botanical factory farming. As was the case with similar plantations and industries elsewhere in colonised Asia, the plantations did little for the prosperity of the Samoan people. The D.H. and P.G., with a presence in other Pacific islands and its head office in Hamburg, was in every sense an early multinational. Profits were repatriated, rather than invested in Samoa for the good of the islanders.

The cultivation process was labour intensive, and since Samoans annoyed the plantation owners with their relaxed attitude towards property and their perceived indolence, the Germans brought in workers from neighbouring places, such as the Solomon Islands. Men, and sometimes women and children, were often forcibly abducted or recruited by deceit to work on the estates in conditions of near slavery. The current colloquial term for the process by which they were brought to the plantations in Samoa, or Latin America, was "blackbird-ing", a word which may derive from the slang description of Polynesians as "blackbirds". There were several attempts to legislate against such people-trafficking. The Slave Trade in the Atlantic had been outlawed by the U.K. in 1807 and the U.S.A. in the year following, but the Pacific in the middle years of the century was still a lawless place. Both nations sent ships there to patrol the seas and intercept vessels involved in blackbirding, but their efforts were not particularly successful. In her journal,

Fanny tells of the wary welcome they received in the Ellice Islands until the people were confident of the peaceful intentions of the Stevenson party. According to the story recounted by her on the authority of a "half-caste", in 1886 two American vessels flying the Peruvian flag

> came to the island and distributed presents right and left to all who came to receive them. Naturally the people were delighted, and when it was proposed that as many as liked could go to Peru to be educated by these kind people, they flocked on board in crowds. The King, anxious that as many as possible of his people should participate in this good fortune, blew his horn, which is the royal summons . . . It is needless to add that these vessels were slavers, and the entrapped islanders were never seen again.[53]

The core activity of Weber's company was the production and export of copra, a business whose workings Stevenson had kept under close observation ever since his earliest days in the Pacific. The *Equator*, on which he sailed from Hawaii, was a working schooner trading in copra between the islands, while John Wiltshire, the protagonist of the novella "The Beach of Falesá", is a copra trader. The product itself is the dried meat of the coconut from which an oil can be extracted. Western firms moved in to export it to Europe in great quantities as its commercial uses became apparent. It could be used in the manufacture of soap, cosmetics, and medicines, and could even provide cattle fodder. The inventive Weber made his mark both

53 Fanny Stevenson, *Cruise of the "Janet Nichol"*, op. cit., p. 121.

on manufacturing techniques and trading methods. In the traditional, domestic method, the coconut was left to dry in the sun, the kernel was ground down, and oil extracted from it. Weber decided this system was inefficient, so, instead of producing oil locally, he devised a revolutionary system for drying the coconut and preserving it whereby the meat itself could be exported in its crude form for processing at plants in Europe or America.

In spite of himself, R.L.S. was impressed by the scale and ambition of the German workings, and saluted the restlessness of mind and the initiative behind the company's operations. He could not deny that on their estates "experiment is continually afoot" and reported that coffee and cacao were being introduced. But the ethical impulse and humanitarian imperative, always strong in R.L.S., led him to denounce the misuse by the company of its power on Samoa. "The true centre of trouble, the head of the boil of which Samoa languishes, is the German firm." He did not exculpate other countries or other individuals, but there is more than a tinge of anti-German xenophobia in Stevenson's railings even if he rushes to remind readers that "three nations were engaged in this infinitesimal affray, and not one emerges with credit" (Tusitala, XXI, 89).

It may be difficult to recall that in this age Samoa was officially independent, and its sovereignty legally recognised by the same Great Powers that interfered increasingly in its affairs. In 1873 the American government decided it needed more information on the state of things and President Ulysses S. Grant dispatched an envoy to the island in the person of Colonel Albert Barnes Steinberger, another of the enigmatic figures who strut across the stage and leave observers then and now bewildered and not a little dazzled. Steinberger manoeuvred himself into a position of prime minister in the government of the Malietoa, which still had an official existence and to which the consuls and traders were in principle subject. He combined whatever duties he had with carrying out the enquiry commissioned by the American president, and his report is a meticulously detailed source of information on all aspects of Samoan life and nature. It is all-encompassing, discussing social customs, native dances, music, food and drink, flora and fauna, illnesses – including venereal disease and elephantiasis – trade, the impact of the missions, language, politics, and the conflicts between rival Samoans. His controversial career is of interest not only because it displays the seriousness of American inter- est in Samoa, but also because it demonstrates in dramatic fashion the opportunities open to white men who, in a border- land where law was erratically enforced and ethical imperatives ignored, could create positions of prestige and power for themselves. Perhaps he was fortunate to have left Samoa before the arrival of R.L.S. He merits only one brief mention in *Footnote*, but had he remained longer on the island he might well have been the object of satirical sallies or indignant letters to London. Equally, he might have become the model for one of those devious, morally ambiguous characters who appear in Stevenson's South Seas fiction.

Steinberger was the last of the mavericks. Bureaucrats in far-off ministries and chancelleries, and their representatives in Apia, began to assume control, to Stevenson's dismay. As a product of the stern Calvinism of Scotland, he felt an obligation to intervene. His parents, especially Thomas, represented the reinvigorated Victorian code which inculcated a sense of public responsibility. It was a lonely impulse of duty, quite divorced from expediency or calculation, which made R.L.S. take the plight of Samoa to heart. He lamented to Sidney Colvin that he felt "wretched" as he witnessed in Samoa the "dance of folly and injustice and unconscious rapacity go forward from day to day" (VII, 2347). His sense of duty mystified his opponents in the colonial administration in the South Seas. His impulse was ethical and humanitarian, but its expression was often despairing.

> The huge majority of Samoans, like other God-fearing folk in other countries, are perfectly content with their own manners. And upon one condition, it is plain that they might enjoy themselves far beyond the average of man. Seated in islands very rich in food, the idleness of the many idle would scarcely matter . . . But that one condition – that they should be left alone – is now no longer possible. (Tusitala, XXI, 81)

This doleful consideration did not lead him to a state of inertia. There was work to be done.

CHAPTER 7

In the Margins of A Footnote to History

Italo Calvino, a great admirer of Stevenson's work, wrote that it was better to "go carefully with Rousseau's myths. Just because someone likes the South Seas, it is not necessarily the case that he has to be an unthinking escapist. If instead one goes there seriously, maybe one feels good there, and finds just what he wanted: that's what happened to Stevenson and Gauguin."[54]

They wanted, and found, different things. In 1892, on Tahiti, Gauguin produced "Manao Tupapau" (The Spirit of the Dead Keeping Watch). The dominant colours in the painting are reds and pinks, but in spite of the delicate shading of tone and the brightness of the floral decoration glimpsed under the couch in the centre of the canvas, the work is subdued and the atmosphere unsettling. There are two human figures: in the background a person of uncertain sex, dressed in a dark cape with a hood, standing with his or her elbow on the couch where a naked girl lies on her stomach, expressionless face turned towards a putative viewer, hands resting on a pillow on either side of her head. Recent critics have been troubled by the fact

54 Italo Calvino, *Letters 1941–1985*, selected and with an introduction by Michael Wood, New Jersey, Princeton University Press, 2013, p. 58.

that the model may have been the artist's "child bride", Teha'mana, who was only thirteen, but, at the time, the work was viewed as erotic and enigmatic, or as an enigma conveyed erotically. In some quarters it was taken as allegorical, with the spirit of a dying Tahiti mournfully observing the inert but still beguiling condition to which she has been reduced. Gauguin did not encourage any such reading. Around the time of its creation he wrote to his wife, Mette-Sophie, saying he was "preparing a book on Tahiti, which will facilitate the under-standing of my painting".[55] It is a limited and typically egoistic ambition. The book was not to help understand the Tahitians and their ways, but to use Tahiti as a tool for the appreciation of the painting of Paul Gauguin.

There is no doubt that R.L.S. felt good in the South Seas and even found much, perhaps all, he wanted, but he was no escapist from the demands made on his conscience. At the same time that Gauguin was executing his painting, on an island in the same sea, between November 1891 and May 1893, R.L.S. was at work on *Footnote*, a book which caused him much torment. He had been initially unsure about whether to tackle the subject. In late October 1891, he was able to announce to Colvin that his novel, *The Wrecker*, was completed and that he wished a rest from fiction. The idea of writing a historical work attracted him, but on which subject? The choice was between a historical work for children, a book on the Stevenson family, or one on Samoan affairs. The idea of a children's history book was enticing because he could use material he had prepared in giving tuition to his stepson Austin, but any such work had the

55 David Sweetman, *Paul Gauguin*, London, Hodder & Stoughton, 1995, p. 358.

disadvantage of bringing him into competition with Walter Scott, with all "his damned defects and his hopeless merit". A more conventional history book had its attractions, but "Scotch is the only history I know." He added the intriguing comment that Scottish history was of special interest to him at that moment "owing to two civilisations having been face to face throughout – or rather Roman civilisation face to face with an ancient barbaric life and government, down to yester-day, or 1750 anyway" (VII, 2357). He left unstated the parallel confrontation between two civilisations in Samoa.

In the event, he plumped for both family history, *Records of a Family of Engineers* (1896), and Samoan history, *Footnote*. His motivation could not have been more different from Gauguin's. His aim was to discuss Samoa, not himself. He told his publisher, Cassell, that it was a book whose worth he was unable to judge but which he felt obliged to write: "I thought it my business to bring certain facts clearly together and lay them before the public" (VII, 2397). Shortly before, he had told Colvin even more explicitly that he was motivated by a sense of duty: "God knows if the book will do any good – or harm; but I judge it right to try . . . I must not stand and slouch, but do my best as best as I can" (VII, 2368).

He was an admirer of Montaigne and given to quoting the phrase from the *Essays* that he undertook nothing "*sans joie*", so it was important to R.L.S. that, while seriously publicising the problems facing Samoa, he could still work in a spirit of "capital fun". Duty and pleasure combined, as so often in him, but these words are used in a letter dated January 1, 1892, so perhaps he was in a frolicsome mood after celebrating a trad-itional Scottish Hogmanay, as are many Scots at that season.

The following day, he wrote to his American publisher in more mellow tones. "Herewith go three more chapters of the wretched *History*; as you see I approach the climax. I expect the book to be some 70,000 words of which you now have 45 . . . 'tis a long piece of journalism, and full of difficulties here and there, of this kind and that, and will make me a power of friends to be sure." This last remark was plainly ironical, and he identified as the two men most likely to be offended the German consul Becker, "who will probably put up a window to me in the church where he was baptised", and Captain Hand of a Royal Navy ship then in port, from whom he expected "a testimonial" (VII, 2382).

Footnote is probably the least read of all R.L.S.' works, as he feared. It covers the period between 1883 and 1892, which is not exactly eight years, but it does cover the "trouble" unfolding before and after his arrival. Initially he wondered if some wry and humorous formula of words would make an appropriate title. "I recoil from serious names, they seem so much too pretentious for a pamphlet," he wrote (VII, 201). His first suggestion was *Tempest in a Teapot*, later rejected as too whimsical. The term *Footnote* avoided all hint of pomposity and kept a sense of historical proportion while avoiding condescension towards the people whose history he was discussing.

The literary critic David Daiches wrote that the two genres which predominate in Stevenson's work were the adventure story and the essay, but he did publish several works of history, and in 1881 actually applied for the post of Professor of History at the University of Edinburgh. This application has, as with other events in R.L.S.' life, prompted capricious and hypothetical reflections of the "what might have been" type, had the authorities in the university responded differently to his request.

He also contemplated writing a history of the Highlands, and of the Appin Murder, but never did. There is, however, a deep similarity between *Footnote* and his first work, *The Pentland Rising*, subtitled *A Page in History*, published at his father's expense in 1866, when the author was sixteen (Tusitala, XXVIII). The subject is the Covenanters' rebellion, their defeat at the Battle of Rullion Green and the execution of their leaders by Bluidy Tam Dalzell. The subtitle, motivation, and approach strongly and strangely resemble *Footnote*. Both works were thoroughly researched, both written with passionate commitment and partisanship, and both focused on episodes which were marginal in the grand sweep of world events, but which were, in the term he employed in *The Rising*, "tragedies" for the people involved. These tragedies had been "in large measure lost or obscured", buried in the wider processes involving the greater powers of the day and the illustrious figures who dominated their own times.

Injustices casually perpetrated in Samoa, like similar acts of oppression on native peoples in far-off lands, would have passed unobserved then, as they scarcely merit a mention in histories of Empire now, had they not aroused the indignation of this man, or had he chosen to live in seclusion in Vailima, unseeing and unhearing, as did so many of his contemporaries in Calcutta or Simla. *Footnote* can take its place alongside *Heart of Darkness* as a radical, deeply felt critique of foreign intrusion and dominance. His near-contemporary and fellow Scot, R.B. Cunninghame Graham, writing of the conduct of the Spaniards towards the native peoples in South America, showed the same measure of anger. He wrote that all men of every nationality are courageous in the main, but can be "pretty brutal when they are let loose among those they hold to be members of an inferior race, especially when far removed from public opinion and its salutary check."[56]

In *Footnote*, R.L.S. provides that salutary check. He rarely raises his voice, and prefers to indicate dissent by satire and mockery rather than vociferous outrage. The acts which appal him are mainly those of fellow white men, but he is free of facile romanticism and subjects the behaviour of Samoans to criticism too. The drift towards warfare by competing factions among Samoans left him baffled and distraught. Since his target audience is in the West, he explains as best he can native rites and customs, never ridiculing them but aware of their oddness to people in London or New York. When dealing with the disputes between (Malietoa) Laupepa and (Tupua) Tamasese, both pretenders to power in Samoa, both holders of titles and symbols supporting their rival claims, he has to expatiate on the symbolic value of mats in Samoan notions of rank. "I despair to make it thinkable to Europeans. Certain old mats are handed down, and set huge store by: they may be compared to coats of arms or heirlooms among ourselves; and to the horror of more than one half of Samoa, Tamasese, the head of the Tupua, began collecting Malietoa mats. It was felt that the cup was full and men began preparing for rebellion" (Tusitala, XXI, 130).

His aim was not to write a neutral chronicle, but to influence decisions and change the course of events. In the opening words, he pointed out that the story he had to tell "is still going on as I write it; the characters are alive and active; it is a piece of contemporary history in the most exact sense." He could

56 R.B. Cunninghame Graham, *Conquest of the River Plate*, London, Heinemann, 1924, p. ix.

not have written with greater commitment had the central characters been not Mata'afa, Tamasese, and Laupepa but Napoleon,
Wellington, and Blücher. The core questions addressed by R.L.S.
concern submission or resistance to the vexations of power.
Issues of autonomy of decision-making, freedom of action,
ownership of resources, and of the right of a people to live in
accordance with their own traditions are as vital to a community living in what are viewed as the margins as for those who
inhabit what is viewed as the centre.

With his knowledge of French, R.L.S. would have understood the term *engagé*, and while he might have been surprised
at the literary-political sense it acquired in the years following
World War II, in *Footnote* Stevenson was *engagé*. He would
have found a more receptive audience had two later notions –
micro-history and racism – been current at the time. The concept of micro-history was introduced only a century later by the
French *Annales* School, but if the term can be taken to indicate
a focused, detailed, intensive study of a supposedly minor
community, or of events or developments which are viewed as
of value in themselves and not as representative of wider move-
ments, R.L.S. was writing such a study *avant la lettre*. For an
island folk whose peace had been shattered and whose interests
had been disregarded, the colonial imperium and the civil wars
which tore the land apart over decades were as decisive for
their future as were the campaigns in Europe led by the French
Revolutionary and Napoleonic armies. The notion of "racism"
was unknown in Victorian times, but it was a reality in imperial
days and denoted an attitude R.L.S. abominated instinctively.

The overriding difficulty he faced in *Footnote* is that the
issues of sovereignty, power, and authority in Samoa have all

the complexity of the Schleswig-Holstein question in Europe. It may be stated that any work which treats this subject comprehensibly will be inaccurate, and any work which treats the subject accurately will be incomprehensible. The complexity of the question bewildered diplomatic envoys and frustrated down-to-earth businessmen, accustomed to Western societies ruled by democratic or monarchic governments. Samoa was none of these things, but nor was it anarchic. There were rules, there was authority, there were kin groups, there was a hierarchy involving the *aiga* (clan), the village, and sometimes even the district; and there was a recognition of some overall entity called Samoa which spread over an archipelago of several islands. Samoa was neither a despotism nor a democracy, although it had features of both. Authority could also be exercised by a spiritual power known as the *taboo*, a force which intrigued Freud, and which was expressed as a veto imposed on certain kinds of action, on frequenting certain individuals, or on trespassing in certain spaces. Samoa had an elaborate system of etiquette, which meant that there was even a parallel language for addressing men and women of higher rank. The *matai* (chieftains) were recognised as superior, but there was no system of automatic inheritance of power, and the *matai* could be removed.

Above all, there were several different "names", approximately equivalent to aristocratic titles in Europe, and a prerequisite to holding power. Samoa was bedevilled by disputes, which often exploded into open warfare, over who had rights to which title and which should be supreme. Europeans translated some of these, especially the purportedly supreme designation "Malietoa", as "king". R.L.S. explained the matter with all the clarity at his command:

The idea of a sovereign pervades the air. The name we have; the thing we are not so sure of. And the process of election to the chief power is a mystery . . . to be indubitable king, they say – some of them say, I find few in perfect harmony – a man should resume five of these names in his own person. But the case is purely hypothetical; local jealousy forbids its occurrence. (*Footnote*, 72)

If that was as much of an explanation of the process as was available, R.L.S. then recomplicated the subject by admitting that the man chosen as sovereign would not dispose of unopposed power. The island of Upolu enjoyed some form of higher position, but Apia became the capital only after the arrival of the Europeans, chosen because of its harbour. The promontory of Mulinu'u near Apia was a recognised seat of authority, and several of the native claimants of power migrated there, as did the German consular rulers. The same promontory was also where in the late twentieth century the parliament of the independent republic was built.

Power was neither totally centralised nor totally devolved. Historians point to an original ruler, a female named Salamasina, whose power extended to all Samoa. She was probably a historical figure even if her biography indicates that she had connections with the goddess Nafanua. After her, power was divided and it was established that there were four supremely important names or titles, called *papa*, a word which means "bedrock" and denotes the fundamental, or more properly foundational, titles. The titles themselves were linked, like European dukedoms, to particular places – for instance the town of Malie with the Malietoa – but there was no royal palace or special residence there. The most prestigious title was Malietoa, but another was Tupua. Someone who managed to collect all four could be called Tafa'ifa, and would exercise universal sovereignty. This situation rarely occurred, and power was generally dispersed between three, four, or five separate names and domains. R.L.S. explained:

> Let us conceive that there are five separate kingships in Samoa, although not necessarily five separate kings; and that though one man by holding the five royal names, might become king *in all parts* of Samoa, there is no such matter as a kingship of all Samoa. He who holds one royal name would be, upon this view, as much a royal person as he who would chance to hold the other four; he would have less territory and fewer subjects, but the like independence and an equal royalty. (Tusitala, XXI, 73)

Not all agree on the figure of five. In some works, Malietoa is written as a proper name rather than a rank, but strictly speaking, to avoid confusion the correct form would be, for instance, Malietoa Laupepa, the man who in R.L.S.' day occupied the post, but was opposed by Mata'afa Iosefo, whom R.L.S. supported. Mata'afa was also a title, or name, but Malietoa was viewed, though not universally, as supreme.

This wrangling over power could have been avoided if different decisions had been made earlier. Vaiinu'upo was converted to Christianity by John Williams in 1830, and came to hold all the titles. His predecessor was Tamafaiga, a despot who was assassinated because of his priapic conduct towards other men's wives. Vaiinu'upo gained two titles after killing him and was granted the other two. This meant that there was undoubtedly in history a period of unity, but it ended with Vaiinu'upo's death in 1841, when he left a will sharing out the various titles once again. The reasons why he divided power are much disputed, but it is possible that his decision was dictated by his conversion to Christianity, which led him to believe that an era of universal peace would be ushered in. He may also have entertained the apocalyptic belief that the end of the world was nigh, or may simply not have been convinced that he had the right to dispose of honours which belonged to individual areas and villages, and were not really his to give away. Consultations were inconclusive and war broke out the following year. The succeeding decades, perhaps until the second Treaty of Berlin in 1899, can be regarded either as a time of warfare interrupted by periods of truce, sometimes lengthy, or as a time of successive but separate wars. The historian Mackenzie Watson confidently identifies seven.

In 1851 Moli, the elder son of Vaiinu'upo, succeeded him as Malietoa, and was recognised as such by the growing European community. This was a heavily disguised blessing, for during his reign the power and insolence of the British, Germans, and Americans increased, and he was held personally responsible for transgressions by his supposed subjects. On several occasions, he was unceremoniously kidnapped and taken on board the warship of whatever nation happened to be berthed in Apia, and kept captive until compelled to cede to demands for "reparations". He died in 1860, and his tomb, which stands in solitary grandeur in the public green in Malie, is still a place of pilgrimage for Samoans.

New figures appeared on the scene. Moli's son Laupepa, to whom R.L.S. devotes a chapter of *Footnote*, claimed the succession in 1868, but was immediately contested by his half-uncle, Talavou. Stevenson's judgement of Laupepa's personality was harsh and dismissive, but Laupepa lived in a time of strife and crisis. He was an unfortunate figure who would have been treated with respect in a more peaceful age, but he lacked the strength of character or the gifts of diplomacy to deal with the intricacies of politics in the imperial age. Often, his right to govern was recognised by the Great Powers only in the breach. R.L.S. regarded him as simply not up to the demands of his elevated position in the complex conditions he inherited. William B. Churchward, missionary and British consul in the 1880s, left a more sympathetic portrait of a well-intentioned, slightly dull man:

> I found him to be an intellectual and pleasant-looking man of about forty years of age, with a very agreeable and subdued manner of address, without the slightest suggestion of the savage about him . . . he was educated at the London Mission College at Malua, and wished to lead a peaceful life; but his high birth would not permit it. By force of circumstance he was obliged to put himself at the head of his family.[57]

The decentralisation of political power in the islands, often paradoxically expressed by the struggles to accumulate "names", meant that Samoa was singularly unprepared to understand, much less resist, the Western entrepreneurs and traders who saw opportunities hidden to the Samoans. Irrespective of what he might become later, Laupepa initially showed some energy

57 William B. Churchward, *My Consulate in Samoa*, op. cit., p. 63.

and foresight, and proposed setting up what Europeans were happy to regard as a parliament which would have its seat in Apia, perhaps as part of a confederal structure, but this proposal did not meet the approval of his rival, Talavou.

From mid century on, every policy of any substance was determined by the resident consuls of the three Great Powers, and these policies were, especially in the case of Germany, dictated by the interests of the companies engaged in exploiting the resources of the islands. The only writ which ran was that of the three consuls acting in unison, although they were in fact rarely able to agree. In 1878, the British High Commissioner for the Western Pacific visited Apia, and during his stay met with the other consuls to establish a local council in Apia, which meant that the wealth-producing centre was for administrative and fiscal purposes separated from the rest of the country. A magistrate was appointed, and his first edicts forbade the sale of alcohol and firearms to native Samoans, provisions which were impossible to enforce granted the number of quasi-pirate ships on the seas willing to sell to anyone. R.L.S. wryly noted that where there is war, there will be traders.

D.H. & P.G. became increasingly exercised over questions of theft from its property, or at least of acts which were such in Western eyes but which were judged differently by Samoans, who had no concept of private possession. In 1883, the Germans imposed a convention whereby Samoans convicted of offences against German citizens or their property were to be detained in the private jail of the German firm. A de facto colonial situation existed, to some extent all over the islands, but explicitly so in Upolu. At the same time, sporadic fighting among Samoans continued around the islands throughout the 1870s and '80s, with armed parties from the Western warships occasionally intervening to stop hostilities or to support one side. The disputes between Laupepa and Talavou ended with the death of the latter in 1880, but hopes for peace were dashed when Mata'afa Iosefo and Tamasese advanced their claims.

These were the "native and domestic" forces whose disagreements, pacts, and shifting alliances created the situation R.L.S. found when he arrived in Samoa. Acting in concert, the consuls proclaimed Laupepa as Malietoa in 1880, but he quickly incurred the wrath of his Samoan opponents. Mata'afa Iosefo seemed to R.L.S. the figure most equipped to rule and to oppose the pretensions of the colonial forces, but other tribes and factions chose Tamasese as ruler. The Americans moved to resolve this situation, and convened on the U.S.S. *Lackawanna* in 1881 a conference, from which it emerged that Laupepa would be recognised as King, Tamasese Vice-King, and Mata'afa Premier. It was good Yankee common sense – which floundered almost immediately.

In 1885, a group of prominent Samoan chiefs requested Britain to make Samoa part of the British Empire. The petition was declined, but the move irritated the German authorities. Theodor Weber, a man disinclined to brook any nonsense from people who upset him, expelled Laupepa from his own house on the Mulinu'u peninsula and moved into it himself. He also raised the German flag there, leading to a declaration by the British and American consuls of the "international status" of the islands. These were futile, even childish, gestures, and it is interesting that the infantile behaviour came from the Europeans. However, the situation was deteriorating rapidly, as was noted in the lucid and disenchanted accounts given by

R.L.S. Traders deplored the instability which made the daily conduct of commercial activity awkward, and the German authorities moved to protect the property of D.H. & P.G. Relations between Britain and Germany in the Pacific, as in Europe, were taut, and several books published at the time were stridently anti-German in tone, warning the Anglo-Saxons to wake up to the imperial threat of a newly united Germany.

The 1880s were a decade of war and rumours of war, the raising of banners, the gathering of forces, the issuing of indignant notes, the summoning of assemblies and councils on Samoa, and of exchanges of diplomatic missives between Washington, London, and Berlin. The three governments sent warships or flotillas to anchor in Apia and reinforce their power locally. At times these vessels undertook punitive expeditions which went beyond sabre rattling, and both British and German warships were guilty of firing cannonades at villages, especially on the Mulinu'u peninsula, where important Samoans had their residence.

The year 1887 was particularly lively and incident-packed, and in many respects a turning point. No-one in Samoa knew it, but that year, in far-off Edinburgh, Thomas Stevenson died, leaving R.L.S. financially independent and giving him the means, ultimately, to travel in the Pacific. That was also the year of the Hawaiian expedition to Samoa to explore the possibility of a Polynesian federation, a mission which upset the Germans mightily. A new manager of the D.H. & P.G., Eugen Brandeis, described by R.L.S. as being "of a romantic and adventurous character", arrived. Officially, he was a manager in the employ of the German firm, but had a military background, and he took charge of training troops on a company estate at Leulumoega.

Samoa was now firmly established as an International Problem, requiring international action at the highest level, and that same year a conference was called in Washington to determine its future, the first of a series of such meetings. It adjourned in July without agreement. The participation of Samoans was deemed unnecessary at discussions on the future of their lands, and their consent was viewed as inessential. In August, five German warships anchored in the harbour of Apia. In Stevenson's words, "by 24 August, Germany had practically seized Samoa" (Tusitala, XXI, 106). Laupepa was officially Malietoa, but the claims of Tamasese had not been renounced, although he was little more than a German puppet. Skirmishes were occurring from time to time, arms were circulating, but their consignment to Laupepa, even though he was the official ruler, was forbidden by the Germans. Lewis Becke, a British-Australian adventurer and scoundrel who turned his hand to literature in later life, recounts a tale of derring-do by which he had guns and ammunition officially given over to the German consul, to be held in secure conditions in the town jail. The consul was duped, for he was the only man who was unaware that they would be spirited away by Laupepa's men once darkness fell. Becke was no philanthropist, and was well paid for his troubles.[58]

War broke out, and it was the desire to collect first-hand materials for his "big book" which brought R.L.S. to Samoa in the first place. The representatives of the Great Powers were in a state of hostile frenzy, and the spark to this particular powder keg was supplied by a ludicrous incident when a German nose

---

58 Lewis Becke, *My South Sea Log*, Glasgow, Collins, n.d., pp. 49–54.

was broken during a boozy reception in a hotel to celebrate the Kaiser's birthday. The insult to imperial dignity was hardly the fault of the unfortunate Laupepa, but the German consul demanded reparation of $1,200. R.L.S. devoted a chapter in *Footnote*, entitled "The Sorrows of Laupepa", to the subsequent events. A German contingent landed, government buildings were stormed, German flags raised, and Laupepa was called on to surrender. He did so, but only after issuing a dignified proclamation, "To all Samoa: On account of my great love for my country, I deliver up my body to the German government. That government may do as they wish to me. The reason of this is, because I do not desire that the blood of Samoa shall be spilt for me again. But I do not know what is my offence which has caused their anger to me and to my country." R.L.S. added that "the sheep departed with the halo of a saint" (Tusitala, XXI, 112). He could have used more magnanimous words.

The immediate problem for Laupepa's captors was to decide what to do with him. Since they had no idea, the unfortunate man spent the next two years shuffled about in German hands, mainly on board ship. R.L.S. got to know him well after his return, and from an interview with him he reconstructed the story of his years in captivity. Laupepa had been shipped to the German colony of Cameroon, to Germany itself, and then to a point within sight of England although probably without landing there, before being taken back to the South Seas and disembarked on the Marshall Islands, where he remained in exile. Meantime, in Samoa, both Tamasese and Mata'afa claimed the title of Malietoa. Mata'afa supported his claim by pointing out that Laupepa had appointed him his successor, but Tamasese had the backing of the Germans. With Brandeis as his premier, he was given the title, but hardly the power. He was regarded as a German quisling.

Both the U.S.A. and the U.K. sent ships from their own navy to take up position in the crowded harbour of Apia. The squabbling, marching, and denouncing continued. A German warship, the *Adler*, bombarded the island of Manono, famed for the skill of its armed canoe sailors. The fortunes of war turned in December 1888, when the Germans landed a large force to deal with Mata'afa once and for all. The armies met at Falagii, but to the astonishment of Samoa, the Germans were defeated with the loss of fourteen men. A monument still stands on Mulinu'u to the fallen German soldiers, but none to the Samoans. R.L.S. regretted that "brave men should stand to be so exposed upon so poor a quarrel or lives cast away upon an enterprise so hopeless," but he adds that "all Samoa drew a breath of wonder and delight. The invincible had fallen; the men of the vaunted war-ships had been met in the field by the braves of Mata'afa: a superstition was no more" (Tusitala, XXI, 183 and 185).

A wider war now seemed inevitable, one which would engulf the islands, setting the various Samoan factions against each other and possibly against the colonising forces, or at least against the Germans. The British, Americans, and Germans made due preparations. Ministers at the highest levels in foreign capitals glowered at each other and dispatched flotillas of fighting ships. In March 1889, the harbour at Apia was host to one British, three American, and three German warships, not to mention six merchant ships and an uncounted number of smaller craft, fishing boats, and trading vessels. The harbour is a circular stretch of water, with two claws stretching out from the twin headlands. This inland sea is bounded by a barrier reef which acts as a breakwater but has a natural fault in the coral allowing ingress and egress. With a more poetic turn of phrase, R.L.S. describes the harbour as a "bottle with a funnel mouth". On land, the sandless beach snakes round from the finger of land which is the promontory of Mulinu'u towards the more fertile fields where the Germans had their estates, with the houses and stores of Apia in between. The captains on the naval ships had, in that time of poor communication with the ministries in the capitals, total autonomy of action. The Great Powers looked on warily, and it is no exaggeration to say that Apia had at that moment all the potential to unleash global savagery equal to that caused later by a solitary act in the city of Sarajevo.

This potential man-made catastrophe was averted by a natural calamity, the hurricane of March 15–16, 1889. Although it left the town largely untouched, it whipped up the seas around the island, causing devastation among the ships in the harbour and death for the men on board. R.L.S. had not yet arrived when the disaster occurred, so for the chapter entitled simply "The Hurricane" he was unable to provide an eyewitness report, but he reconstructed the events using the tools of a journalist, interviewing, listening, taking notes, making calculations, hazarding conjectures, drawing conclusions, and producing with this material one of the most extended pieces of vivid, descriptive, and harrowing prose which even he ever wrote. Taken as an account of a disaster, it can stand comparison with Daniel Defoe's accounts of the Great Fire of London, and taken as a chronicle of human impotence at sea, it is the equal of anything written by Joseph Conrad. R.L.S. said several times during the voyage in the Pacific that he loved the sea, unlike

Fanny who hated it, but coming from a family of lighthouse engineers he was also desperately aware of the savage menace of storms. He had travelled around the coasts of Scotland to visit lighthouses designed by his father and grandfather to stand sentinel in remote spots and provide protection from the sea, and had listened to tales of the disasters which had befallen communities whose lives had been wrecked by storms, squalls, or the collision of ships on rocks. The event in Apia was a tragedy arising, he said, from "man's animosities", in the sense that the ships were crowded in the harbour because of the human inability to conduct their affairs rationally and peacefully. R.L.S.' depiction, which balances compassion for the sailors and awe at the natural forces unleashed, merits the Sophoclean definition of tragedy as the struggle of "man at odds with more than man".

Stevenson's chronicle is beyond compare, so only the briefest summary of the disaster will be offered here. The hurricane was a work of nature, its impact heightened by human ineptitude and indecision and by the atmosphere of suspicion of the commanders of the three flotillas towards each other. The barometers the day before indicated the imminence of the hurricane and thus the advisability of raising anchor and moving to safety in the open sea, but no captain or admiral was prepared to make the first move for fear of what their adversaries might do in their absence. They each vacillated and hesitated, until the storm blew at an intensity which left them trapped. Only the H.M.S. *Calliope* was able to manoeuvre in the teeth of the winds and waves through the opening in the reef and avoid battering the other ships. She returned to the harbour two days later to find she was "the only survivor of the thirteen sail", and the only one which had suffered no loss of life. For the rest, in Stevenson's words, "the morning of the 17th displayed a scene of devastation rarely equalled: the *Adler* (German) high and dry, the *Olga* (German) and the *Nipsic* (American) beached, the *Trenton* partly piled on the *Vandalia* (both American), and herself sunk to the gundeck; no sail afloat; and the beach piled high with the *débris* of ships and the wreck of mountain forests." He attempts no overall estimate of the number of human casualties, although they were high. The Samoans responded with bravery and altruism, setting aside their enmity towards the Germans in their efforts to bring ashore as many men as could be saved. The Germans and the Americans found it more difficult to set aside their animosities, and, when ashore, the lawless crews of the two nations had to be berthed some way apart. Martial law was imposed to prevent the sale of alcohol for fear of the consequences.

R.L.S.' conclusions are cast in quasi-biblical terms. The cyclone gave rise, almost inevitably, to metaphysical musings on man and nature, on human folly and cosmic futility, and on the puniness of human strength when faced with the power of natural forces. For the warring foreign nations, "both paused aghast: both had time to recognise that not the whole Samoan Archipelago was worth the loss in men and costly ships already suffered." On a geopolitical scale, he believed that the events of those days marked an "epoch in world history". The main effects were two: it led to the summoning of the Congress of Berlin to resolve the Samoan issue, while reflection in Washington on their inadequate sea power led to the foundation of "the modern navy of the States", with consequences he leaves it to later generations to evaluate.

The disaster jolted the ministries and chancelleries on both continents, leading to the unremarkable conclusion that this situation could not continue. The German foreign minister, Count Herbert von Bismarck, son of the Iron Chancellor, invited Britain and America to send envoys to Berlin to resolve what was now termed the Samoan Crisis. The conclusions of the 1889 Treaty of Berlin were a perfect application of the logic of nineteenth-century imperialism. The main provision was the maintenance of the rights and privileges which the three Powers had acquired by their separate treaties. It was also decided to establish a Supreme Court, whose main purpose was to adjudicate on land disputes, these being the main worry of the companies. A neutral figure was judged to be necessary, so the King of Norway was invited to make the appointment of a Chief Justice. He chose the Swede Conrad Cedercrantz, whom Stevenson liked as a person but abominated as a judge. The municipal council for Apia, where most of the whites lived, was re-established, and it was decreed that it would consist of six elected representatives: three Samoans, and three members chosen by the consuls, but with a president appointed by the Powers. In the event he was the Austrian aristocrat, Baron Senff von Pilsach, another object of Stevenson's scorn. The property and commercial dealings of resident foreign companies were protected. The intentions of the signatories of the treaty towards the Samoans were professedly benevolent and their "free right" to elect their chief or king according to their traditions was recognised in the final charter; but since Laupepa, who had been dethroned in 1881, was restored by a decree issued in Berlin, this right was nugatory. Great play was made of the fact that the final document was signed not only by the Powers but also by the Samoan government, but since that government was a puppet administration, its assent was worthless.

The provisions of the treaty were unworkable and self-contradictory, and led to increased conflict, particularly over who was to be regarded as "king", or Malietoa. R.L.S. ridiculed the treaty, which was perhaps the most ludicrous international document ever signed. Officially, Samoa was still independent, but this status was a sham. Authority was divided between the three Great Powers in the way it had been among Samoan *aigas*, and each tried to manipulate the Samoan authority figures. The settlement was inherently unstable, and the whole question had to be revisited only a decade later by a second Treaty of Berlin of 1899, when Samoa, whose consent was still not sought, was partitioned, with the western islands becoming a German colony and the eastern coming under American jurisdiction. Partition is still in force, and if the western islands now form the Republic of Samoa, the eastern islands remain American territory to this day.

CHAPTER 8

Civil and Uncivil Life in Samoa

During his time in Samoa, R.L.S. put to himself from various angles the one question – What does it feel like to be a Samoan, particularly in an age when the islands are peopled by foreigners who have assumed power, pursue their own interests, and regard the native inhabitants as inferior? He did not deal systematically with civil society in *Footnote*, but was never less than an intrigued onlooker into their practices and customs. To access their beliefs, one approach was to seek out parallels between their history and Scotland's, but that could only take him so far. His experiences in Samoa gave him the shock of the new, and the abiding impression is that, however receptive and open-minded he was, he frequently found it easier to love the Samoans than to understand them.

Far from being some objective, dry-as-dust observer, he allowed himself to be overwhelmed by the *joie de vivre* of Samoan life. "They are easy, merry, and pleasure loving," he wrote, adding that they were

> . . . the gayest, though by far from either the most capable or the most beautiful of Polynesians. Fine dress is a passion, and makes a Samoan festival a thing of beauty. Song is almost ceaseless. The boatman sings at the oar,

the family at evening worship, the girls at night in the guest house, sometimes the workman at his toil. No occasion is too small for poets and musicians . . . song goes hand in hand with the dance, and both shade into the drama . . . Games are popular . . . fishing, the daily bath, flirtation . . . conversation, which is largely political . . . and the delights of public oratory; fill in the long hours. (Tusitala, XXI, 76)

How very unlike the home life of Victorian Scotland! This description, which makes Samoa resemble Eden before the Fall, was not the complete representation of their life. R.L.S. never shied away from criticism or exposure of the darker side of life. In foreign eyes there were three aspects of Samoan existence which were regarded as blemishes, or even vices, all objects of appalled disapproval. These were given blunt names – idleness, lewdness, and communism. R.L.S. examined all three, but was also perplexed and unsettled by a fourth – the frequent recourse to warfare.

He regarded with amusement the readiness to indulge in feasting, and was entranced by the people's joy in *dolce far niente*, but even here he was assailed by the worry that indulgence in easeful living could go too far and descend into mere indolence. In the Victorian perspective, sloth aroused in observers a complex response of visceral envy and moral disapproval. William B. Churchward was ambivalent about the fact that intense labour was never required of Samoans, since the climate was favourable, coconut and breadfruit required little or no cultivation, while the sea teemed with fish. Even the clothing could be made "from leaves plucked in the bush, or from the back of a paper mulberry-tree," and in any case this is essentially female work, leaving "the men plenty of time to sleep". Cutting timber for house-building and the building work itself was men's responsibility, but the thatching of the roofs and the plaiting of the blinds on the sides was left to the women.[59] It was a style of living which could hardly be further removed from the rhythms of life in industrialised Britain, and could hardly fail to irk a man of R.L.S.' background.

He too showed concern over the lack of the industrious spirit among Samoans. Having grown up in a family of engineers for whom the Protestant work ethic was a prime moral impulse, he was accustomed to other values. One of the prayers he composed for evening worship with family and staff in the grand hall in Vailima requested divine assistance to "let cheerfulness combine with industry". In a talk R.L.S. gave to church students in the college of Malua, he told them to encourage more industrious habits among their fellow citizens, not just because it was a good thing in itself but also because their leisurely ways left them defenceless against nations of greater determination and a more energetic turn of mind. Habits which had been acceptable when Samoa was left to itself, isolated and undisturbed, became dangerous when ships carrying men set on exploiting Samoa's resources anchored in the port.

At the same time, he could not understand the objections of other white men to longstanding traditions which were merely unfamiliar. The basic wear was the *lavalava*, which R.L.S. translated, not inaccurately, as kilt. Other parts of the body were tattooed so heavily and intricately as to appear at first sight like

59 William B. Churchward, *My Consulate in Samoa,* op. cit., p. 318.

clothing. Protestant missionaries set their face against tattoo-
ing, but the Catholic priests had no objection. The practice
had a central place in Samoan culture and was an indispensable
rite of passage between boyhood and manhood. The process
took several days, during which the young man went into the
bush with friends who comforted and encouraged him in what
was an extremely painful ordeal.

The problems which really tormented Europeans concerned
dress, or undress, especially as regards women. Female tattoos
were sparser than men's, and in Nuka-hiva, Maggie wrote
approvingly that the women "tattoo their legs all over . . . they
had the appearance of wearing open-work silk stockings."
However the *lavalava* and tattoo still left much of the female
body uncovered, to the dismay of missionaries. There is a
photograph of Fanny seated by the fireside in Vailima, while a
Samoan maid sits on the floor, bare-breasted. The young woman
is sufficiently beguiling to ensure that the image has been
reproduced on many occasions, but captions from the early
editions offer the reassuring information that had it been a
more official occasion, the young lady would have been more
modestly attired.

In the same photo, Fanny was attired in the long "Mother
Hubbard" to which she had been introduced in San Francisco
by Belle. The odd name indicates a long, loose, shapeless dress
which hung straight from the shoulders with no tuck at the
waist, and which did not require a corset. Its design ensured that
it was cool in a warm climate, but while it may have been liberat-
ing for Fanny and Maggie, it was hardly so for Samoan women.
Missionaries saw it as a duty to compel women in the South
Seas to dress with due modesty, and viewed the Mother

Hubbard as the ideal solution. On their part, Samoan women were mystified by the reluctance of white women to attire themselves in the way they did. The Rev. John Williams provided an account of the dilemma:

> They [Samoan women] are continually wishing the teachers and wives to lay aside their garments and *faasamoa*, do as the Samoan ladies do, gird a shaggy mat round their loins as low down as they can, tuck up a corner in order to expose the whole front and side of the left thigh, anoint themselves beautifully with scented oil, tinge themselves with turmeric, put a string of blue beads around their neck and then *faariaria*, walk about to show themselves. You will have all the *manaia*, the handsome young men of the town, loving you then . . . They could not be induced to cover their persons, of which they were exceedingly proud, especially their breasts which are generally very large.

Williams faced embarrassment of his own over fashions of attire on various occasions, but dealt manfully with the problem. He was invited to dine with a king and his five wives who, when called to table, formed a circle around him and dropped their *lavalavas* to the ground. "This is the first time I have had the honour of eating with *five naked* queens," he said.[60] The nature of the dancing which followed the meal was too much for him, and indeed for all writers on Polynesian ways, including R.L.S., who all make dumbfounded, overtly

60 Richard M. Moyle (editor), *The Samoan Journals of John Williams, 1830 and 1832*, Canberra, Australian National University, 1984, pp. 117 and 144 (emphasis in the original).

disapproving, reference to the lasciviousness of the display. At an earlier stop in the Marquesas, Maggie opined thoughtfully that the explicitness of the dance persuaded her of the wisdom of the Indian custom of early marriage. There are no descriptions of such dancing, since the writers self-censored events they found unacceptably lewd.

R.L.S. too held back from giving such a description in his essay on his visit to the island of Tutuila, part of the Samoan archipelago. He met an eight-year-old boy with precocious ability as an artist, but his actual designs left R.L.S. "without words to tell of what he drew and said". It was not so much the indecency of his drawing that left him speechless, for R.L.S. admitted boys of his age "in God-fearing England" could have done the like, but the fact that he had "no shame or fear before his elders". His exhibition preceded a dance led by the *taupou*, the young woman selected as leader in public festivities. She was, R.L.S. underlines, a church member and a married woman, which should have made her ineligible for the role, but she was young and pretty, and in her bearing "a nobler woman it is scarce possible to conceive, being shaped like a divinity upon huge lines." When the dance began, the space filled with onlookers, including children who joined in the singing and kept time to the dance, but for R.L.S., "when the indecent part came it was singular to look about on all these shaven heads of children wagging and all their little hands clapping the tattoo to such an unsuitable and ugly business." Stevenson struggled to make sense of it, and to distance himself from facile judgements, but could not succeed. "No sense of shame in this race is the word of the superficial, but the point of the indecent dance is to trifle with the sense of shame: and that very particularity that the child actor should be a maid further discloses the corrupt element which has created and so much loves this diversion"(Tusitala, XXI, 49–50).

Such dissolution in leisure activities was bad enough, but economic questions regarding ownership and property rights were of a higher order of seriousness. R.L.S. was initially baffled and later horrified at the social practice which he, like other observers, termed "communism". It was a source of deep irritation to the colonial traders to discover that objects needed on plantations could be casually taken for their own use by employees or passers-by who could not see any wrongdoing in their actions. The merchants pressed for legal measures against what they viewed as sanctioned theft. R.L.S. yet again made his own efforts to understand the Samoan point of view, and proposed that their "communism" was a consequence of retarded development: "in most points they are contemporaries of our painted ancestors who drove their chariots on the wrong side of the Roman wall. We have passed the feudal system; they are not yet clear of the patriarchal. We are in the thick of an age of finance; they are in a period of communism. And this makes them hard to understand" (Tusitala, XXI, 7).

Hard to understand from a Western perspective, and more so when this facet of Samoan culture is concealed, or even travestied, under a term, communism, unknown to Samoans and fearsome to the Western bourgeoisie. The lines quoted appear in the first paragraph of the first chapter of *Footnote*, and so serve to set the scene for further discussion. Communism is here presented as a symptom of backwardness, and as such is the basis of a plea made by R.L.S. for understanding and tolerance. There is, he says, a profound historical-cultural clash between settlers who make use of the most advanced Victorian innovations, "mails and telegraphs and iron war-ships", and "the native actors (whose) ideas and manners date back before the Roman Empire". It could be noted that once again the antithetical point is not London or Berlin but ancient Rome, the eternal legislator of Western civilisation, culture, and standards.

It is with a full awareness of this disparity that he issues his challenge to his contemporaries back home. How are the Samoans to be regarded and treated by Western civilisation, which has the advantages of more developed technology and of a more advanced system of ideas and beliefs? What rights do the Samoans have? What respect does their civilisation deserve? R.L.S. denounced the misuse of mechanical expertise and advanced ideas for exploitative purposes, but he never questioned, as later writers would do, the fact of Western advancement, not only in technology but in outlook. He is watching the race between the hare and the tortoise and knows it was only in Aesop that the tortoise won. If it was impossible to make the hare slow down, he wanted it to look back sympathetically, while he urged the tortoise to speed up.

At the same time, he issues an implicit, later explicit, challenge to the Samoans. How do they view themselves? Does their self-image require to be modified in view of prevailing circumstances in the modern, globalised world? He did not hesitate to criticise what he felt to be backward or damaging to their interests, and "communism" was a prime example. The question may seem to later generations like a singularly crass example of cross-cultural misunderstanding. In the Samoan perspective, property was not the possession of a single person. It was a community resource, to be borrowed, taken, and used, perhaps temporarily, but not necessarily so. To men reared on Western political economy, this outlook was unacceptable, indeed unimaginable. Some commentators were more positive than R.L.S. In his valuable report to the American government on life in Samoa, Albert B. Steinberger stated that "communism is a creed among them", although he unexpectedly added that this had "never been an effectual bar to the accumulation of property".[61] In the introduction to George Turner's book, the writer reveals his own hesitations and mental confusion. He opens with seeming enthusiasm for Samoan altruism, but, as a good Victorian bourgeois, is compelled to come down on the other side:

> Even in the field of practical politics we may learn something from the Samoans. Political theorists among us have been speculating about communism, but the Samoans, like other peoples near the same level of culture, have been living it. Among them there might be, and perhaps in some measure still may be seen, practical common property, where each may freely borrow another's boat or tools or clothes, and live as long as he pleases freely in the house of a clansman. Here is a people who hear with wonder that among the white men the poor can be hungry and houseless. From this sorrow and disgrace the Samoans are free; but they pay dearly for this good in a social state where work is unprofitable and progress is checked because the earnings of the industrious pass into the common property of worker and idlers.[62]

61 Albert B. Steinberger, *Report Upon Samoa*, op. cit., p. 50.
62 George Turner, *An Hundred Years Ago*, op. cit., p. xii.

R.L.S. was sceptical about the advantages Turner identified, and the latter too concluded that communism supports idleness, a dangerous vice. Incomprehension was deepened by the fact that the very word "communism" carried sinister connotations for the European bourgeoisie in the nineteenth century, especially after the spectacle of the Paris Commune. Communism was, in the opening words of the *Communist Manifesto*, the spectre that haunted Europe. It created apprehension in the propertied classes, a fear given a moral dimension by preachers and religious thinkers from Pius IX to Dostoevsky. The version of communism dominant in Samoa was neither of the scientific type Marx advocated nor the ethical model advanced by William Morris and familiar to Stevenson. It was what Marx dubbed "primitive communism", that is, an instinctive tribal sense of community expressed in economic association. The single person or family was more than a monadic unit, and was of their very nature part of a greater whole. In Samoa, such community living did not end with death. Corpses were not, are not, buried in separate fields away from the places where the living have their being, but alongside the house where they had lived.

Society in Samoa, based on blood groups, was of its nature communitarian, not individualist. There was no concept of country or state, but the alternative was not the rule of mere force, nor was it lawless anarchy. Goods, including tools, domestic items, and agricultural or fishing implements were not exactly held in common, but they were in the public sphere, so that even when crafted by a specific family for their own use, they had to be ceded when requested. To demonstrate the limitations of Samoan communism, Churchward tells of a fishing trip where the work of the fishermen was exploited by "an awful old pirate of a Samoan called Johnny Adams". He took no part in the fishing itself, but waited slothfully until the first boats were making for shore with their catch. He pulled up alongside them and took the best fish from their canoes, a practice "justified by Samoan custom".[63]

R.L.S. returned to the question on several occasions, underlining what he saw as communism's negative consequences on economic activity and on the prospect of future progress:

> . . . property stands bound in the midst of chartered marauders. What property exists is vested in the family, not the individual; and of the loose communism in which a family dwells, the dictionary may yet again help us to some idea. I find a string of verbs with the following sense: to give away without consulting other members of the family; to take from relatives without permission; to have plantations robbed by relatives . . . the language had recently to borrow from Tahitian a word for debt. (Tusitala, XXI, 77–8)

Samoan *homo* was scarcely an economic animal at all, and that was another aspect of international misunderstanding. The Samoan style of life was for R.L.S. unsustainable in contemporary conditions, and required reform and modernisation. "The particular drawback of the Polynesian system is to depress and stagger industry. To work more is there only to be pillaged; to save is impossible" (Tusitala, XXI, 79). He told of a pastor who had saved up to purchase a boat, only to have to cede possession to relatives who had no claim on the vessel other than the fact

---

63 William B. Churchward, *My Consulate in Samoa*, op. cit., p. 318.

that they liked it and had always wanted a boat. To make matters worse, the boat was not completely paid for and the pastor had to sell off some of his own property to redeem his debt for an item he could no longer use. The final twist in the tale was that some months later the new owners smashed some part of the boat, and returned it to the original owner with the demand that he repair it. R.L.S. gave another example, of a serving girl in their employ at Vailima to whom they gave some fine clothes for her to wear when serving at table, as well as some warm garments to protect her from the cold she experienced in the fields. After her first visit home to her family, she returned clad in an old tablecloth, her whole wardrobe having been claimed by her relatives. R.L.S. was baffled and disturbed.

This encounter with an alien political viewpoint was a challenge to R.L.S., who never subscribed systematically to any ideology. He was by instinct a conservative and a Conservative, but no conventional designation does justice to a political outlook such as his, defined by moral opposition to actions and situations he found incompatible with his sense of justice. It is difficult to make R.L.S.' outlook even over imperialism wholly consistent or coherent. During the Boer War, he can be regarded as being among that small band of dissidents who were not merely anti-war but defiantly pro-Boer. "This is a damned, dirty foul job of ours in the Transvaal," he wrote to Henley in March 1881. He went on, "the cause seems to sit heavy on the scientific soldiery. God forgive this rotten old England" (III, 776). In an article, "Protest on Behalf of Boer Independence", he says, "it is no affair of ours if the Boers are capable of self-government or not" (Tusitala, XXVIII, 217). This notion is in general harmony with his view of the Samoan situation, and on that basis he could be taken as an anti-imperialist, but in 1885 his references to General Gordon during the siege in Khartoum, and his scathing comments on Gladstone's refusal to send reinforcements to Sudan, would put him on the other side. He regarded Gordon as a hero and dismissed Gladstone with withering words. He did not side with the native peoples in Khartoum. When discussing Gordon and Gladstone, he was an observer on the sidelines, but in Samoa he was a witness, as well as a public intellectual with influence and responsibilities. His defence of Samoa was conscience-based but his public awareness was deeper. The supremacy of personal conscience, expressed as a belief in decency, was central to the standards he advocated. Decency was an inchoate hope that the values of private life should be extended to public conduct.

However, decency is in short supply. Human beings demonstrate a genius for devising justifications for conflict. Men of such widely differing viewpoints as Dante and Marx were drawn to the belief that if the lust for possessions could be eliminated, an era of peace would follow. A familiarity with Samoan history would have disabused them. There were disputes between villages or branches of families over rights to land, and, when such quarrels had been resolved, other concerns which might seem trifles to outsiders provided reasons for warriors to blacken their faces, oil their bodies, issue terrifying whoops, and form war parties. It was no matter that the *casus belli* might seem to outsiders a trifling issue over ceremonial procedures, privileges carrying no material advantage, or the entitlement to use titles. Mackenzie Watson seems in his classic history to have put warfare on the island down to the exuberance of youthful males: "Warfare has ever been a

Robert Louis Stevenson with Chief Tui Malealiifano.

Kava was traditionally prepared by young women, who chewed the root of the pepper plant, spat it into the dish (*tanoa*) and mixed it with water before serving. The drink was an indispensable preliminary to all ceremonial meetings.

Mata'afa Iosefo stands in front of a hut. R.L.S. considered him the Samoan leader most equipped to rule and to oppose the depredations of the colonial forces.

The young woman is *taupou*, or village maiden, usually the daughter of the chief, with a jester at her side.

The Vailima house in its original form, before the extension was added. Mount Vaea in the background.

A feast on the verandah at Vailima. On the house side Fanny, Robert Louis Stevenson, Lloyd Osbourne, Austin Strong and Margaret Stevenson sit among Samoan guests.

Family and household staff gather on the verandah at Vailima. All the people are named below in ink. In the back row are Joe Strong with a parrot on his shoulder; Margaret Stevenson; Lloyd Osbourne; Robert Louis Stevenson; Fanny Stevenson; Simi the butler. In front of them sit Elena the laundress; Taloja the cook; Belle and Austin Strong; Lafaele the cattleman and Tomasi the assistant cook. At the front are Savea the plantation boy; Arrick the pantryman and another boy.

Stevenson sits at a dining table in the middle of the Great Hall at Vailima. Also visible is the staircase that so delighted the Samoan staff.

FORTUNATE FOLKS.—No. 4: ROBERT LOUIS THE FIRST OF SAMOA.

" The latest Australian papers leave no room for doubt that by general consent Mr. Stevenson is now regarded as the first citizen of Samoa, and if events should develop in the direction of the choice of a ruler by the popular will, the author of 'Treasure Island' would assuredly head the poll."

An engraving in an Australian newspaper depicting Stevenson as a popularly appointed ruler of Samoa.

Chief Tamasese and other Samoan war-chiefs gather around a *kava* bowl. Tamasese enjoyed the German patronage during his struggle with rival chief Mata'afa Iosefo.

Stevenson sitting up in bed having a conversation with Joe Strong, his stepson-in-law, who is perched on the end of his bed. Lloyd Osbourne sits on the floor in a stripy jacket.

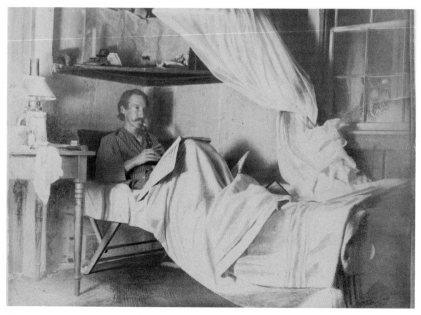

Stevenson sitting up in bed, playing a flageolet.

Mourners, mostly Samoan, gathered round Stevenson's grave on top of Vaea Mountain. Belle Strong and Lloyd and Austin Osbourne stand to the right.

A view of Stevenson's tomb showing its inscription in English.

recognised occupation of the younger men. The causes were often trivial, the methods a curious admixture of childish regard for ceremony and of craft, of careless generosity and of cruelty."[64] The great satirists, such as Voltaire and Swift, have looked with outrage or wry humour on the tendency to endow trivia with great significance, and it is all the easier for commentators to take a lofty view when the land is no bigger than Lilliput.

R.L.S. struggled to make comprehensible the "trivial" matters which during his lifetime led to war in Samoa. "The Battle of Matautu", a chapter in *Footnote*, is a bulletin on a conflict in 1888 before his arrival. It is masterly in its attention to detail and in its explanation of the military campaign. The war pitched two rivals to the throne against each other, Tamasese with German support and Brandeis as his supposed prime minister, and Mata'afa, the eternal rebel and champion of independent Samoans. The opposing sides were backed up by European warships, which never came into conflict with each other but which fired on villages. No-one emerged as victor, and armed conflict was replaced by a distrustful truce. R.L.S. would witness the next outbreak from closer at hand.

He could not complacently take the view that war was an act of youthful exuberance. He examined the conduct of the foreign forces but also the civil society which produced it. John Williams had been baffled before him: "A mere trifle is sufficient to create war among them, such as the running away of a purchased wife and her falling into the hands of another."[65]

64 Robert Mackenzie Watson, *History of Samoa*, op. cit., pp. 22–3.
65 Richard M. Moyle (editor), *The Samoan Journals of John Williams*, op. cit., p. 84.

It is a curious judgement in itself. Sexual jealousy and male possessiveness have unleashed hostilities ever since the Trojan War. Both Williams and Watson were ambiguous about the actual ferocity with which armed engagements were conducted. Watson said "clubs and spears of various patterns and slings were the usual weapons", while Williams suggested that there was an agreed etiquette which limited the destruction caused by military actions. "It does not appear that their wars are bloody. Five or six killed would be reckoned a great number. Their weapons appeared far from formidable. Little clubs three or four feet long and little spears about six feet long, some parts not thicker than a finger were the principal weapons we saw."

Williams' statements on the number of dead in warfare are belied by other sources. Defeated enemies were decapitated where they fell, the bloody torso abandoned, and the severed heads brought back in triumph to be piled up as proof of bravery before the chieftain of the victorious side. R.L.S. tells of a Wesleyan missionary who visited a camp to remonstrate against this barbarity, but had no answer when the chief asked him to explain the difference between their acts and that of David after slaying Goliath. The missionaries preached compliance with the gospel of peace, but with no greater success than clergymen in Europe and America. R.L.S. was incapable of insouciance about war and its prosecution, but enjoyed no greater success than the clergymen.

CHAPTER 9

A Deeply Interesting Time

A letter sent in late 1892 to Henry James is remarkable for the clash between its high-spirited levity of tone and the gravity of the impending crisis he was describing.

> It is likely by my judgment that this epoch of gaiety in Samoa will soon cease: and the fierce white light of history will beat no more on yours sincerely and his fellows here on the beach. We ask ourselves whether the reason will more rejoice over the end of a disgraceful business, or the unregenerate man more sorrow over the stoppage of the fun. For, say what you please, it has been a deeply interesting time. You don't know what news is, nor what politics, nor what the life of man, till you see it on so small a scale and with your own liberty on the board for stake ... And anxious friends beg me to stay at home and study human nature in Brompton drawing-rooms. *Farceurs!* (VII, 2502)

There was a Mozartian puckishness to Stevenson's character which could lead him to behave in the most unpredictable, and sometimes most inappropriate, ways. He was heedless of the Chinese curse, if he had ever heard it, about living in interesting times, and the times following his arrival had certainly been interesting. In surveying the scene in Samoa, with the ever-present threat of warfare, he was prey to two oddly clashing moods. The first, to which he gives voice in the letter, is a mood of bubbling, personal excitement at living in an "epoch of gaiety" or being in the front line during some light adventure. He gives the impression of looking on in the spirit of a schoolboy reading *Treasure Island*. The second frame of mind is more sober and more in keeping with the gravity of unfolding events, and gives evidence of a man in the grips of pain and anxiety over national and international conduct as the settlement imposed by the Treaty of Berlin aggravated an already deleterious situation for the Samoans. The second mood was dominant during his years of residence, as the crisis in Samoa deepened and worsened.

Samoa had never been officially annexed by any Western power, and its successive requests to be made part of the British Empire, to be given the status of an American protectorate, or annexed by New Zealand had all been rejected. In spite of that, it was an occupied country under de facto colonial rule, but with the twist that it was not ruled from any one capital. Britain and Germany eyed each other with deep distrust, while the Americans muscled in to guard their own interests. The dominant economic power in Apia was Germany, and personal relations between inhabitants in Samoa reflected the tensions between the British and German empires worldwide. Warships from the three countries were still frequent visitors to Apia, in principle to ensure that peace was maintained but mainly to protect the interests of their nationals.

R.L.S. was participant as much as witness, and attempted to halt the process of deterioration by using his influence both in person on the island and by making representations to London. He had been informed, however inadequately, about the Samoan situation while in Hawaii, and wrote the first of a series of letters to *The Times* while there, so he felt himself entitled to plunge head first on arrival into the political affairs of Samoa. By January 1890, he was writing to Malietoa Laupepa, to advise him, on the basis of experiences in the Marquesas, to take action to stop the growing consumption of opium in Samoa (VI, 2200). The issue had nothing to do with R.L.S. or his circle, but it established him either as a self-opinionated interferer or a crusading do-gooder, depending on the stance of the observer. He was serving notice that he had no intention of staying on the sidelines.

In the same month, he delivered an address to students of the Malua Theological College, established in 1844 by the London Missionary Society to educate native clergymen for churches in the Pacific. The speech is passionate, infused with keen concern for the future of Samoa, and must have made a powerful impact when delivered, although Harry Moors writes that R.L.S. was not an effective public speaker. It is striking that R.L.S. speaks from inside a Christian framework, as though he were a staunch believer and not the sceptic whose disbelief had so outraged his father. His knowledge of the Bible stood him in good stead and provided him with a ready stock of references familiar to his congregation. Part religious sermon and part political manifesto, the core of the talk is a restatement of the Protestant work ethic applied to the Samoan situation. In his interpretation, an important distinction between Judaism and Christianity was that the former required only observance of the law, while the moral code of the latter demanded work, endeavour, and labour. R.L.S. admired Samuel Smiles' famous work *Self-Help*, and numbered its author among his correspondents. Smiles' robust teaching, and the "muscular Christianity" of such eminent Victorians as Thomas Arnold, could clearly be heard behind R.L.S.' warning to his listeners that the principal danger facing them was "the loss of your land to foreigners", and that the remedy lay in hard work.

> I will say to you plainly, if you cannot get your own people to be a little more industrious, to make a little more money, and to save a little money, you may make all the good laws on earth, still your land will be sold – when your land is sold, your people will die – and in these lands where your children might have lived for a hundred centuries, another race will sit and they will ask themselves, "What were the Samoans?" . . . It is for the king to make laws; it is for you to make the people industrious and saving.[66]

The alternative was not merely subjugation by outsiders but the disappearance of the people and of their way of life. He would repeat the exhortation several times.

At the same time, he was fully aware of the realities of power. Samoa was divided between its own factions, while the three consuls retained their influence. Colonel Henry Watts Russell Coetlogon had served in the British army in various parts of the Empire before being appointed British representative in Samoa, but he is remembered for his officious bumbling in shooing away R.L.S. when he turned up to pay his respects on the

66 R.L. Stevenson, "An Address to Samoan Students, Malua", in *Sophia Scarlet and Other Pacific Writings*, edited by Robert Hoskins, Auckland, A.U.T. Media, 2008, pp. 71 and 81.

consul's day off. He was succeeded by Sir Thomas Berry Cusack-Smith, who reacted with exasperation to this novelist for having the gall to interfere in matters which were none of his business. R.L.S. formed better relations initially with Harold Sewall, the American consul, though, by the time he was recalled in late 1892, Sewall informed R.L.S. sarcastically that if blood were spilt, observers might attribute it to a failure by the consuls, whereas in fact the guilt would be his. Relations with Dr Stuebel, the German consul, referred to locally as "the great and wise Stuebel", were always prickly.[67]

In the spring of 1890, after an unhelpful delay, the men appointed to head the institutions established by the Treaty of Berlin took up office. They were well-intentioned and no doubt public-spirited members of the minor European aristocracy who would have lived and worked unremarkably in the shadows of history had not R.L.S. brought them into the light, rarely to their advantage. He dismissed the two main officials as "nincompoops" or asses, and complained about their languid ways, their lack of intelligence, and the large salaries they received. The Swede Baron Conrad Cedercrantz was appointed Chief Justice, while the Austrian Baron Senff von Pilsach arrived to take office as President of the Council of Apia, an autonomous body separate from the government of Samoa, de facto run by the white men in their own interests and given responsibility for all administrative and fiscal matters in the capital. Officially, the Council was answerable to a conclave of the three consuls. The third authority established by Treaty was

67 This description is found in *Cyclopedia of Samoa*, op. cit., an invaluable source of information for the characters and events discussed in this chapter.

the Land Court, which had one commissioner from each of the Powers as well as a Natives' Advocate, all under the general authority of Cedercrantz. Its central remit was to adjudicate in the many disputes over ownership of land between Samoans and incomers, and it was the one unquestionably fair and respected institution. The American Commissioner, Henry C. Ide, became a firm friend of R.L.S.', who made Ide's daughter Annie the gift of his birthday when he discovered that hers fell on Christmas day, thereby causing her to lose a round of presents. He made friends too with the British Commissioner, Bazett Haggard, brother of the novelist, despite being troubled by his excessive drinking.

R.L.S. had fun in private, caricaturing and mocking the new office-bearers, but his talent for friendship and a correspondingly low ability to nurture feelings of hatred or even antipathy complicated matters for him. He found himself liking men whose policies he detested. He gave a brief résumé of the complexity of his situation in March 1892. "I am now on terms again with the German Consulate, I know not for how long; not of course with the President, which I find a relief; still with the Chief Justice; always with the English Consul, though I do not care for him. For Haggard I have a genuine affection; he is a lovable man" (VII, 2393). Politics and personality were in conflict for the rest of his life. In July 1894, he informed Colvin that he was "on fair terms with two Treaty officials, although all such intimacies are precarious: with the Consuls I need not say my position is deplorable. The President [by that time, Herr Emil Schmidt] is a dreamy, rather dreary man, whom I like, *bien qu'il m'impatiente continuellement*" (VIII, 2762). The Chief Justice aroused in him feelings stronger than impatience.

As R.L.S. tentatively felt his way into the native life and culture of Samoa, he relied on a wide circle of friends and acquaintances, especially among missionaries, for information and insight. Even if he maintained doubts about the missionary enterprise as such, he trusted the advice received from Rev. James Chalmers, whom he praised as one of the most admirable men he had ever met, and from a Wesleyan, Rev. George Brown, both of whom wrote books on Samoa. The Rev. Clarke, the man he met on landing in Samoa, became a friend and source of information. He also made friends among the mainly French Catholic missionaries on the island. He recognised that missionaries lived among Samoans, offered education to their children, and familiarised themselves with their language and thought in a way few traders did. Harry Moors, although a trader, was an exception.

It is worth underlining the exceptional nature of R.L.S.' position. He could have turned away, he could have regarded the activities of the Three Powers in Samoa as no business of his, he could have expressed a general trust in the goodwill of administrators and traders, he could have placed his belief in some historical process to bring about improvements to Asian and African peoples, he could have withdrawn to his study in Vailima, but he did none of these things.

His opposition to policies proposed by the consuls or by the Chief Justice and President was deeply resented in official circles, and meant that for years he lived under the threat of deportation. When, in October 1892, H.M.S. *Ringarooma* arrived in Apia, it was widely assumed that its mission was to deliver an order of expulsion to R.L.S. A few months later, Sir John Thurston, who boasted the grand title of High

Commissioner of the Western Pacific, issued an edict, clearly aimed at R.L.S., establishing the crime of sedition for all those who "by word, deed or writing", bring about "discontent or dissatisfaction, public disturbance, civil war, hatred or contempt towards King or Government of Samoa or the laws or constitution of the country, and generally to promote public disorder in Samoa." Not even Lord Braxfield, the model for Lord Justice Clerk in *Weir of Hermiston*, had used the charge of sedition in such a wide-ranging spirit when condemning reformers to Botany Bay. R.L.S. had to pull strings in London and ask Colvin, using his title as Sir Sidney, to intercede with Foreign Secretary, Lord Rosebery, to have the edict reversed.

At the same time, he was frequently impatient with the state of chronic unrest that existed inside the native Samoan community as they circled suspiciously around each other, vying for supremacy. His prime goal was reconciliation and the maintenance of peace. There were three main factions, each claiming the supreme title of Malietoa: the first was headed by Laupepa, back in Samoa after a period of exile imposed by the Germans; the leader of the second was Mata'afa Iosefo, who had been left in charge by Laupepa when he was taken from the archipelago; the third, more amorphous in 1890, was headed by Tamasese the younger, whose family was among the most powerful in Samoa.

Laupepa had returned to Samoa a broken man, and announced his wish to abdicate. At a great meeting in 1889, the chieftains confirmed Mata'afa as his successor, but this election was overruled by the consuls, who reinstated Laupepa in spite of his declared wishes. The decision was dubious in law, but respect for law was weak among the white authorities in Samoa, as was trenchantly stated in an editorial in a Samoan journal, officially anonymous but universally attributed to R.L.S. It is one of his most outraged and contemptuous denunciations of imperial interference, as well as of a consular decision which flew in the face of the agreements made at Berlin.

> The conference drew up a document which was dubbed its final act, but Samoa was not made acquainted with the contents of this production. Three Great Powers had kindly taken Samoa in hand, and her part was humbly to submit to be led blindfold along the way which was pointed out to her . . . Yet, to give the gentlemen who composed that conference justice, we must acknowledge that they had been jealous for the freedom and independence of Samoa . . . They proceed to declare that "the Three Powers recognise the independence of the Samoan Government and the free right of the natives to elect their chief or king and choose their own form of government according to their own laws and customs" . . .

His indignation was aroused by the fact that in spite of this supposed recognition of Samoan sovereignty and right to choose a ruler, their decision, their exercise of that right was overruled by an "invitation" from the consuls to restore Laupepa. R.L.S. continued, "in this instance, the word 'invite' actually meant 'command'; it was simply the velvet glove concealing the mailed hand of arbitrary dictation." Laupepa was restored to a throne he did not want. "This episode is absolutely without parallel in history," he concluded.[68] Tamasese assented to the imposed agreement and was given a position

68 (Samoan) *Weekly Herald,* July 15, 1893. The full article is quoted in *Cyclopedia of Samoa,* op. cit., pp. 49–52.

as Vice-King, an office which did not exist. Mata'afa was ostracised. The consuls proceeded to issue an announcement accepting the very pact they had imposed in the first place. Laupepa remained in Apia, where he was under the thumb of the white authorities, while Mata'afa moved to Malie, the traditional seat of power of the Malietoa, and lived there in succeeding years in resentful exile. There were now two centres of power in Samoa, meaning that a state of civil strife existed, with the possibility of an explosion into open warfare at any moment. R.L.S. wrote bitterly to say that had the appropriate steps been taken at the right time, the two men could have been coaxed into coming to a peaceful settlement. He attacked those in power, whom he blamed for fomenting division. He was especially contemptuous of clergymen who took the official anti-Mata'afa line and preached "sermons against the sin of rebellion" (VII, 2435).

Laupepa was never a strong ruler and was treated by R.L.S. at varying times with pity or contempt. Mata'afa lost much of his authority and his rights were disputed, but R.L.S. supported him unwaveringly as the best defender of Samoa. He nicknamed him "the king over the water", a title given to the Stuart sovereigns by their Jacobite supporters in eighteenth-century Scotland. There were many reasons why Mata'afa could not summon general support, not the least his being Catholic at a time when that religion was still viewed with widespread distaste. Fanny too in her diary was unstinting in her praise of him. There were attempts to have him deported, moves she regarded as "a terrible mistake". She complimented him on "behaving extremely well" in refusing to take the war to his enemies, although from a military point of view he would have been better advised to take the initiative. However, Fanny also noted the military realities, and was worried by reports that "the captain of the *Sperber* is ready to help in case of necessity", help which would have taken the form of resisting any attempt by Mata'afa to march on Apia.[69] She also noted that he had ordered his followers to continue paying their taxes at a time when the arrangements put in place by the treaty were breaking down and both dissident whites, including R.L.S., and native Samoans refused to make payments. One reason for this tax strike was that the income went largely to pay the bloated salaries of the new officials and to construct luxury residences for them.

In spite of his support for one party, R.L.S. made every effort to remain even-handed and act as peacemaker. The path to Vailima was well trodden by emissaries, intermediaries, and messengers bearing gifts, most in good faith but some by self-important poseurs or mischief-makers anxious to report back to hostile authorities anything that might damage R.L.S. "I am swallowed up by politics . . . much drafting, addressing, deputationising has eaten up all my time," leaving him short of time to complete *The Wrecker*, he told Burlingame (VII, 2354). The wonder is that in such an atmosphere he was at all able to maintain any semblance of a normal routine, to continue writing, throwing parties, attending official functions, entertaining guests, or going to dances in the Public Hall in Apia; somehow, in spite of the febrile atmosphere, life for him and the white community went on. Some of the incidents which led to heightened, inter-community strife were ludicrous, and these R.L.S.

69 Stevenson and Stevenson, *Our Samoan Adventure*, op. cit., p. 117.

savoured. Haggard supposedly shot a hen belonging to a German resident and was threatened with reprisals. His German colleague on the Land Commission visited him to say, "You have shot a German hen and you will be turned out of your house." There was no evidence that any hen, German or other, had been shot, and even less evidence of Haggard's responsibility, but tensions rose. R.L.S. commented, "It made the fellows ill to live wi'" (VII, 2357).

Both Laupepa and Mata'afa were among R.L.S.' guests in spring 1892. Aunt Maggie is all the more useful as a witness of thinking at Vailima: since she confesses to having little understanding of Samoan politics, her comments can be taken as reflecting the thinking around her. She recounts a surprise visit from Laupepa, accompanied by an armed guard, and describes him as "a pleasant-mannered, mild-looking elderly gentleman [who] made himself most agreeable." He requested that he be shown around the house and was "loud in his praise of all". His wife turned up a few days later, so a ceremonial escort had to be provided once again for a view of the house. The royal couple extended an invitation to the Stevensons, and this inevitably sparked a similar invitation from Mata'afa in Malie. She writes that "although Malietoa (Laupepa) is supported by the three protecting powers, the greater number are in favour of Mata'afa, who is indubitably the abler man of the two, and (as many hold) the rightful king. We believe that peace might easily have been maintained if the reigning king had been wisely advised, but the moment was allowed to pass."

The response to these invitations required diplomatic caution, and it was decided the hosts had to be visited in order of official priority, "the king in possession first, and 'Charlie ower the water' later". The party which went to see Laupepa included R.L.S., Fanny, Belle, and Aunt Maggie. They found the official royal residence a modest building, since, in Aunt Maggie's words, "the present advisers of his majesty spend all the revenue on fine houses and large salaries for themselves, and do as little as may be for the nominal ruler." R.L.S. put the matter more strongly, referring to the "king's wretched shanty, full in view of the President's fine new house". He added the comment: "It made my heart burn" (VII, 2408). Samoan ceremony is as elaborate as anything in Versailles, so the guests were greeted first by the queen outside the house, then by the king indoors. After pleasantries, the *kava* bowl was introduced, but there was some anxious discussion before it was decided whether Tusitala's mother or wife should be served first. The meal was gargantuan, as is the *faa samoa* way, but although R.L.S. managed to fix an appointment with Laupepa for the following day to discuss official business, the meeting did not take place, apparently because the king was deliberately detained by the Powers.

Some days later, the Vailima delegation set off to visit Mata'afa in the more distant town of Malie. Aunt Maggie stayed at home, but Fanny and Belle went along. Their presence once again caused official embarrassment at the *kava* ceremony, since it was assumed they were both wives and it was unclear which one had priority. Mata'afa's house had all the accoutrements of grandeur, including guards posted at the door. The banquet was equally grand, but this time a private political discussion did take place. Mata'afa expressed gratitude to R.L.S. for his efforts to ensure peace, even to the extent of risking deportation, and said he was willing to meet Laupepa. The meeting between the two rivals could not be arranged, but R.L.S.' preference for Mata'afa was confirmed.

The third member of the tangled Samoan royalty was not neglected. Tamasese, son of the man who had been made king by the Germans but later dethroned, arrived in Vailima in July. "A fine powerful fellow with a very pleasant smile," wrote Maggie. She believed that he had renounced all claim to be anything more than "a Samoan chief, pure and simple". He was not at that point a main player in the disputes for supreme power, but would re-emerge later. Meanwhile, he was happy to be treated with due respect at Vailima and given the now obligatory tour of the house.[70]

Shortly afterwards, Mata'afa was officially declared a rebel, although he was not actively pursued. The declaration was viewed by R.L.S. as an act of unpardonable folly since Mata'afa was the only man who had held the rebel party in check and prevented carnage. Intrigues among the white community reached depths of outright perfidy when a clergyman named A.E. Claxton, who had translated "The Bottle Imp" (1891) into Samoan but whose relations with R.L.S. later foundered, devised a duplicitous plot to have Mata'afa kidnapped and deported. Claxton, who was also Natives' Advocate, proposed to the American consul that Mata'afa be given a promise of safe conduct to visit Apia and then be seized and carried off. The consul refused to countenance the idea, saying that he "was a gentleman". Gossip was rife in the small society of Apia, and the story made the rounds.[71] If it had been carried out, it would,

70 M.I. Stevenson, *Letters from Samoa*, op. cit., pp. 157–69, and 208–10.
71 Harry J. Moors, *With Stevenson in Samoa*, Boston, Small, Maynard & Co., 1910, p. 134. R.L.S. reports the matter in *Footnote* and in various letters, without naming names.

in R.L.S.' view, "have loosed the avalanche at once" (VII, 2335).

R.L.S. found himself entangled in a legal action in which Cedercrantz and von Pilsach threatened to summon him as witness in an action for libel against one W.H. Yandal, a man of mixed race who was one of Moors' retainers. He acted as interpreter for Mata'afa and was alleged, probably accurately, to have entered into a conspiracy with him. The officials saw this case as an opportunity to question R.L.S., who was reluctant to have his own relations with Mata'afa, or his actions over the non-payment of taxes, made any more public. The accused's solicitor had the inspired idea of using R.L.S.' long-forgotten membership of the Faculty of Advocates in Edinburgh to invite him to take a brief in Samoa. He had no intention of using him in court, but a lawyer cannot be put in the witness box in a case in which he has some professional involvement. R.L.S. was relieved when Yandal was acquitted, but even more relieved to avoid cross-examination, as he admitted that "the dogs were on the right scent, and might have made a rainy day for some of us had they persevered" (VII, 2500).

A more grim event was recounted in the letter to *The Times* dated October 12, 1891. Some of Mata'afa's followers were arrested and jailed, but the Chief Justice, Cedercrantz, chose this moment to sail off to Fiji, washing his hands of the unrest in the islands, and leaving von Pilsach to deal with the problems. Having got word of an attempt to spring the men from jail, the authorities actually mined the premises with dynamite obtained from one of the wrecked ships in the harbour. If any escape were attempted, the building and those in it would be blown up. When word got out, the President went into a state of panic over the enormity of the acts he had authorised, and retired to his own house with a fever. R.L.S. reported these matters soberly to *The Times*, but then switched tone and demanded the dismissal of the President, "so that if I be fined a dollar tomorrow for fast riding in Apia street, I may not awake next morning to find my sentence increased to one of banishment or death by dynamite" (VII, 2355).

Fanny's journal in early 1892 is witness to her fear that the outbreak of war was imminent, and that the first battle would be fought near Vailima. In that event, their servants would be called on to leave and fight alongside their families, leaving the Stevensons defenceless. She was informed that her family had been marked out for revenge attacks by Laupepa's men, since they were considered, rightly, to be supporters of Mata'afa. Portents of war reported by the servants included darkening skies and the sighting of a headless eel on land.[72] Meantime, R.L.S.' time was taken up writing letters, attending meetings, and joining deputations. He faced renewed threats of deportation, told Samoans in one district not to pay their taxes and received lavish gifts from them in return, opposed the proposal to have a white man appointed as dictator of the islands, participated in debates over who should pay the salary of the Natives' Advocate in the Land Commission, and ran into difficulties following the publication of *Footnote*, which was, not unreasonably, regarded by the Germans as a hostile tract. The feeling over this publication was so strong that he even faced the prospect of being challenged to a duel by the German consul, Karl Bierman. Having heard that the consul had been briefed on the book, he took him a copy so that he might read for himself.

---

72 Stevenson and Stevenson, *Our Samoan Adventure*, op. cit., p. 169.

The consul returned the book the following day, saying he had spent one whole evening "perusing" it. R.L.S., still in the spirit of gaiety he had described to Henry James, described the consul as "a little fatted bald insignificant soul, of an astonishing aridity and power of tedium," but concluded that "it seemed the right thing to let him have a crack at me." There were, he reflected, three people in Apia whom he could shoot at "with a considerable amount of grim satisfaction, aye, and from behind a hedge," but Bierman was not one of them (VII, 2496). Perhaps the consul felt the same way because, in the event, the challenge was not delivered. The image of R.L.S., gun in hand, accompanied by a second, facing an armed opponent at dawn, is startling and beguiling, paralleling in a farcical key the drama of the duel between the brothers in *Master of Ballantrae*.

Several letters written by him to *The Times* were published in the course of 1892. In April, he wrote in mischievously Gilbertian tones, but with meticulously documented respect for fact, about the financial and fiscal chicanery perpetrated by the C.J. (Chief Justice) and the President. Customs duties, if not taxes, had been paid, but the clauses of the treaty left it unclear whether they should go to the government headed by the Malietoa and his "advisers", or to the white men's municipality presided over by the President. The matter was referred to the C.J., and judgment given in favour of the municipality, leaving the government coffers empty, public works unfunded, and salaries unpaid. Laupepa's government faced bankruptcy, so, one year after the initial judgment was handed down, it was reversed in an empty courtroom, where the C.J. heard representations for both sides delivered by the same man, Senff von Pilsach, who appeared both as adviser to the Malietoa and as

President of the municipality. "Is this English law? Is it law at all?" asked R.L.S. He reported that dissatisfaction was now widespread and that one of the native orators at an official function asked who had appointed the Great Powers to make law for them. Was armed insurrection at hand?

The Times was left in a state of perplexity over these letters, and in a leader wondered whether the passion which evidently motivated R.L.S. had "warped his judgement", and suggested that he return to writing his romances. However, the paper went on to agree that the gravity of the accusation merited a "prompt and impartial enquiry". R.L.S. was delighted when he got wind of this evaluation from a New Zealand newspaper, and wrote again to repeat his earlier accusation, setting out another unfolding scandal involving the use of public money to purchase the *Samoa Times.* The white authorities in Samoa, troubled by press criticism, went so far as to buy over the island's only existing newspaper. In an attempt to keep the move secret, they paid in gold bullion, but regrettably neglected to remove the official government wrapping from the bundles in which the gold was tied, and gave away their identity as plotters. R.L.S. actually assisted in establishing a rival journal. Meantime, the native government had suggested a way out of the impasse over tax collection by proposing to the municipality of Apia that white men too should pay tax. The request was rejected (VII, 2426 and 2440).

Cedercrantz intrigued to establish the nature and frequency of R.L.S.' contact with Mata'afa, and even attempted by threat of deportation to intimidate one of Harry Moors' clerks into divulging any information he had. R.L.S. wrote an indignant letter to him, reiterating that his only purpose was peace. He was aware of the absurdity of having to write to London to have news about Samoa circulate in Samoa, but one more letter was sent to *The Times* before the year's end. His commitment was not half-hearted, but he was afraid of trying the patience of civil servants and ministers and ended his letter with the promise that this would be the last expression of "these twopenny concerns". The earlier part of the letter exposed a grotesque situation which had arisen inside the white community, following the decision of the C.J. to take up residence on land in the Mulinu'u promontory which the German firm claimed as theirs. It transpired that while his right to the house was covered by the Berlin Treaty, his title to the land it stood on was not. It further emerged that he had never paid rent, making "the Chief Justice a squatter". He declined to move and procrastinated as long as possible. The final situation, R.L.S. said, could have come from Offenbach's operettas – works with which he was familiar and to which he made frequent reference – since the firm threatened to go to law, but could only raise an action against the C.J. in the court over which the same man presided.

R.L.S. composed his final piece of mocking doggerel about Cedercrantz in a letter to Charles Baxter in December 1892, a mock request to the King of Sweden to recall his subject home. In fact, in May the following year both Cedercrantz and von Pilsach were removed from office, at which point, typically, R.L.S. began to feel sorry for them (VIII, 2514). Their departure did not materially alleviate the situation. To see if his vision for the future of Samoa would find approval, and to gain deeper insight into British policy, he met some colonial satraps, all graced with knighthoods for their services. In Auckland in 1893, after *Footnote* had been published, he enjoyed a long conversation with Sir George Grey, who had served twice as

Governor of New Zealand. Although showered with official honours during his career, he had still come into conflict with the Colonial Office in London, and was viewed by R.L.S. as a refined expert on the politics of the Pacific and on British attitudes. He was heartened by Grey's encouragement to continue as he had been doing, although the knight advised him to work through the normal channels and avoid writing to the press. R.L.S. also respected the work of Sir Arthur Gordon, the first Governor of Fiji when it became a British colony in 1875, and in that role defender of the land rights of Fijian people against the claims of white settlers. He admired even more Sir William MacGregor, originally Gordon's medical officer but later Governor of New Guinea. MacGregor was his preferred candidate to head a colonial administration if Samoa were ever annexed, as he at times concluded, however reluctantly, might be necessary. His support for MacGregor was based on the unremarkable belief that "it is nonsense and will prove cruel nonsense to bring anybody here who does not know the islands" (VIII, 2697). But that was not all. On another occasion, we find R.L.S. stating, "If only we could have MacGregor here with his schooner, you would hear no more of troubles here in Samoa. That is what we want; a man who knows and likes the natives, *qui pait de sa personne* (sic), and is not afraid of hanging when necessary. We don't want bland Swedish swindlers, and fussy, footering German Barons. That way the maelstrom lies, and we shall soon be in it" (VIII, 2577).

This language and these thoughts are somewhat at odds with R.L.S.' more humane views, but he was no Liberal and certainly no opponent of capital punishment. He did not cultivate a taste for footling euphemism, so when he believed that hanging was necessary for the public good, or to avoid "the maelstrom", he expressed himself as strenuously as did Lord Braxfield, or his fictional counterpart, Lord Weir of Hermiston. The picture of MacGregor on his schooner, overseeing a policy of "hanging when necessary", is unpleasantly Machiavellian – but the Machiavelli who invited readers of *The Prince* to question who had in reality been more humane: Florence, whose desire to be loved had the unintended result of allowing Pistoia to be devastated, or the notorious Cesare Borgia, whose relentless severity and savagery brought a period of peace to the citizens of Romagna. R.L.S. feared the storm which seemed likely to break over Samoa, and while he was convinced that the original sin had been perpetrated by the white men who had disturbed an established equilibrium, he had to confront the reality which faced him there and then.

He was subject to sudden swings of mood and approach. In the same year, 1893, he spoke in radically different terms in an article which appeared in a Sydney periodical, the *Presbyterian*:

> On the whole the influence of whites on islanders strikes me as far from beneficial, and the more whites, the worse the effect. A single trader, even the most atrocious scoundrel, is rapidly conquered by his medium, adopts island civility and decorum, even if he had none of his own when he came there. But so soon as the whites are in a considerable body, the work of decivilisation proceeds merrily. I said "decivilisation", but if you insist on it, I will say "debarbarisation". At least, it is a process towards the worse.[73]

73 R.L. Stevenson, "The Labour Traffic", in *Sophia Scarlet*, op. cit., p. 116.

CHAPTER 10

Outbreak of War

In Samoa itself, the situation was deteriorating rapidly. Orders were issued that the collection of taxes was to be imposed by the crews of a warship, the followers of Mata'afa to be disarmed, and R.L.S. himself deported. Skirmishing between the two sides was now occurring with some regularity, and in April 1893 Mata'afa hoisted his flag and made a formal claim to be Malietoa. Both the island and the community at Vailima were in an uproar, and it was believed that this time the whites were in danger. R.L.S. was galvanised into action, but, faced with war, his first internal reaction was, astonishingly, of almost orgiastic glee. He reported to Colvin a conversation with Balfour in which he expressed "the sentiment that was in the air, 'after all, there are only two things worth while – to have women and to kill men'" (VIII, 2595).

His actual efforts were aimed at preventing the killing of men and the violation of women. Fanny, emerging from her prolonged period of illness, took up the cause of Mata'afa with a fervour bordering on frenzy. "I wonder at the forbearance of these Samoans. Were I a Samoan, I would agitate for a massacre of the whites."[74] Unsure whether Vailima would be left

74 Stevenson and Stevenson, *Our Samoan Adventure*, op. cit., p. 232.

untouched in the event of warfare, R.L.S. purchased a supply of rifles. Fanny raged against the restrictions imposed on her as a woman in the event of hostilities breaking out, and swore that, in the event of an attack on Vailima, she would refuse to be locked away from the fighting. She filled her diary with polemics against the consuls, though she knew they would be compromising for both of them if her writings fell into enemy hands. R.L.S. warned Fanny and Belle against attending routine social events, which went on as before. He told them not to go to a ball in Apia in early July, but they "made a strike for freedom" and went of their own accord, leaving R.L.S. "in deep sulks at [our] attitude".

R.L.S. visited chiefs on both sides, noting as he went the gathering of armed warriors in the bush, but recording that they all saluted him as he rode past. Once again, however curiously, he worked himself into a state of exhilaration. "War is such an *entraînement*," he wrote, slipping into French as though to provide respectable cover for his feelings. Fanny noted that her husband and Balfour came back from an expedition to see the rebel outposts "quite wild with excitement". She commented that it was going to be "a difficult task to keep Louis from losing his head altogether".[75] Belle too was carried away by the febrile atmosphere. Once she went with him to do sketches of the pickets, and was disappointed to find none.

War broke out in July. It was short but brutal. The Mata'afan forces made the first move, but were driven back and never regained the initiative. Laupepa's army moved forward relentlessly and soon were able to organise a victory march in Apia.

75 Ibid., p. 213.

R.L.S. noted that there were friends and even family members on either side, and that while they had broken ranks to take *kava* together before the shooting began, these links did nothing to attenuate what he regarded as the more savage customs of the people. It was customary for women to march with the army, not to take part in the actual fighting but to carry ammunition and generally spur on the men. He saw one woman drag her husband out of a ditch and chase him back into battle with jeers. He also recorded watching the village jester leap about in the vanguard of the approaching army. The *taupou* – the ceremonial village maiden chosen for her personality and looks – had a special role in this martial ritual, and walked in the front line cajoling, encouraging, and stiffening the resolve of the men. Granted their exposed position, casualties among the women were not unknown, but they were exempt from a practice to which R.L.S. and Fanny objected with great vehemence, that of chopping off the heads of fallen soldiers and carrying them in triumph back to lay in a pile in front of the leader. On this occasion, Laupepa's forces brought back eleven heads, one of which was discovered to be a woman's.

R.L.S. and Fanny offered their assistance in the ad hoc hospital set up in the Public Hall in Apia, but retired to Vailima in the evening. In some respects, life went on as normal. R.L.S. mentions playing a game of tennis one day before going to the hospital. Under pressure, Mata'afa retreated to a neighbouring island, but found himself still under assault. A British warship, the *Katoomba*, arrived with orders to crush the rebellion, but Captain Bickford had been on other occasions a guest at Vailima, so R.L.S. was able to intercede with him. He found him sympathetic to Mata'afa and critical of the inactivity of the Three Powers. The two men reached an agreement that if Mata'afa gave himself up to him, the captain would guarantee his safety. The rebel chief and his lieutenants duly surrendered and were subsequently deported to the German Marshall Islands. Some of his other followers were imprisoned in Apia. Laupepa was left as Malietoa of Samoa, but was more than ever a puppet ruler. The hoped-for era of peace did not ensue, for shortly afterwards Tamasese rose in rebellion in pursuance of his own claim. The islands were, according to R.L.S.' final, lengthy, and detailed letter to *The Times*, reduced to a state of anarchy. Mata'afa remained in exile until 1898.

The outcome represented the ruin of everything R.L.S. had hoped for in Samoa. The brightest and best were in exile or in detention, their aspirations drowned in blood, and foreigners now in uncontested control in the archipelago, even if they still had to use proxies as camouflage. Samoa limped along with further periods of bloodshed until the second Treaty of Berlin in 1899 formalised its situation as subaltern. All that he had warned against ever since his 1890 address to the students in Malua was now a reality. The land had been "sold". To make matters worse, R.L.S. worried that by supporting one side rather than staying silently in the shadows, he carried part of the guilt. The failure tormented him deeply, perhaps all the more so as Fanny became stridently polemical in her denunciations of the victorious side and in her expressions of support for Mata'afa, whom she took to describing as "my king".

"You will see that I am not in a good humour," R.L.S. told Colvin in August, and that was an understatement. "Life is not all Beer and Skittles; and mine is closing in dark enough. Where does blame come in? Nowhere, I believe, or very little.

Only the inherent tragedy of things works itself out from white to black and blacker, and the poor things of a day look ruefully on. Does it shake my cast-iron faith? I cannot say it does. I believe in an ultimate decency of things." This last much-quoted sentence was as firm and fundamental a statement of Stevenson's worldview as he ever made, and has all the greater force because it was made when he was himself at his lowest ebb. It established him to later generations as an existential optimist in an age of philosophical, Schopenhauerian pessimism. The landscape he now looked on was grim and profoundly changed. "It is hard walking, and I can see my own share of the mis-steps, and bow my head to the result, like an old, stern, unhappy devil of a Norseman" (VIII, 2646).

He was experiencing the dark night of the soul as he re-examined his own advice and conduct. Specific events, like the flawed military strategy, also worried him. He wrote several times during his life that, had his health not made it unthinkable, he would have liked to have followed an army career, but now he was faced with defeat and the *vae victis* realities of the battlefield. J.L. Borges divided Europe between those for whom Waterloo was a defeat and those for whom it was a victory. Years previously, R.L.S. had, like Scott before him, walked over the fields of Waterloo, and that battle was for him undoubtedly a victory. Equally, there was no doubt that the outcome of the battles on the fields at Vaitele between Mata'afa and Laupepa was for him a defeat. If it was on a smaller scale than Waterloo, that did nothing to lessen the sense of tragic waste he felt. But it was in this state of dejection and discouragement that the true, moral grandeur of Robert Louis Stevenson asserted itself. A lesser man would have trimmed and compromised, denied responsibility or sought an accommodation with the victors, but that was never his way. He had risked incrimination and deportation, he had alienated men who had been his friends, he had upset authorities in Britain and Samoa, he had seen his reputation trashed in newspaper columns and had even been told that his political-moral convictions put his life and that of his family at risk, but still he stood by the man who was his friend and whom he had viewed as the best hope for Samoa. There had never been one iota of self-interest in his policy, and now consistency, compassion, and a sense of justice made him remain faithful and loyal.

He assumed personal responsibility for the defeated and scattered followers of Mata'afa. He sent Graham Balfour to the Marshalls with gifts, and took care of the Apia prisoners. The director of the jail was the same Baron Wurmbrand who had earlier been his guest, and it was no fault of his if life inside the prison was degrading. There were accounts of prisoners being left to wander about or even return home for family feasts while supposedly serving their sentence, but on a day-to-day basis conditions were dire. Dissatisfied with the cramped cells, the prisoners had built for the chiefs traditional homes inside the compound. Resources to pay the guards or to feed and clothe the prisoners arrived erratically, leaving them often exposed to hunger, if not actual starvation. R.L.S. described them as "voluntary prisoners" who had proved their loyalty on two occasions when the guards had deserted, and in yet another letter to London added the plea, "at least let them be fed!" Large fines had been imposed on families and villages, meaning that they lacked adequate resources to feed their imprisoned relatives. R.L.S. protested, "I have paid taxes to the Samoan

Government for some four years, and the most sensible benefit I have received in return has been to be allowed to feed their prisoners" (Tusitala, XXI, 295).

Wurmbrand was happy to turn a blind eye on occasion, and permitted the holding of feasts inside the prison, in which he cheerfully participated. Two in particular stand out. The first was a delayed celebration of R.L.S.' birthday in 1893, where he provided the *kava* and the tobacco, and the second a feast at Christmas that year. On this second occasion, the prisoners, who had now taken on the daily task of feeding their unpaid and desperate jailers, invited the Stevenson party from Vailima, and they themselves provided hospitality on a lavish scale. Full Samoan ceremonial was observed, and crowds gathered outside the gates to goggle. Inside there were eighteen chiefs with one recognised as Head. For the feast, girls had been summoned from the villages to serve *kava* and distribute the various dishes to guests in order of established priority. Speeches followed the feasting, and R.L.S. heard himself described as the "only friend" of the imprisoned Samoans who were in a condition of slavery. Presents of cups, fans, and necklaces were given out, followed by the more serious distribution of foods, including five pigs and masses of fish, to be taken home. When the last words had been spoken, the party marched triumphantly along the main street, provocatively passing the palace of Laupepa and the headquarters of the German firm. "No such feast was ever made for a single family, and no such present ever given to a single white man. It is something to have been a hero of it" (VIII, 2677).

This token of recognition was outshone by a later gesture made by the chiefs. R.L.S. interceded with the Malietoa and the Chief Justice, and wrote to *The Times*, pleading for an amnesty for the exiles and release of the men detained in Apia. Eventually, a pardon was granted. Days later, the freed men made their way to Vailima and offered, in gratitude for his kindness and support, to construct a road to join his property to the main road some quarter of a mile distant. R.L.S. was overwhelmed by the gratitude shown, even if in private he remained wryly sceptical, for he assumed that as part of the deal he would have to provide food and drink to the workers. The chiefs declined all his offers and insisted that they would be satisfied with what their wives could supply. All the ex-prisoners took part in the labour, including, against all Samoan tradition, the chiefs, for whom manual labour was commonly viewed as beneath their dignity. The work was completed in slightly more than a month, and was given the name Road of the Loving Hearts.

The completion was, inevitably, marked by a feast at Vailima which surpassed all others. R.L.S. invited all the authorities, including the Land Commissioners, the American Chief Justice, the consuls, the officers of the *Curaçao* which happened to be in port, as well as the chiefs and the men who had done the actual labour. The evening closed with a speech delivered by R.L.S. and translated by Lloyd. He could not know that it would be his last testament to Samoa, but there is a curious completeness to a cycle that opened with the lecture in Malua and closed with the address at Vailima. Once again, the talk was a supremely crafted exercise of the skills of the preacher and the orator, allowing him to draw on his knowledge of the history of Scotland and Rome, as well as of biblical texts, as he set out to encourage, plead, inspire, and embolden his listeners, and also to issue his now customary admonition to them. His first plea was for peace, to ensure that Samoa would avoid the fate of the Scottish Highlands after the Clearances. "There is a time to fight, and a time to dig. You Samoans may fight, you may conquer twenty times, and thirty times and it will all be in vain. There is but one way to defend Samoa. Hear it before it is too late. It is to make roads, and gardens, and care for your trees, and, in one word, to occupy and use your country." This rhetorical flourish led to the final warning. "If you do not others will."

The history of the Covenanters was well known to him, and the elegiac lyricism of this talk recalls the words of preachers addressing their flocks on the moors of Scotland. Knowing his audience's Christian convictions, he reinforced his arguments by reminding them of the parable of the talents.

> What are you doing with your talent, Samoa? Your three talents, Savaii, Upolu and Tutuila? Have you buried it in a napkin? Not Upolu at least. You have rather given it out to be trodden under feet of swine, or of that much worse animal, foolish man, acting according to his folly . . . God has both sown and strawed for you here in Samoa. He has given you rich soil and a splendid sun, copious rain; all is ready, half done. And I repeat to you that thing which is sure; if you do not continue to use and occupy your country, others will. It will not continue to be yours or your children's, if you occupy it for nothing. You and your children will in that case be cast out into the outer darkness, where shall be weeping and gnashing of teeth.

Employing well-tried rhetorical tropes, he ended with a series of paragraphs each beginning – Chiefs! He appealed to them to work and build, to be inspired by the permanency of the Roman roads, and to consider that the road they had built for him would be remembered by "far-away descendants who will bless those who built it". However, his most moving and personal passage came in the centre of the speech, when he spoke of himself and his relations with Samoa. He saw "the day of the great battle" approaching when it will be decided whether Samoans "are to pass away like other races, or to stand fast". He added: "I do not speak of this lightly, because I love Samoa and her people. I love the land, I have chosen it to be my home while I live and my grave when I am dead. And I love the people, and have chosen them to be my people to live with and die with."[76]

Only some months after the construction of the Road of Loving Hearts, the same labourers were called out to cut by night a path up the side of Mount Vaea to allow the coffin containing the body of R.L.S. to be carried for burial on the spot he had chosen.

76 R.L. Stevenson, "Address to the Samoan Chiefs", in *Sophia Scarlet*, op. cit., pp. 121–5.

PART III

Home at Vailima

CHAPTER 11

A Real Domestic Man

"It was in Samoa that the word 'home' first began to have a real meaning for these gypsy wanderers," writes Nellie Vandegrift Sanchez in her biography of her sister, Fanny.[77] The other towns where they settled after their marriage all had a temporary feel, a stop along life's way, a resting place in the quest for somewhere likely to improve R.L.S.' precarious health. Referring to his time in Hyères, Sanchez says she had never thought of R.L.S. "as a real domestic man but now I find that all he wanted was a house of his own". It was in Samoa that he found it. On the downside, it became quickly clear both to him and Fanny that there would be no question of taking up residence in Madeira and commuting to London, or indeed of seeing again his "own precipitous city", or of "taking that walk by the Fisher's Tryst and Glencorse".

There were other reservations to be overcome. The first impression of the island was not wholly favourable: "Samoa, Apia at least, is far less beautiful than the Marquesas or Tahiti . . . I am not especially attracted by the people; they are courteous, pretty chaste, but thieves and beggars, to the weariness of those involved," he wrote (VI, 2194). Fanny was even more forthright.

77 Nellie Vandegrift Sanchez, *Life of Mrs. Robert Louis Stevenson,* London, Chatto & Windus, 1920, p. 167.

During a sojourn in Sydney, she added a lengthy coda to a letter to Colvin complaining about the prospect of life in Samoa, and stating that she accepted it out of a sense of love and duty. She firmly disabused Colvin of the notion, which he had never entertained, that she was making an act of self-sacrifice "with flowers on head". It was not so. "The climate does not agree with me. Louis knows that, and yet he is willing to stay . . . the Samoan people are picturesque, yet I do not like them. I do not trust them. My time must be so arranged that I do not clash with them" (VI, 2240). She was plainly piqued at the time of writing, but this was far from her last word on Samoa.

Judging by the rapidity with which initial doubts about Samoa were jettisoned, R.L.S. did not take much persuading. Under Moors' guidance, he began looking for property, initially considering a Spanish-style villa in Apia itself, until he was put off by the marshland behind it.[78] Moors had other suggestions, and by January 1890 R.L.S. was able to tell Lady Taylor that he was now "the owner of an estate on Upolu, some two or three miles behind and above Apia". He described the terrain in some detail, pointing out that the house was yet to be built and that "as a climax, we may have to stand a siege in the next native war" (VI, 2198). Fanny needed more convincing, but was finally reconciled to the idea, with what level of enthusiasm it is impossible to say. R.L.S. conveyed her assent to Moors with words taken, oddly, from the passage in *David Copperfield* where Barkis the carter asks David to convey to Peggotty his proposal of marriage. "Barkis is willin'", were the unromantic words, and in Samoa these words indicated that Fanny agreed

78 Stevenson and Stevenson, *Our Samoan Adventure*, op. cit., p. 126.

on the choice of place of residence. In March, he told Charles Baxter in Edinburgh that he was sure he would "never come home except to die" (VI, 2215).

This was one of several letters Baxter received that month as R.L.S. pondered his decision and explained his equivocations over the friendship he had formed with Moors. "The man himself is a curious being, not of the best character . . . the most infamous trader in these waters, the man who is accused of paying natives with whist money . . . you may wonder why I should become at all intimate with a man of a past so doubtful; but in the South Seas any exclusiveness becomes impossible; they are all in the same boat" (VI, 2219). It is interesting to see R.L.S. suspending normal moral criteria on the grounds that different standards apply in the South Seas, and that he has to take life as he finds it. These are dilemmas dramatised on a deeper level in his later fiction. In the same letter, he writes of Moors that "it's my belief he won't cheat me", but that belief has been subsequently, if inconclusively, questioned. A shrewd businessman, Moors sold him the estate of 314½ acres at a stiff price. Happy though R.L.S. was on his new land, and much as he relished his status as laird, the upkeep of it and of his family, or clan, was a burden and a worry to him all his days.

Aware of the parallels with Walter Scott's construction of his home in the Borders, he referred semi-jocularly to his new purchase as sub-Priorsford. He informed Baxter that he had acquired "from 600 to 1500 feet, have five streams, waterfalls, precipices, profound ravines, rich tablelands, fifty head of cattle on the ground (if anyone could catch them), a great view of forest, sea, mountains, the warship in the haven: really a noble place" (VI, 2203). The estate was named Vailima, meaning in

Samoan "five streams", although there were fewer than five – estimates of the actual number differ – by the time the family took up residence. No matter. Later his mother paid for the installation of pipes which gave the house a ready supply of water. For a tropical island, Samoa has an abundance of fresh water, and the estate included a small rock pool constantly refilled with water flowing down Mount Vaea, which the family used for bathing. The beetling high, tree-covered Mount Vaea itself towered over their "big, beautiful, windy house". The mountain has a place in local folklore, since it was believed to be the petrified remnant of a warrior who married a Fijian princess. She bore him a child whom she wanted to take back to Fiji to show to her family. She was so long away and he stood so still watching for her return that he turned to stone, and when she did finally come back, she embraced his unmoving form and the two shed such an abundance of tears as to form a stream and fill the pool below. The family bathed there regularly.

Once the choice had been made, R.L.S. made every effort to put down roots and establish friendships, acquaintances, involvements, and alliances. But he experienced his own version of the Scottish anti-syzygy, the splintered sensibility or fractured consciousness which caused his mind and his imagination to operate in different spheres. Initially at least his imagination remained in Scotland while his conscience was active in Samoa. From the start, he was uneasy about the way in which the Samoans were being dispossessed by strangers who disrespected them. Having decided it was good to integrate, he set out to learn Samoan, and arranged with Henry Simele, a chieftain who joined the Vailima staff, a series of language sessions in which they taught each other their native tongues. He had no truck with those, not only Germans, who lived segregated from the islanders. His support for the Samoans made him enemies among the white residents.

In addition to the climate, Samoa had the advantage over Honolulu, another possible residence, that it was "more savage" but not more remote, in the sense that steamers bound for New Zealand, Australia, and California stopped regularly, allowing R.L.S. to keep in contact with publishers and friends. He was an indefatigable correspondent. There was an established ritual when the mail arrived. He kept an eye on the harbour, dispatched one of the staff to pick up mail, arranged the family group in a circle while he handed out the post to each one, but forbade them from opening a single letter until the distribution was complete. He set himself immediately to penning replies while the ship was in port. There were some regular correspondents, notably Sidney Colvin, letters to whom had a special status because they were intended for eventual publication. Often they were written over days or even weeks, in the style of entries in a journal. Colvin did publish an edition of the *Vailima Letters* after R.L.S.' death, but he was squeamish or even old-maidish in his approach and excised sections which he believed might be damaging to the reputation of the great man.[79] There were other passages he cut out for no reason that can now be deciphered. The full range of R.L.S.' correspondence was only made clear when Bradford A. Booth and Ernest Mehew published the definitive, eight-volume edition, an unsurpassable labour of love and scholarship.

79 Sidney Colvin (editor), *Vailima Letters; Being Correspondence Addressed by Robert Louis Stevenson to Sidney Colvin, November, 1890–October 1894*, 2 volumes, New York, Charles Scribner's Sons, 1896.

Victorians like Queen Victoria herself or Mr Gladstone (how R.L.S. would have hated any comparison with his arch-enemy!) were correspondents on a heroic scale, and R.L.S. stands alongside them. Given their output, it is astonishing that they found time for anything else. Fanny and Aunt Maggie too were dedicated letter-writers, so the scene when a ship anchored down in Apia must have been one of silent, focused industry. R.L.S. was a master of the art or craft of letter-writing, and deserves the respect shown to such as Lord Byron or Jonathan Swift, even if his letters do not have the intimacy of the poet's or the psychological mystery of the Dean's. In spite of having to write at speed while the ship was at anchor and not having the liberty for revision, the letters are captivating and display all the stylishness for which his prose is celebrated. His letters to his friends show immense warmth, humour, vivacity, quirkiness, and shrewdness of judgement, qualities not always apparent in his fiction. He also had the courtesy to answer letters from people not known to him, including requests for autographs, with the one precondition that his name be spelt correctly. Those who addressed their request to a Stephenson could expect short shrift. He had little patience with time-wasters. One anonymous young man who pondered about coming to Samoa in the belief that he could live there without working was dismissed with a few sharp words. "There is no part of the world where a young man with the curse of improvidence can hope to live with decency or can be sure of not dying on the gallows – Samoa is no exception" (VIII, 2541).

He had a ready armoury of satirical jibes and barbs when upset, mainly at the expense of political opponents, such as Gladstone, but the bulk of his correspondence is chatty and gossipy. He can be amused and whimsical when discussing affairs at Vailima, enraged and polemical when on politics, and thoughtful and incisive when the subject is literature. The letters also keep readers, now as then, abreast of the course of day-to-day events and of the frustrations of family life, so that his life can be read in his correspondence. Few other writers have provided quite so much information on the progress of their own books, expressing doubt over moments when things are going badly or elation when all is proceeding smoothly. Often the letters are mini-essays of criticism on contemporary writers, ranging from Zola to Hardy and Meredith. He and Henry James, whom R.L.S. described in a poem as "the prince of men", exchanged novels as they were published, and invariably expressed their judgements with candour, so that their correspondence provides keen critical insight on their own work and on that of their contemporaries. Emerging writers, such as Rudyard Kipling, J.M. Barrie, and S.R. Crockett, received admiring or encouraging mail when their early works appeared. R.L.S. wrote to Yeats to congratulate him when he published the "Lake Isle of Innisfree".

For Stevenson himself, it seems that these letters were a means by which he maintained for himself a fiction that he was still enrolled in a community or club in London or Edinburgh, whose members were his friends from other days. He kept in touch with writers and men of letters such as Edmund Gosse, and the poet and critic W.E. Henley, with whom he was on the friendliest of terms until their relationship was ruptured in 1888 when Henley virtually accused Fanny of plagiarism over a story she had written. Among personal friends were Charles Baxter, whom he had known since university days in Edinburgh and who became an advocate; Frances Sitwell, with whom the youthful R.L.S. had fallen in love but who later married Colvin; Bob Stevenson, his cousin, an unreliable correspondent. The polemical letters to the authorities in Samoa, whether consuls or officials appointed after the Treaty of Berlin, belong in a category of their own, as do his incisive letters to *The Times* and to various London publications.

Being a domestic as well as a literary man involved hiring staff and helping to tend the land. In some accounts, Vailima was an untamed wilderness which had never been occupied, while in other versions there had been a previous resident, who may even have been, in Stevenson's own words, a "blind Scots blacksmith" (VI, 2233). The couple at least half-believed in the existence of this mysterious earlier landowner, and once cut their way into the woods to locate a banana patch, the remnants of a supposed plantation placed there by human agency. The really well-attested inhabitants of the area were the *aitu*, spirits of some malignity and power, whose presence had both advantages and disadvantages. They kept hostile prowlers at a distance but made the Samoan workforce apprehensive. Their unease would constitute a problem for Fanny in her efforts to cultivate the estate, for many of the servants could not be persuaded to venture into the bush, or to stay there for long enough to complete specific tasks.

She was not the only one to encounter such problems. In an essay written to accompany a book of photographs by Joe Strong, which was never actually published, R.L.S. tells of an expedition by Joe into the forest in Samoa to visit a stone house inhabited by a devil which represented a mortal peril to Samoans, but not to white men. The unfortunate servant who accompanied him went forward in fear and trembling, and finally sat down and refused to go any further. Joe forged ahead on his own until he too was forced back by the thick undergrowth, but found that the servant, overcome by dread, had already fled.[80]

R.L.S. delighted in the land which made up his estate, and the time he spent working on it inspired one of his best poems, "The Woodman", which both describes his efforts and draws on Samoan superstition. He was intrigued by the reaction of a Samoan servant who was evidently at work with him domesticating the woodland, but who was overcome by an abiding ancestral fear of the *aitu*:

> With lowered axe, with backward head,
> Late from this scene my labourer fled,
> And with a travelled tale to tell,
> Returned. Some denizen of hell,
> Dead man or disinvested god,
> Had close behind him peered and trod,
> And triumphed when he turned to flee.

There are echoes here of Coleridge's "Ancient Mariner". R.L.S. looks on with sympathy and bemused interest at his servant's plight, but cannot endow these spectral forces with any mystical reality. This is strange, since some of R.L.S.' own stories, "Thrawn Janet" in particular, draw on similar beliefs. Celtic folklore as recited by the bards was populated by brownies, fairies, kelpies, ghosts, mutants, stolen babies, witches, and warlocks, and at other times R.L.S. used these weird legends to

80 R.L. Stevenson, "A Samoan Scrapbook", in *Sophia Scarlet*, op. cit., p. 59.

establish relations with the Polynesians. In *Ballads* (1890), he writes from inside the minds of the islanders, but here he positions himself as an observer looking on with rationalist scepticism at the Samoan who sees *aitu* concealed in trees. R.L.S. was even moved in a letter to Colvin to "lament [my] insensibility of superstition", although in the same letter he wondered if he was "being drawn in" as he had felt a chill settle on his heart when he worked. He persuaded himself he heard laughter and the sound of blows (VII, 2266).[81] The poem continues:

> How different fell the lines with me!
> Whose eyes explored the dim arcade
> Impatient of the uncoming shade –
> Shy elf, or dryad pale and cold,
> Or mystic lingerer from of old:
> Vainly. The fair and stately things,
> Impassive as departed kings,
> All still in the wood's stillness stood,
> And dumb. The rooted multitude
> Nodded and brooded, bloomed and dreamed,
> Unmeaning, undivined . . .

He employs a poetic conceit to transform the wild lands into an enemy with whom he and his "wife, the tender, kind and gay", are at war, but the force he was tangling with was the brute strength of a natural power which, however delicately he personifies it in his rhymes, is far removed from the incorporeal spectres which haunt the Samoan imagination.

81 Alberto Manguel used the episode in his intriguing novella on R.L.S. in Samoa: *Stevenson Under the Palm Trees*, Edinburgh, Canongate, 2004.

Bursting across the tangled math
A ruin that I called a path,
A Golgotha that, later on,
When rains had watered, and suns shone,
And seeds enriched the place, should bear
And be called garden . . . (Tusitala, XXII, 161)

"The Beach of Falesá", written at about the same time would disappoint some critics because the element of bewitchment would turn out to be a ruse dreamed up by a villain to deceive the islanders, not a phantom presence.

It is hard now to imagine the prospect from Vailima as a wilderness, but the landscape and views, with the mountain on the one hand and the sea a distant vision over the leaves of palm and coconut trees on the other, offer still a vision of unspoiled beauty. Apia itself, some three miles away down a bumpy track, through a forest which was forbidding after dark, was not visible. R.L.S. often made the journey there, and even his mother jogged down frequently on horseback. It was in some ways similar to the frontier towns Fanny had known in the days when she lived with her first husband, but the differences were significant. She complained that although the shops were often short of the necessities of life, it was always possible to buy a bottle of vintage champagne. R.L.S. had a taste for good wine, and frequently dined either with Moors or the resident consuls, at their homes or at the Tivoli Hotel. He was equally liable to drop in at the more suspect haunts where the beach-combers drank and smoked.

In London, Colvin took on the role of literary agent but R.L.S. complained that he was a poor negotiator who ended up making unfavourable agreements with publishers in both Britain and the U.S.A. He often disregarded explicit instructions, as when he permitted "The Bottle Imp" and "The Beach of Falesá", two novellas which R.L.S. judged incompatible in inspiration, to be published in the same volume. R.L.S. was unforgiving and replaced him as agent with Charles Baxter, who operated more skilfully in the publishers' market. Colvin was also frequently critical of the quality of R.L.S.' writing in the South Seas, and tended in letters to express too unequivocally the worry that he was squandering his talents on second-rate material when he should be producing something more in keeping with conventional ideas of literature. Other metropolitan literary friends had the same concerns, sometimes betraying an intellectual snobbery and provincialism of their own. Living in such a remote, uncivilised spot would, they believed, prove damaging for his reputation as a writer, and starting from that premise they found their fears amply confirmed by the novels and poems he wrote. At times, R.L.S. responded with exasperation tempered by the genuine affection he felt for them. Few men have ever had such a vocation for friendship as R.L.S., and the warmth and effusive vocabulary he sometimes used, even if common in Victorian times, jars with contemporary sensibility. It created problems for biographers of a later generation at a time when affection between heterosexual males could only be expressed in more restrained terms, leading them to see, however ludicrously, traces of subdued homoeroticism. R.L.S.' regret at separation from his friends was genuine and fulsomely expressed. He was dismayed when they held Fanny responsible for settling in the South Seas, and begged Colvin not "to start in to blame Fanny", telling him she had wept all night after hearing of his disapproval of their plans, and putting responsibility onto her. "When it came to this Samoa business, I was averse, only for your sake . . . Know this: I love you" (VI, 2240).

The stop at Samoa, intended as a short break in a longer voyage, had become a life-changing event, but actually settling took some time. The first period there lasted only two months, from December 1889 until February 4 the following year. During that time they completed the purchase of the land, but there was no shelter available on the estate, making it impossible to take up residence immediately. Moors agreed to take responsibility for the building operations, leaving the Stevensons free to continue on their way to Sydney. Apart from securing property, R.L.S. had made friends, engaged with the politics of Samoa, familiarised himself with the commercial and political incursions of the Europeans and Americans, and witnessed the extent of German power on the islands. He had acquired shrewd insights into the issues facing the islands, and corrected some of the misapprehensions he had gathered in Honolulu.

It was also at this period that he wrote the first version of the fable recounted to him on Hawaii, "The Bottle Imp", a tale that would have an importance for him – and for the literature of the South Seas – which outweighs its intrinsic merits, considerable though they are. It was the first literary work translated into Samoan and would, in quite unexpected ways, help determine and enhance the writer's image and status among Samoans. Although it is set on Hawaii, and although the subject has an unmistakable resemblance to the South Sea *Ballads*, the story has European origins. Oddly, R.L.S. and Fanny give different versions of the source. In an introductory note, he suggests that the tale had turned up "in that very unliterary product, the English drama of the early part of the century", having been reworked by "the redoubtable O. Smith", while she says that they had seen the melodrama acted in a private theatre in the house belonging to their friend of Bournemouth days, Sir Percy Shelley. She attributes it to "an author, even then, almost forgotten, named Fitzball". She also claims that the play had German derivations (Tusitala XIII, x–xii).

She may be right about the antecedents, for the work reads like a medieval morality tale. Down on his luck, Keawe is informed about an imp who, though locked in a bottle of unbreakable glass, yet has the power to grant any wish the owner makes. There is of course a moral catch. Whoever ends up in final possession of the bottle will be condemned to the everlasting fires of hell, and ownership can be changed only by selling the bottle at a price lower than had been paid for it. It had passed though many hands, so the price is already perilously low. Along the way, Keawe falls in love with Kokua, and uses the magical powers of the imp to construct the Bright House for them, but on account of the sentence of damnation which hangs over the possessor of the bottle they cannot live happily ever after. Love and sin are in competition with each other in an atmosphere which, for all its glittering allure, is marked by the presence of evil: quintessentially Stevensonian territory. There is no need to apply too heavy a hand and seek out traces of the dire bedtime stories recounted by Cummy to her infant charge, but the consciousness of lurking evil hangs over much of R.L.S.' storytelling, as it does over much of Scottish fiction. The couple exchange ownership of the bottle between themselves, but one of them is faced with damnation. Fortunately, a *deus ex machina*, the sort of wicked wretch of a man who peoples improving, religious tales, and who reckons he is bound for hell anyway, calmly accepts the bottle and the fate that accompanies it.

The tale as it is retold is undoubtedly a beautiful piece of professional craftsmanship, and the style has the lilt of the fairy stories of the Brothers Grimm, but was there some moral message behind the dilemma, or did its appeal for R.L.S. lie in its dramatic narrative for its own sake? The tale met the approval of missionaries, who seemingly believed that it carried a Christian message, while also seeing it as in keeping with pre-Christian, Samoan cultural notions. They had it translated into Samoan and distributed as a serial in their news-sheets, but its impact was not what they had hoped. Written fiction was unknown in Samoa, so it was assumed by native readers that the tale was factual, and that the real protagonist was R.L.S. himself, even if he was not yet known as Tusitala. The magical power of the imp provided an answer to questions which puzzled Samoans. Where did Stevenson's wealth come from, since he neither ploughed nor fished? In a letter to Conan Doyle, he explained that the islanders had no problem believing in the existence of a spirit of arbitrary power and genuine malevolence, of the sort which populated the woods of Samoa, but they did struggle to come to terms with the idea that a man could earn his living merely by putting words on a page (VIII, 2624). Many visitors to Vailima begged to be shown the bottle with the imprisoned imp, while others who saw the safe in the main hall assumed that this was its abode. The popularity of the tale endowed R.L.S. with the status of a magus. He became, though not only by virtue of this tale, a chieftain of some standing.

In Sydney they were reunited with Belle. Her husband Joe had been on the *Equator*, but as a consequence of R.L.S.' disapproval of her conduct, Belle had been dispatched with Austin to Australia to await the arrival of the others. Stevenson's affections for Joe and Belle wavered, causing him at times to disapprove of both, or to side now with one, now with the other. Joe was plainly a rogue, an untrustworthy, unreliable sponger, given to pilfering and hard drinking, but R.L.S. was well disposed towards him, and Fanny too described him as lovable. However, the days in Hawaii and on the *Equator* were his moment of maximum favour in R.L.S.' eyes. Belle, on the other had, had aroused R.L.S.' displeasure in Hawaii, causing her to be refused, in spite of her pleas, permission to travel with her mother and husband on the yacht. When they arrived in Samoa, Joe gave every appearance of illness, and was sent to join his wife in Sydney and recuperate, which he did very rapidly, if indeed he had ever suffered from any genuine, medical ailment.

R.L.S. and Fanny had to arrange accommodation in Sydney, and faced an embarrassing contretemps. The dishevelled couple presented themselves at a respectable hotel, only to find them-selves treated condescendingly by the receptionist. Self-control was not one of Stevenson's more notable characteristics, and he threw a tantrum and stormed off to book a room in another establishment. The embarrassment was on the other foot when the hotel discovered the nature of their gaffe with a man whom they discovered to be a celebrity of some standing, and offered to make amends. R.L.S. was implacable.

It was during this stay that he came across the disparaging remarks made in a published letter by the Rev. Dr Hyde about Father Damien, whose work with the lepers on Molokai R.L.S. had so admired. The priest had gone to the leper colony on the island to tend to those suffering from the disease, but contracted leprosy, from which he died. R.L.S. visited the same island in May 1889, and wrote at the time ambiguous words of half-hearted praise of Damien, but he was indignant when he read Hyde's sneering attack and wrote a fiery, unrestrained satirical response in his defence (Tusitala, XXI). His pamphlet was a savage *ad hominem* philippic which could have given Hyde grounds for raising a libel case, and any damages awarded would have been ruinous for a man whose finances were in a precarious state. The construction of Vailima would scarcely have been possible, nor would debts incurred to Moors have been repayable, but Hyde preferred the high ground of patrician disdain and took no legal steps. R.L.S. quickly regretted his intemperance, but said so only in private correspondence. He never apologised to Hyde.

He made a start to *The Wrecker*, but his health collapsed. He had a further attack of "bluidy Jack", as he referred to his haemorrhages, but this one so serious that Fanny doubted, not for the first time, whether he would survive. Lloyd was sent to lodge with the Strongs, although this too caused further dissent, with the Strongs convinced, perhaps not inaccurately, that he had been planted to spy on them. At that time, R.L.S. declared himself pleased with the conduct of Joe and Belle, who "had been behaving excellently", as he reported to Baxter. He was sure Joe had been "in a critical state of health, but he still lives . . . and Belle has been a kind nurse to him". His own condition was less promising, and he wrote that "this visit to Sydney has smashed me handsomely" (VI, 2215). Everyone believed that a return to the sea would assist his recovery, and Fanny, undeterred by the strike which was paralysing shipping in New South Wales, managed to persuade the Scottish owners of the *Janet Nicoll* to take on board a sickly, possibly moribund, passenger. They set sail on April 11, 1890, not sure where they would call since the vessel was engaged in trading, and the agreement was that guests on board would have to take their chances. They stopped at Auckland, and while at sea a box of fireworks, an unwise purchase, exploded, causing a fire on board. One crew member, in accordance with best maritime practice, picked up a smoking box to throw overboard. Fanny intervened to prevent R.L.S.' papers from ending up at the bottom of the ocean. One of their fellow passengers, Jack Buckland, an exuberant drunk with a wealth of stories, provided the model for Tommy Madden of *The Wrecker*.

As it happened the next place at which the *Janet Nicoll* made a call was Samoa, which gave them the opportunity to examine progress on the construction of Vailima. They were not entirely pleased with what they saw. "Obliging natives from the Cannibal Islands" were engaged in cutting down the forest, and a house "the size of a manufacturer's lodge" was more or less prepared for them. R.L.S. was happy to consider it "the egg of a future palace", but Fanny was less positive, so he was forced to add the words that "over the details on paper Mrs Stevenson and I have already shed real tears". He still harboured no romantic notions about the characters or behaviour of the Samoans themselves, and expressed his doubts forthrightly: "the native population, very genteel, very songful, very agreeable, very good-looking, fairly false, absolutely, hopelessly dishonest, chronically spoiling for a fight (a circumstance not to be entirely neglected in the design of the palace)" (VI, 2232).

The visit was brief, and they continued on their way through the South Seas, leaving the work of reclamation and construction once again in the hands of Moors. They stopped at some other islands until, somewhat strangely in view of his failing health, R.L.S. was left on his own on the island of Noumea while Fanny and Lloyd continued on their way. He claimed the reason was that he wished to study the convict system, but it may be that the couple needed a break from each other, since their relationship was uneven. The party met up again in Sydney in August. He took up residence in the Union Club but had immediately to take to his bed as his infirmity returned. It was here in Sydney that he confirmed definitively his decision about his and his family's future. If his health was so poor in Australia, how would it be in England, he asked Henry James. Lloyd was dispatched to Britain to sell off Skerryvore in Bournemouth, and to arrange to send much of the furniture to Samoa. He was also instructed to go to Edinburgh to help Aunt Maggie make her own preparations for the journey to Samoa. Once again, one must marvel at the pluck and energy of this woman, widowed and elderly by the standards of her time, as she prepared to uproot from all that was familiar to her and set off for a far-off land of which she knew little. R.L.S. was doubtful about Lloyd's abilities for this task, since he did not view him as "a man of business", and recruited friends to keep an eye on him.

In Sydney, he had an uncompromising tête-à-tête with Joe. The early promise had not been maintained. Joe's behaviour had "swollen his [Stevenson's] spleen", as evidence, not denied, emerged of his having returned to his old, dissolute ways, spending money advanced by R.L.S. in ways not intended, including on drinking and visits to brothels. Joe had taken up his painting once again, and had even managed to sell some of his works, but he spoiled any positive impression by keeping the profits for his own purposes, while still drawing an allowance from R.L.S., whose exasperation with Joe and revised opinion of Belle were given free expression in a letter to Charles Baxter. "Belle has behaved really well this time," but as for Joe, "Oh Christ Jesus! It is sometimes too much to have to support this creature." The puzzled bystander might wonder what did persuade him to continue supporting such a wretch, but R.L.S. was driven by his own imperatives. "And yet withal he's a kind of innocent" (VI, 2249). Perhaps the real innocent was R.L.S. himself, or perhaps he was that rare being, a genuinely generous-minded man, always prepared to dip his hand deep into any mud to find a diamond hidden to all others. The kind of *faux* innocent Joe really was would become clearer and clearer in the coming years when the family, Belle, Joe, and Austin, were in residence on Samoa.

R.L.S.' troubles with his health and travails with his extended family had not caused him to set aside writing, even temporarily. Marcel Schwob wrote to him to request authorisation to translate *The Black Arrow* into French. Permission was granted, although the author said he had no high view of that work himself. He had much else on his mind:

I am just now overloaded with work. I have two huge novels on hand – *The Wrecker* and *The Pearl Fisher*, in collaboration with my stepson – the latter I think highly of, for a black, ugly trampling, violent story, full of strange scenes and striking characters. And then I am about waist-deep in my big book about the South Seas: *the* big book on the South Seas it ought to be, and shall, and besides, I have some verses in the press which, however, I hesitate to publish. For I am no judge of my own verse; self-deception is there so facile. All this and the cares of an impending settlement in Samoa keep me very busy, and a cold (as usual) keeps me in bed. (VI, 2238)

The Pearl Fisher was later entitled *The Ebb-Tide*, but perhaps because Schwob was discouraged by Stevenson's low opinion of his own work, the translation of *The Black Arrow* never appeared. In September 1890, R.L.S. and Fanny set off for Samoa and their *vita nova*. The time at sea did him good and once he was back on the island, R.L.S.' health recovered. The wind seemed set fair.

CHAPTER 12

Residents and Visitors

R.L.S. gave various accounts of his routine at Vailima, even if he never stuck rigidly to it. In a letter in March 1891, he invited his correspondent to admire his "busyness". He rose early and had his coffee or orange juice brought to his room, and so he was ready to start writing before the rest of the house was stirring. About two years into his residence in Vailima, he began to suffer from cramps in his hand, and employed Belle as his amanuensis, even for his correspondence. This displeased Fanny, who was uneasy about any other woman, even her own daughter, getting too close to her man. Previously he wrote sitting up in his bed, but when Belle assumed the task of scribe, he would spend time preparing developments of plot and clearing his thoughts for the morning's dictation. He explained that in a normal day at that time he worked between 6.00 and 10.30, when he stopped to give lessons to Austin. After the split between Joe and Belle, Austin was sent first to California, and later to New Zealand, to continue his education. Lunch was at 11.00, after which R.L.S. played some music. His favourite instrument was the flageolet, which he played so badly that people fled from the sound. He allowed himself time for leisure after lunch, often bathing in his pool on Mount Vaea. He feared that Fanny, whose health was often poor, was over-exerting herself, but she "gives herself no chance, being always out *fighting* in her garden." The following year, he added that they usually played cards in the evening, but once a week there was a dancing club to go to.

One of his greatest delights was to set off alone on his horse, Jack. Graham Balfour wrote that Jack "reigned alone in Stevenson's affection"; Moors says R.L.S. was not "a daring rider" but one who preferred to jog and enjoy the scenery. During his travels in the Cévennes, he found that one of the supreme pleasures of life was to sit in the evening leaning against a tree, smoking and reflecting. In Upolu, he enjoyed tethering his horse and giving himself the opportunities for the same enjoyments, perhaps even rewriting what he had earlier committed to paper. All the inhabitants of Vailima were inveterate smokers, whose consumption of cigarettes amazed Moors. R.L.S. rode Jack once in an exhilarating paperchase which took place on a Sunday. He was reproached later in the week in the main street in Apia by Rev. Clarke's wife for breaking the Sabbath, a rebuke he accepted meekly. Altogether, he wrote, "it is a life that suits [me]" (VII, 2395). He liked a certain formality of dress at dinner, the main communal activity of the day. He was also fairly strict about topics of conversation at table, preferring to avoid anything too serious, although conditions in Samoan society did not always permit that. By all accounts, he was a magnetic conversationalist, a splendid raconteur, and a fine wit. Both Balfour and Belle seem to have aspired to be his Boswell, and made copious notes of his conversations.[82]

R.L.S. was, as far as the vicissitudes of life and health

---

82 Balfour's papers are now lodged in the National Library of Scotland.

permitted, happy in Samoa. His mother writes that as he returned to Vailima after going to Sydney to meet her, "his love of the place was strong in his eyes". In another of her letters, she sets out the essence of what she terms "his own gospel", that while "it is our duty to be good ourselves, our duty to our neighbour is to make him happy."[83] R.L.S. identified a similar state of mind in Walt Whitman, and it was one of the factors which he found most attractive in Whitman's verse, while its absence went some way to explain his distaste for writers as diverse as Emile Zola and Thomas Hardy. His anxieties over the political strife in Samoa and rage with the unjust pseudo-colonial rule to which the archipelago was subjected were heart-felt and intense, and his championing of the native cause also gave him an added *raison d'être*. He told Edmund Gosse, "our home, our estate, and our boys, and the politics of the island keep us perpetually amused and busy" (VIII, 2585). There was little in the current affairs of the island to cause amusement in any conventional sense, but they did keep R.L.S. charged with fire and purpose.

Following the arrival of his mother, he introduced the ritual of evening family prayer into the Vailima routine. He wrote some of the prayers himself, and a few were later published individually, complete with reverential illuminated letters. The majority of the staff was Catholic, known in Samoa as "popeys". Aunt Maggie, while personally kind to everyone, retained a Presbyterian prejudice against Catholic "idolatry", but when she insisted that the Catholics be brought to the prayer meeting, she came into conflict with Fanny, who was not keen on the

83 M.I. Stevenson, *Letters from Samoa*, op. cit., pp. 34 and 257.

idea of collective prayer in any circumstances. They came anyway. By the time she wrote a preface to the prayers for the Tusitala edition, Fanny had forgotten this disagreement and wrote that the omission of a prayer session would have been shameful in any Samoan household. The ceremony was conducted in accordance with a strict liturgy. A conch, normally a vessel summoning warriors to arms, was sounded, and the family and servants trooped into the great hall. The family took their regular places at table and the staff gathered in a semicircle. Lloyd read a chapter from the Bible in Samoan, R.L.S. recited a prayer which might be improvised to refer to some events in the day, and the session concluded with a hymn, also in Samoan.

In Edinburgh decades previously R.L.S. had quarrelled bitterly with his father over his loss of faith. The prayer ceremony has led enthusiastic believers to see signs of R.L.S.' return to religion, some even suggesting that he was on the point of converting to Catholicism. This is unlikely in the extreme. The prayers are addressed to the Lord in the Christian style in which R.L.S. had been brought up and which would be familiar to Samoan converts, but they show little sense of the numinous, and are limited to expressing in appropriately quasi-religious tones essentially moral secular aspirations. Lloyd Osbourne said it was characteristic of R.L.S. to say: "Christ was always such a great gentleman: you could always count on His doing the right thing" (Tusitala, I, xvi). R.L.S. had similar ambitions. The Lord to whom these prayers are addressed is a largely benevolent but unpredictable, shamanic force, and above all a capable distributor of benefits. His prayer entitled "Sunday" opens with the words, "We beseech Thee, Lord, to behold us with favour, folk of many families and nations gathered together in the peace of this roof, weak men and women subsisting under the covert of Thy patience." The slightly archaic vocabulary is indispensable to the lofty tone.

R.L.S. lived without regaining a creed but also without being able to renounce entirely a transcendental view of life. He was never a materialist. His beloved nurse Cummy had done her work thoroughly and transmitted to him a religious worldview. In his adulthood that once magnificent structure was a ruin, but the remnants were as recognisably religious as the ruins of Border Abbeys he had visited in his youth. His religious sense was a form of lapsed Calvinism, a quintessentially Scottish state of mind. "The Scottish atheists were unmistakable children of the Kirk," in Chesterton's words.[84] Lapsed Catholicism is a state of mind with a code of morals made familiar by Graham Greene and François Mauriac, but lapsed Calvinism has not found its spokesperson. The lapsed believer comes from a strong tradition of faith, and gropes all his life among the rubble of past belief. Theology did not interest R.L.S., but many of his novels are imbued with a Calvinist sense of life and morality, focusing on the power of conscience and the sense of duty. *The Master of Ballantrae* dramatises a dispute between the merry, carefree devil dreaded by the Calvinist imagination, incarnate in the Master, and the dreary, dutiful slave of conscience who is his brother, Henry.[85] The deeply rooted ethical outlook which underpinned all his writings made him conscious of the existence of an evil which was cosmic rather than social. His mental

84 G.K. Chesterton, *Stevenson*, op. cit., p. 127.
85 James McCearney, *Le Pays Stevenson*, Paris, Christian de Bartillat, 1995, p. 136.

universe was founded on an imprecise mysticism without a creed.

The first of the prayers is "For Success", and another is "For Continued Favours", a notion which had been parodied by Robert Burns in "Holy Willie's Prayer" a century before. The most common plea is for decency, for the observance of moderate behaviour, or for that gentleness of spirit which will soothe pain and resolve conflicts. The prayers are all to do with the here and now, and could be recited by anyone with or without a creed. Other prayers are "For Renewed Power", "Before a Temporary Separation", and "For the Renewal of Joy". Such words could have been, and probably were, intoned by holy men on Samoa before the coming of Christianity. There is no denying that R.L.S. was a good man, but the prayer ceremony was only formally a religious rite. He once agreed to preach at a Sunday School on the island, and told his charges that God had created everything. When he was asked by one of his brighter pupils, Who created God, he turned and fled.

While they do not feature in his prayers, his sexual morals were rigid and implacably Calvinist. His attitude to Robert Burns was coloured by his distaste for Burns' philandering ways, while in an essay on John Knox, uncompromisingly entitled "John Knox and Women", he took the reformer to task for his semi-suppressed libidinous outlook on women. He never deviated from this early Puritanism. In Samoa, he was appalled to discover that an employee of the lawyer Carruthers, with whom he became friendly, was having an affair with a Samoan woman, and refused to dine with Moors if the man was likely to be there. Carruthers was compelled to dismiss him. His rage with Joe, when he found out that Joe was conducting an affair in Apia with a Samoan woman while married to Belle, was "titanic", and was the final blow in his relationship with Fanny's son-in-law, who was expelled from the house in spite of his promises to reform. His discovery that Lloyd was similarly involved with a Samoan woman presented him with a dilemma of a different order. He could hardly expel his wife's son, so he told Lloyd to marry the girl. Lloyd refused, and while R.L.S. had no option but to accept, his disapproval was forcibly expressed.

Callers to Vailima over the years were legion, and different categories can be distinguished: invited guests, groups of native Samoans arriving spontaneously on a *malaga* (tour), crew members of British ships, European or American residents of Apia, and individual travellers from overseas who were driven by curiosity or admiration. Many of those who received hospitality in Vailima, even for short periods, wrote about the experience, some offering descriptions which shine welcome light on private life. Belle recorded an evening in February 1892. "We danced this evening after dinner in the big hall. Mamma sat on the table and turned the hurdy gurdy, and Louis waltzed to triple time. He can also dance the Highland *schottische*, which he does with much earnestness. We had great fun teaching it to Captain Wurmbrand who, being an Austrian, is also a beautiful dancer."[86] Baron von Wurmbrand, to give him his full title, was a guest at Vailima and given the room previously occupied by R.L.S.' mother. He was one of that pack of elite, eccentric drifters who fetched up in Samoa and sought out R.L.S. Wurmbrand had been an aristocrat in Austria-Hungary and seen service in

86 Belle Field (Osbourne) and Lloyd Osbourne, *Memories of Vailima*, New York, Charles Scribner, 1902, p. 56.

the imperial army, but seems to have committed some social solecism which compelled him to leave court circles. R.L.S. brought Wurmbrand to vivid life with a few strokes of the pen, recounting that post-Vienna he had been a rough rider and shepherd in Australia, and describing him as "an intensely excitable little man, with the appearance of a bandit and the manners of a French jack-in-the-box" (VIII, 2698). He was followed by a Hungarian count, Festetics de Tolna, a "very pleasant simple boyish creature", who arrived on his yacht with his American wife. He too was invited to Vailima, but when another Hungarian turned up, Festetics de Tolna departed hurriedly, leaving behind speculation as to his past. He wrote a work in French on his acquaintance with R.L.S., as everyone did.

Not all visitors were star-struck by the experience of being admitted to the presence of R.L.S. In October 1890, Henry Adams made his way to Vailima. A scion of the patrician New England family which had produced two presidents of the United States, he had published anonymously two novels, *Democracy* and *Esther*, in which he worried about the future of civilisation in view of the emancipation of women. In the same decade, he wrote the nine-volume history of the U.S.A. on which his reputation then rested. His most enduring work, the recondite, probing examination of medieval culture in *Mont Saint-Michel and Chartres* was still ahead of him, but he was in his own view a sensitive man of letters. Adams was in the South Seas recovering from the death of his wife and resting after the labour of completing the history, and was travelling in the company of the artist, John La Farge, whom R.L.S. had known in New York. Adams was an intolerable snob. Although the Stevensons showed him friendship, his judgement on them was acid, and would continue to be delivered in the same terms over the coming decades. He made no allowance for the fact that R.L.S. and Fanny had just moved in to their new estate when he turned up, and recoiled in horror when he was invited to breakfast but asked to bring some food with him. The supplies were sent ahead in a grand basket, a gesture which R.L.S. told Henry James he viewed as a snub. Adams described R.L.S. and Fanny's appearance disdainfully, emphasising their grubbiness and ignoring the fact that they were engaged in "weeding". After his first visit, he wrote:

> In the middle (of the clearing), stood a two-storey Irish shanty with steps outside to the upper floor, and a galvanised iron roof. A pervasive atmosphere of dirt seemed to hang about it, and the squalor is like a railroad navvy's board hut. As we reached the steps, a figure came out that I cannot do justice to . . . he was costumed in very dirty striped cotton pyjamas, the baggy legs tucked into coarse knit woollen stockings, one of which was bright brown in colour, the other a purplish dark tone. With him was a woman . . . [who] wore the usual missionary nightgown which was no cleaner than her husband's shirt and drawers, but she omitted the stockings . . . when the conversation began, though I could not forget the dirt and discomfort, I found Stevenson extremely entertaining.

The two men "came round to a sort of liking for Mrs Stevenson, who is more human than her husband. Stevenson is an *aitu*, uncanny." Adams pouted in a style worthy of Louis XIV in Versailles when he discovered that R.L.S. knew La Farge by reputation but had no idea of the grandeur of Adams himself.

When Colvin's edition of the Vailima letters was published, Adams wrote that they made him "crawl with creepy horror, as he did when he was alive".[87] In a letter written in Paris long after Stevenson's death, he said that he used

> to feel sympathy, naturally repressed, with poor old Louis Stevenson when he came down to chat with La Farge. Stevenson's mind was as Scotch as mine was Yankee . . . Stevenson's view of the South Seas was that of a serious-minded Scotchman who is consumed with desire to understand his wayward and fanciful and immoral children. La Farge, I knew, never was in the least perplexed, though often amused, by the way Stevenson saw things, and the pathetic desire he had to see them differently.[88]

At least in that final point he was more or less correct, although there was nothing pathetic about his wish, nor is it clear in what way he wished to see Samoan ways "differently" rather than accurately. Adams could not fathom the Samoans. "They are the least imaginative people I have ever met. They have almost no arts or literature. Their songs are mere catches . . . even their superstitions are practical."[89]

Marie Fraser arrived with her mother in Samoa in 1892 and wrote a book of recollections which has received only patronising or sneering notices. She was an actress, but the only record of her career is in a review by George Bernard Shaw, who saw her in Ibsen's A Doll's House and damned her as "very bad".

87 Worthington Chauncey Ford (editor), *Letters of Henry Adams*, Boston, Houghton Mifflin, 1938, p. 269.
88 Ibid., p. 139.
89 Elizabeth Stevenson, *Henry Adams*, New York, Macmillan, 1955, p. 216.

Her book is somewhat giddy and excitable in tone, but if she was no critic or analyst, she provided memorable, first-hand accounts of interesting episodes. Their stay in Vailima ended unhappily, with R.L.S. dismissing them as "exceptionally silly women", and the others glad to see them go. However, Marie's book is a worthwhile record of social life. The lavishness of the feasts at Vailima awed her, particularly the party held to celebrate R.L.S.' birthday. Interestingly, she noted that "the gathering consisted almost entirely of natives, very few white people being present." After the introductory pleasantries, the group were led off to be attired in the appropriate style. "Ropes of many-coloured, sweet-smelling flowers were twisted round our necks and waists and wreaths placed on our heads." The group were then escorted to a specially constructed native house thatched with coconut palms, with palm leaves on the floor and these in their turn covered by the mats which are such an indispensable part of Samoan life and etiquette. Seats are unknown in Samoa, so the company sat cross-legged on the floor. The quantity of foods astonished Miss Fraser: "dozens of pigs, varying in size from a rabbit to an immense creature which formed the centrepiece, quantities of chickens and ducks, every kind of native fruit and vegetable, and before each guest a leaf of large pink prawns." This was not all, although Miss Fraser baulked at sampling the mysterious dish which "consisted of green worms that appear in the sea at certain intervals according to the state of the moon."[90]

Samoan ceremonial invariably demanded the consumption of *kava*, a non-alcoholic drink which R.L.S. discusses frequently

90 Marie Fraser, *In Stevenson's Samoa*, London, Smith, Elder & Co, 1895, p. 28.

in his letters. To say it is an acquired taste is an understatement. The basic ingredient is the root of a pepper plant, and traditionally this root had to be chewed by a female, preferably the *taupou* or village maiden, but in her absence any woman would do. After chewing it, she spat it into the concave *tanoa* (bowl), where it was mixed with water and strained through a fibre made from the inner bark of the fau plant. It retained a muddy appearance, was served in a half-coconut shell, and distributed among the company according to rank. Fanny's status in Vailima puzzled the Samoans on several such grand occasions, for normally the *taupou* would take priority as second in rank to the chieftain, and the younger woman on the premises, Belle, seemed to fit the part, but they agreed with Stevenson's insistence that Fanny be given the higher status. Speeches and singing followed the *kava*, or happened later, after the meal. For R.L.S., the arrival uninvited of a group led by their chieftain was often an unwelcome interruption of his work, but he was always willing to descend to the verandah and participate in the ceremony.

Fraser also gave a vivid description of the costume in which the servants at Vailima were arrayed – white linen shirts, a *lava-lava* in Royal Stuart tartan, and a sky-blue and purple-striped blazer. Hair was combed straight back, with a few flowers stuck in. Apart from the flowers, the outfit resembles the uniform of a Scots private fee-paying school. The servants were also taken by any item of Western clothing they could find, however incongruous, so the widow's caps Aunt Maggie felt obliged to wear were systematically purloined and donned by the boys who marched about wearing them. To avoid such scenes, the family took to burying unwanted items of clothing. In her widow's weeds, Aunt Maggie in photographs has an uncanny resemblance to Queen Victoria.

August 1892 saw the arrival of two very different people. Graham Balfour, R.L.S.' cousin, had come into an inheritance with the death of his father and set off on a tour of the world, with Japan his principal destination. None of the family had seen him since he was a boy, and so were unsure what to expect or even what he looked like. As they waited by the pier watching travellers disembark, "we chose some awful cads," R.L.S. admitted, and were relieved to find he was "as nice a young fellow as you would want". Belle plainly agreed with that assessment and promptly fell in love with him, a sentiment which was not, alas, reciprocated. He was lodged with Lloyd in the cottage, and was by all accounts a highly welcome addition to the Vailima clan. He showed he fitted in with domestic ways by going barefoot, like the others, and making himself useful by helping Fanny in the garden and playing chess with R.L.S. He even acquired some fluency in Samoan. His initial plan was to stay a month, but in the event he was with them for about a year. Later, after R.L.S.' death, when the original invitation to Sidney Colvin to write R.L.S.' official biography was withdrawn by Fanny, he was entrusted with that delicate task. His biography has the stateliness of Victorian architecture but is masterly and invaluable.

The other was Lady Jersey, wife of the Governor of New South Wales and the very incarnation of the "new woman" who was then making an appearance in London in suffragette marches and in the plays of Bernard Shaw. No-one could have been more calculated to stir the already none too calm waters in Vailima, and indeed in Samoa as a whole at a time when consular and international relations were precariously balanced. Officially she was there to visit Bazett Haggard, the British Land Commissioner, but, the moment she arrived, Haggard introduced her to R.L.S., who was instantly attracted to her. This of itself meant that she was bound to arouse the ire of Fanny, who denounced her roundly in her diary as a member of the "champagne Charley set", and vented her spleen more fully in a portrait of her as "tall and leggy and awkward, with bold black eyes and sensual mouth; very selfish and greedy of admiration, a touch of vulgarity, courageous as a man, and reckless as a woman."[91]

Reckless she may have been, and she certainly appealed to the puckish side of R.L.S.' nature. Her presence and personality gave him licence to indulge in the sort of pranks he had enjoyed as a student in Edinburgh, but the political situation in Samoa, and her status, meant that the stakes were higher. Her entourage included her brother, Captain Leigh, whom R.L.S. dismissed as "a very nice stupid glass-in-the-eye kind of fellow". R.L.S. was due to make a visit to Mata'afa, and Leigh asked if he could go along. Since Mata'afa was viewed by the authorities as a rebel and an opponent of the official Malietoa, it was agreed Leigh would have to travel incognito. R.L.S. promptly created a Jacobite name and sent off a letter to him dated 1745. The matter became more complex when Lady Jersey expressed a wish to join the party. Her status as wife of an imperial office-bearer made this awkward, but R.L.S. was delighted. She too needed a new identity, so he named her Amelia Balfour, and told Mata'afa she was his cousin. Lady Jersey got into the spirit by writing

91 Stevenson and Stevenson, *Our Samoan Adventure,* op. cit., p. 208.

some poems in the name of Amelia, but Mata'afa was not deceived. R.L.S. wrote to Colvin that "the lark is huge", but went on: "I would not in the least wonder if the visit proved the signal of war." His next comment rings false and genuinely reckless: "With this I have no concern, not yet with the feelings of the Earl of Jersey; I am not his wife's keeper, and the thing wholly suits my book and fits my predilections for Samoa."

He tempered his indiscretion by ensuring that Lady Jersey met the other two pretenders to the supreme position in Samoa, but the concealment of the visit to Mata'afa required some nifty footwork by Haggard, and presumably the earl. R.L.S. was able to report later that month that "the round of gaiety continues . . . I ought to say how much we all like the Jersey party." The "we" did not include his wife, who was still, in Burns' words, nursing her wrath to keep it warm. He had reversed his initial impression of Leigh, whom he now viewed as "very amusing in his small way". Compliments were showered on the woman who had turned his head. "Lady Jersey is in all ways admirable: so unfussy, so plucky, so very kind and gracious." He brought her along to assist at the opening of a school in Apia, where she revealed herself to be "really an orator, with a voice of gold". The social whirl while the party was in town included dinners in various houses and a steeplechase. A curiosity of the visit was a pastiche novel, in the style of Ouida, *An Object of Pity or the Man Haggard*, to which five of them, including both Fanny and Lady Jersey as well as R.L.S., Belle, and Graham Balfour, contributed comic portraits of Haggard. The work was published privately (VII, 2452).

Public curiosity about the very idea of R.L.S. making his home on Samoa continued unabated, and some artists sought permission to paint his portrait. Lady Jersey's visit overlapped with that of Count Nerli, son of an Italian nobleman and an artist whom R.L.S. met by chance on the beach and invited to Vailima. He may have regretted his impulsiveness for we find him describing Nerli as someone who is "said to be a good painter, also a drunkard and a sweep, and he looks it" (VII, 2444). R.L.S. agreed to sit for him. Nerli also did a number of pencil and charcoal drawings which are now distributed in galleries around the world. Fanny disliked the oil-colour portrait, which she viewed as flawed because the artist had expended too much effort in an attempt to locate the Hyde underneath the Jekyll. Inevitably, Nerli penned a brief pamphlet on R.L.S. In 1894, an English painter, A.J. Daplyn, whom R.L.S. had known in Barbizon, turned up. He reported to his mother that he found the artist *"reether dreary* but an honest man". To compensate, Fanny and Daplyn got on well, which lightened the atmosphere in the house. The portrait is now in Monterey.

There were many occasions for parties, picnics, dinners, some celebrating birthdays or public holidays in either Britain or America, others simply extemporised. The accounts of these events given by R.L.S.' mother are fluttery with an excitement she could never have experienced in Edinburgh's New Town. She provides disbelieving lists of the frequency of dinners and feasts and of the quantities of food and drink consumed. "I have been quite gay (for me!) this week, having been to no less than two entertainments." The first was a lunch on board the H.M.S. *Curaçoa* and the second a picnic at the volcanic Papaloa pool at the foot of steep surrounding cliffs. She declined to make the dive herself, but was impressed by the Samoan girls and the *Curaçoa* sailors who did. After the bathing came a splendid al fresco Samoan meal, "with no end of pigs, chickens, crayfish, prawns and so on, and quantities of bread-fruit, taro, and coconuts both to eat and drink", all rounded off with Samoan and European dancing. There was a brief moment of panic when a group of armed warriors was espied nearby, but they were well disposed and delighted to be offered a pig as their share of the feast. The realisation that a war was being waged in the vicinity did not disturb the even tenor of life.[92]

Crews of visiting ships were welcome guests at Vailima. The *Curaçoa* seems to have been a special favourite, but the officers of any visiting vessel could expect an invitation, and would return the favour. R.L.S. was amused to note that as soon as a ship docked, the Scots among the crew would instantly make their way uphill to Vailima, "like homing pigeons". On some occasions, the entire crew came for a reception on the verandah, one in particular being described as "the brightest in the annals of Vailima". In September 1893, the British warship *Katoomba* was in the harbour as part of a multi-national peacekeeping force. The island was still reeling from the war between rivals for the position of Malietoa, and privately it was a time of great anxiety for R.L.S., with his wife making an uncertain recovery from a bout of illness, but the show went on. The captain released his band for a day, and "they came fourteen of them with drum, fife, cymbals and bugles, blue jackets, white caps and smiling faces." The house was duly decorated with fragrant flowers and scented greenery, extra staff were taken on, and, as the band proceeded up the hill from Apia, it attracted "a following of children by the way, and we had the picking of

92 M.I. Stevenson, *Letters from Samoa*, op. cit., p. 280.

Samoan ladies to receive them". Delicacies were served, as they "played to us, they danced, they sang, they tumbled. Our boys came in at the end of the verandah, and gave *them* a dance for a while." It was difficult to bring a halt to the proceedings, but R.L.S. pronounced himself and Fanny "the most contented hosts that ever watched the departure of successful guests" (VIII, 2624).

And then there were balls, both at Vailima and in the hotels and clubs in Apia. R.L.S. was modest about his abilities as dancer, realising that the dainty two-step was not for him, but he threw himself into waltzes and quadrilles with a will. He was concerned about the exclusion from society of people of mixed parentage and accepted, with some uncertainty, the proposal made by one of his staff to establish at Vailima a Club – the capital letter is his – which would organise "a sort of weekly ball for half-castes and natives, ourselves to be the only whites". Twenty people turned up at the inaugural meeting to be treated to cake and lemonade and listen to R.L.S. outline the project. Fanny was selected as president, and the one white man and his wife who came along were kept segregated from the rest. Fanny and Belle had been sceptical about the project, and they found that their first task was to deal severely with one lady who "reclined upon the booosom [*sic*] of a gentleman". Whites were excluded because they could not be relied on to behave respectfully. As R.L.S. put it, "a Samoan girl is told she must not mind white gentlemen when they pull her about, because the white gentlemen cannot help it" (VII, 1892). Such insouciant tolerance of male ways!

Dances in town generally passed off quietly but could provide matter for salacious gossip and once provoked a fight which was not conducted according to Queensberry rules. An other-wise unidentified Mrs Kopsch turned up, her mere presence causing other denizens to flee the scene. A letter reporting the fracas that evening appeared in the local *Herald* but, some-what curiously, the editor of the journal who published it took issue in the street with the letter-writer and punched him on the nose. At the same ball, a young lady called Bella Decker appeared, but in Fanny's view she was "showing more of her legs than was *convenable* for a girl of her age". Whether or not this was the motive for his act, the fact is that Macfarlane the printer touched her on the neck. For his act of impropriety, he was taken to task by Mr Harold Chatfield, letters were exchanged, satisfaction demanded, and the two men met in front of a large public, not to exchange bullets, but to face up to each other in fisticuffs. Blows were struck, but fortunately the forces of law and order intervened. Thus are affairs conducted in Lilliput. R.L.S. relished the absurdity of it all and reported it gleefully to his mother (VIII, 2572).

The unstable relations between nationalities in Samoa meant that balls held in the Public Hall were lively affairs, not conducted with the decorum of similar events in Jane Austen's Bath. The "Spinsters of Apia" threw a soirée "for a select crowd", and R.L.S. found himself, to his embarrassment, in a set for a quadrille with Chief Justice Cedercrantz. As he put it, "he had been trying to rake up evidence against me by brow-beating and threatening a half-white interpreter; that very morning, I had been writing the most villainous attacks upon him in *The Times*," but etiquette and a liking for his adversary meant that the two ended up "crossing hands and kicking up and prancing for each other" (VII, 2452). A fancy dress ball held in 1893 in honour of Queen Victoria's birthday was one of the more rumbustious of these gatherings. R.L.S. writes of it in the low-key, detached style of a Mark Twain, informing his correspondent that the event brought together

> the elite and beauty of Samoa. Mr Osbourne [Lloyd] and Mrs Strong [Belle] with powdered heads, Ahrens [a German office-worker] in a court dress of the last century and considerably under the influence of punch: and Frings entirely under ditto and ditto in a Rococo costume and equipped with a long staff with a ball on the end of it (said to be the knob of his brass bedstead) with which he went about vaguely knighting people on the head until it was removed from him and concealed behind the door. His last exploit was to publicly embrace Mrs Isobel Stewart Strong, after which his wife removed him.

Matters deteriorated when diplomatic niceties aggravated alcoholic flirting, and a dispute arose over rank in a square dance. The German consul's wife claimed primacy, supported in her claim by consular officials, while Dr Bernard Funk, *et al.*, took another position. With a display of mock regret, R.L.S. noted that the whole affair passed off bloodlessly, depriving him of another public, entertaining duel. "What a pretty pair Sparrowhawk Ahrens and Beerbarrel Funk would have made on the field of blood and glory" (VIII, 2590). Dr Funk was the doctor who attended R.L.S. after his fatal seizure. Life was not dull.

CHAPTER 13

A Home for Angels

Looking back, R.L.S. recalled days of depression in Edinburgh when he was unsure if, no matter how much he wished it, he would ever have a wife and friends, and compared that state of mind to his happiness when he realised he had attained his wish. In fact, he would never quite enjoy both at the same time. He formed new friendships in Samoa, but his dearest friends were in London, and, when they had been geographically closest to him during his residence in Bournemouth, there were moments of tension between them and his wife. In Samoa, while at times he relished being "away from the little literary bubble of London" (VII, 2314), he repeated in correspondence with his friends how much he missed their company and conversation, and how splendid it would be if Henry James, Sidney Colvin, or Charles Baxter would come to Samoa, or if they could agree to rendezvous at some intermediate point, southern France, Cairo, or Ceylon being favourite phantom destinations.

Relations with Fanny in Samoa were intense but unstable and variable, and she still kept some new friends at bay. In an obituary, the Rev. Clarke wrote that "when she wished, no-one could be more charming or gracious," but added that "she was a woman of many moods and tenses [*sic*], devoted to R.L.S. with a passion so fierce that she was jealous even of his men friends."

He recalled occasions when he went to visit him only to be turned away by Fanny, but would then see R.L.S. waving to him from his room on the first floor and bidding him to come in through his mother's room.[93] More than one friend recorded how astounded they were when Fanny would intervene in a conversation to order R.L.S. off to bed, and even more astounded when he complied.

He gathered his and her family, as well as a group of servants, around him in a structure which resembled a Highland clan. In *Weir of Hermiston*, the elder Kirstie was officially the housekeeper at Hermiston and young Archie Weir her master, but between them there existed an informality of manners bordering on the intimate which, writes R.L.S., "has never been uncommon in Scotland, where the clan spirit survives". Kirstie's feelings "partook of the loyalty of a clanswoman, the hero-worship of a maiden aunt and the idolatry due to a god". These words were written in 1894, when in Vailima R.L.S. was the recipient of comparable sentiments of devotion. On one occasion Sosimo, his personal valet, saw that R.L.S. had risen unusually early to begin his work and brought him not only coffee but also an omelette. R.L.S. was impressed, and replied in the standard ceremonial formula, "great is your wisdom", but was moved when Sosimo abandoned formal etiquette to reply, "great is my love".

There were periods of tension and misery which will be discussed, but for much of the time life in Vailima seems to have flowed peacefully under a regime which mixed the carefree spirit of Rabelais' Abbey of Thélème with the Benedictine rule of division between manual and mental labour: there were even

93 *Daily Chronicle*, February 21, 1914.

prayer sessions. The clan-community was relaxed, but respected a structured order of discipline and dedication to work, providing R.L.S. with the domesticity he craved. For some periods, it is possible to follow in detail the moods, quarrels, conversations, illnesses, parties, sleep patterns, work schedules, menus, relationships, and varying views on local politics of all the inhabitants, not only R.L.S. Home life at Vailima, abundantly documented by Fanny as well as in the voluminous correspondence of Aunt Maggie and R.L.S., is supplemented by Lloyd's introductions to thirteen of the volumes in the Tusitala edition, in which he strayed from literary criticism to biographical reminiscence, while Moors wrote his own memoirs. Floods of articles, interviews, and books were produced by visitors who came to Samoa to pay homage, or to jeer. Newspapers in Samoa itself, as well as in Australia and New Zealand, were interested in news or gossip from Vailima. By comparison, Dickens and Thackeray lived in seclusion and privacy.

When the couple returned from Sydney to take up permanent residence, the main house had yet to be built and, as is clear from the opening words of her Samoa diary, Fanny was not altogether pleased with the temporary, unfurnished cottage Moors had constructed. "Things rather unsatisfactory, more attention having been paid to the ornamental rather than the practical side of affairs," she noted testily, continuing "a very neat and expensive building, very like a bandstand in a German beer garden, has been built in a corner above the small waterfall." The house is no longer there, having been blown down in a storm, but a contemporary photograph shows a fairly sturdy two-storey wooden building, with a staircase leading to an upstairs verandah protected from sun and rain by the overhanging roof.[94] R.L.S.' horse, Jack, is tethered to a post, and if the scene has the look of a pioneer's shack, the building is also a smaller version of the final house which was already in the planning stage. No German beer garden was ever built in that style. The Stevensons slept upstairs, but the downstairs section was crowded with several Samoan servants. The attention paid by Moors to the "ornamental side" did not meet with Fanny's approval, and she was upset at the "cold black paint" and the "still more offensive white" which gave the whole place a "chilling, deathlike aspect".[95] They had limited means and were compelled for a time to eat and live frugally, in conditions similar to those they had known during their honeymoon in a prospector's cottage on the slopes of Mount St Helena. On one occasion, recorded by both and by every biographer, they were reduced to dining on a single avocado.

Fanny's further observation that "there was no shelter for the pigs and no chicken house" indicates the domain that over the years she intended to make her own. She took in hand the decoration of the house and, more importantly, the cultivation and management of the estate. In Oakland and Skerryvore she had tended plants, and even created gardens in soil as unpromising as on any island in the South Seas, such as Apemama, where they stopped for sufficient periods of time. Her interest in gardening and matters botanical dated back to her girlhood, and in Samoa she excelled as housekeeper, estate manager, chatelaine, cook and above all as gardener, botanist, and landscape artist. No dilettante, she maintained contact with the most advanced

94 This photograph is now in the possession of the Edinburgh City Museums.
95 Stevenson and Stevenson, *Our Samoan Adventure*, op. cit., p. 31.

botanists in London and Australia. She had no hesitation in getting her own hands dirty, and led the way in planting, weeding, sowing seeds, and general work on the soil. She would come in "heated and bemired up to the eyebrows, late for every meal", her husband complained. Attempting to develop and improve nature, she scoured pamphlets for unfamiliar plants and seeds, took professional advice on climate and soil, and succeeded in infecting her husband with the same primal attachment to the land and gardening that she felt herself. She pressed her staff into service, but this could be exasperating, as when she found plants put into the ground upside down, and replanted them the correct way, only to find the following morning that the same helpful servant had put them back as they had been. The efforts were herculean. "In three days we have planted more than two thousand cacao plants," reported R.L.S. "The whole family, from myself down to the pantry boy are exhausted" (VII, 2376).

The first task, to make the ground habitable, required not sophisticated skills but the strength and application of a navvy. Trees were to be felled, woodland cleared, undergrowth chopped, and pathways constructed. The tropical trees were covered with creepers, and lianas were an obstacle to anyone attempting to make their way in the woods. The dense dark of the vegetation, made noisy by the cries of the more cacophonous birds and the song of other species, as well as by the croaking of tree frogs "of stentorian voice", brought both Fanny and Louis up short on different occasions, and made them understand how such places could be viewed as inhabited by creatures not, or no longer, of this earth. Their task was to prune and clear, or to do all that came under the general term "weeding", a word which acquires unaccustomed lyrical overtones in R.L.S.'

usage, and which recurs like a musical refrain in his correspondence. "I love weeding even, but clearing bush is heaven to me,"
he told his mother (VII, 2259). True happiness, he opined, comes
from standing in shrubbery or flower bed, encouraging the natural cycle of life, making things grow, and deriving satisfaction
from seeing the results of physical, agricultural labour. Weeding
meant more than uprooting wild vegetation. It involved imposing human order on a wilderness and creating the conditions for
domesticity. The image of this writer of romances sweating,
dirty, standing in mud as he worked with a scythe, or a "cutlass"
as he called it, to clear away the detritus of years is an arresting if
unusual one, and would have amazed and distressed his delicate
literary friends in the Savile Club. He revelled in it, and one letter to Colvin is an extended cry of delight, perhaps heightened
by his returning strength and his discovery of himself as a person capable of real labour.

> This is a hard and interesting and beautiful life that we
> lead now; our place is in a deep cleft of the Vaea Mountain,
> some six hundred feet above the sea, embowered in forest,
> which is our strangling enemy and which we combat with
> axes and dollars. I went crazy over outdoor work, and had
> at last to confine myself to the house, or literature must
> have gone by the board. *Nothing* is so interesting as weed-
> ing, clearing, and path-making; the oversight of labourers
> becomes a disease; it is quite an effort not to drop into the
> farmer; and it does make you feel so well. To come down
> covered with mud and drenched with sweat and rain after
> some hours in the bush, change, rub down and take a chair
> in the verandah, is to taste a quiet conscience (VII, 2266).

The question of conscience always baffled him. He was able to tell Colvin that, since arriving in Samoa, he had completed three chapters of *The Wrecker*, eight of the South Seas book, as well as a "hatful of verses". But did literary activity, he wondered, really constitute work? It is hard not to conclude that the dire spirit of John Knox, reduced to a nagging whisper rather than a condemnatory roar, was seated on his shoulder as he explained: "And the strange thing that I remark is this: if I go out and make sixpence, bossing my labourers and plying my cutlass or spade, idiot conscience applauds me: if I sit in the house and make twenty pounds, idiot conscience wails over my neglect and the day wasted" (VII, 2266). Many of the letters from the early days in Samoa, with their description of the scenery the family inhabited, have the grace of prose poetry, and a tone expressive of everyday happiness. The anxious accounts of impending war were in the future. For the moment R.L.S. was happy at home, in his own home. The sight by day of mountain, sea, woodland, and blue skies, and by night of "real stars and moon overhead, instead of the tin imitations that preside over London" (VII1312), spurred him even in private correspondence to a delicacy of joyful lyricism which must have been a delight to the recipients of his letters, at least for those who could rid themselves of their groaning that he should not have been there in the first place. "I hope you are well," he told Colvin. "I am wonderful, but tired from so much work . . . if you could see this place! But I don't want anyone to see it till my clearing is done, and my house built. It will be a home for angels." If boredom struck, he could saddle Jack and ride down to Apia, sure of a welcome.

The building of their house was under way by January 1891 and largely completed by March. There had been delays as plans were modified to reduce expenditure, which threatened to run out of control. Moors noted that neither Fanny nor Belle had any sense of thrift, so that the building cost more than estimated. Fanny insisted on having Californian redwood imported for the long downstairs room which ran the full length of the house. In April R.L.S. told Edmund Gosse that they were in their house "after a fashion", that is, "without furniture and camping". The main point was that the place was "beautiful beyond dreams". He expatiated a little: "some fifty miles of the Pacific spread in front; deep woods all round; a mountain making in the sky a curded profile of huge trees on our left . . . it amazes me how people can live on in the dirty north" (VII, 2313). It was late 1892 before the house was completed to their satisfaction. The sheer expanse of the place, not to mention the mahogany furniture, the silverware, the dining sets, the crystal glasses, the wine cellar, and the paintings awed Samoan society. The Vailima house museum as it is today has two wings, one added as the family's confidence and prosperity grew, especially when *The Wrecker* brought greater royalties than expected, the other added much later, after the family had moved out. The original house, the central part of today's structure, was a two-storey building with a verandah at ground level and a balcony above. R.L.S. made light of the expense in a letter to Colvin later in April.

We have spent since we have been here £2500 which is not much if you consider we have built on that, three houses, one of them of some size, and a considerable stable, made two miles of road some three times, cleared many acres of bush, made some miles of path, planted

245

quantities of food, and enclosed a horse paddock and some acres of pig run: but 'tis a good deal of money counted as money. (VII, 2317)

The upstairs library and the downstairs "great hall" were linked by the grand staircase, a structure previously unknown on the island. When Fanny asked one of the servants to carry a bucket of water upstairs, he gripped it in his teeth and clambered up the roan pipe. When the purpose of stairs was explained to him, he spent the following hours running delightedly up and down.

There were no interior doors, only mats over entrances, in the Samoan style. Aunt Maggie paid to have running water available, while it was R.L.S. who insisted that, whatever the climate, fireplaces were indispensable for a home worthy of the name. The servant Henry, who had never seen such a thing before, sat happily in front of it, waiting for the opportunity to throw on some logs. R.L.S. had a bedroom-cum-workroom, while Fanny had a room of her own. This is not a matter which either of them discussed in their correspondence, so posterity can make of this what it pleases. The furnishing was tasteful and splendid, containing items from both Heriot Row and Skerryvore, a safe which was believed to be the prison of the imp of the story, as well as a sculpture by Rodin, a Chippendale sideboard, paintings by Bob Stevenson as well as a portrait of R.L.S. by John Singer Sargent.

The cottage where they had lived on first arriving was refurbished for Joe and Belle, and the area in front of the house was transformed into a lawn. Trees, bushes, and flowering plants formed the surround, and from the upper balcony it was possible to look over the treetops to the sea. There was even a tennis court. R.L.S. played a little, but when one particularly energetic game led to a recurrence of his haemorrhaging, he resigned himself to looking on longingly. The lawn was ideal for croquet, and cricket, which was played in the Samoan style, that is, with teams of indefinite size. Some visitors were surprised to see the boys playing cricket with sticks and oranges.

As work got under way in transforming the estate, R.L.S. was able to look with amusement and affection at Fanny as she laboured in their grounds. There is not the same feel of abiding joy in her diary as in his letters, but nor is there any sign of the bouts of the profound, unfocused dissatisfaction she was prone to. She occasionally bawled in frustration at the Samoans on their staff, although she did concede that they were trying to be helpful. Her chief aim being to make Vailima self-sufficient, she purchased farm animals, which she was sorrowful about slaughtering. She also set about creating an orchard. Her ambitions were boundless, as is clear from the lists of everything she planted. With help from R.L.S., she cut into the forest. In the first month, she "dropped a few seeds of melons, tomatoes and bush lima beans . . . I have bought some alfalfa seeds to experiment with." Mangoes, papayas, and pineapples were added to the bowers. The two modified their diet to suit local produce, so they developed a taste for the taro plant, a staple of the Samoan diet. By November, Fanny was able to write that "my garden looks like a real garden". At the insistence of Lafaele, an unusually superstitious member of their staff who was often a nuisance, she was forced to plant cabbages, and she herself identified a sunny spot suitable for lettuce. Becoming bolder as she progressed, she made an attempt to cultivate cacao and later the coffee plant. Moors noted with surprise the vast quantities of coffee consumed at Vailima, so the availability of supplies of their own would have been economically advantageous. Since she wanted more than a vegetable garden, she cultivated frangipani and hibiscus. Some authorities, but not all, credit her with introducing the *teuila*, now the national flower of Samoa, to the islands. All her experiments were discussed with experts in Kew Gardens, and she was careful to burn the soil which brought new plants, for fear of importing diseases to the island.

The animals created greater heartache for her. A fowl house was built for the five Cochin hens and two cocks she had brought from Australia, a paddock created for a cow, and a stable for the horses. An enclosure was constructed for the three pigs, one white boar, and two sows she described as "slab-sided". Pigs ran wild in Samoa, and roasted pork, cooked by digging in the ground an *uma* where the animal was cooked over smouldering twigs, was a prime ingredient in native feasts. The Stevenson table was replenished by birds shot by hunters, and although Fanny confessed to some compunction over consuming them, she repressed her scruples when she realised that, in the early days, they had nothing else available. Later, they would receive presents of livestock, but were not always sure how to cope with them. This problem was particularly acute when, after the house was completed and a lawn laid out in front, one grateful group turned up with a live bull. The more routine problems were that the farm pigs were prone to clamber over the fencing, and the hens were liable to be devoured by wildlife. An ageing cockerel was particularly irritating, since it would stick its beak into a newly laid egg, thereby upsetting the breakfast menu.

However much Fanny prided herself on her proficiency and expertise in farming and botany, the couple had a serious disagreement when R.L.S. described her as having "the soul of a peasant". It is impossible to know the tone of voice in which he spoke these words, whether humorous, sardonic, careless, or even complimentary, but they stung her to the quick. She mentions the remark in her entry for October 23, and returns to it querulously or reflectively several times on subsequent days. The paragraph caused such concern to the anonymous person, possibly Lloyd, who first came into possession of the diary after her death, that he or she deleted it.[96] On the one hand, Fanny was prepared to admit that R.L.S. "may be right. I would as soon think of renting a child to love as a piece of land. When I plant a seed or a root, I plant a bit of my heart with it . . . I do not feel so far from God when the tender leaves put forth and I know that in a manner I am a creator." These are the musings of a somewhat vapid mystic, but the question that nagged her was what kind of creator she was. Her aspirations and doubts on this question went to the heart of her self-identity. She preened herself on her prowess as gardener but did not wish to be seen as primarily a tiller of the land, so she put her dilemma in the form of self-interrogation. "Had I the soul of an artist, the stupidity of possessions would have no power over me." Her driving ambition had always been to become an artist. It was that need which, after separating from Sam Osbourne, had brought her from America to Europe to enrol in an art school in Belgium. It was that quest which had taken her to Grez, where she first met R.L.S. It was that longing which had caused her to write short

96 Charles Neider, "Introduction", in Stevenson and Stevenson, *Our Samoan Adventure*, op. cit., , p. 13.

stories, including the one which Henley dismissed as plagiarism. It was that need which led her to claim to be credited as co-author of *The Dynamiter*. She claimed she had helped with *Prince Otto*, and used her prefatory note to *Kidnapped* to recount her attempted reworking of *The Hanging Judge*, a play R.L.S. had started writing with Henley during their unhappy period of theatrical collaboration. Other plays by the two men were completed, but this one was left in draft form until it was taken up by Fanny. She considered rewriting it as a novel, but eventually left it as a theatre work. It was never performed, but is listed in the Tusitala edition as a collaborative venture with R.L.S. Henley has been written out. She always wished to be seen as an artist of some sort, but now she found out, or believed she had found out, that in his eyes she was no more than a peasant.

On November 5, in another passage which was heavily deleted by the same unknown hand, she wrote that she was "feeling very depressed, for my vanity, like a newly felled tree, lies prone and bleeding. Louis tells me that I am not an artist but a born, natural peasant." The complexity and contradictions of her thoughts that day suggest deep inner turmoil. Being a peasant was, she had often thought, "the happiest life and not one for criticism," but she now had to face the fact that she "could not support a fly by my sort of work, artistic or otherwise." She switches tack and adds that she "so hates being a peasant that I feel a positive pleasure when I fail in peasant occupations". There then follows a list of such failures, including hens which do not lay eggs, or seeing them eaten by cocks when they do, and pigs climbing out of their sty and doing "all manner of mischief". In fact, whatever her dissatisfaction with her achievements, Fanny was not devoid of literary ability or stylistic flair.

Her diaries are written with vigour, fluency, and the occasional flight of fancy. She had a sharp eye and a capacity for vivid visual observation. As she later became more involved in the politics of the island at the time of its civil war, she showed herself a shrewd judge and passionate reporter. Her fortune and misfortune were to live alongside Robert Louis Stevenson, and to measure herself against him. She herself had the benefits and frustrations of the "artistic temperament", but never was able to actually produce art, a common predicament for people who see themselves in that light.

Otherwise, her energy was boundless. If R.L.S. was the chieftain, she was the governess and general overseer who took day-by-day charge of the household, both indoors and outdoors. It was she who oversaw the activities of the squad of servants and labourers, the latter mainly recruited by Moors. The first team contained several Europeans, although later they were viewed as unduly troublesome, and replaced entirely by Samoans. In the accounts given by R.L.S., but also by Fanny, the members of their staff are portrayed as vividly as the slightly bumbling, well-intentioned, serious-minded, comic characters who people light fiction, his or that of others. The first person to turn up at Vailima was Paul Einfurer, a German who in R.L.S.' account could have emerged from an Offenbach operetta. He had been pantry-man on the steamer which had conveyed the Stevensons from Sydney to Samoa, but jumped ship and begged to be taken on by them to tide him over until Christmas, a common deadline for the resolution of all problems. Fanny took him on as general handyman, but, though good-hearted, he turned out to be wholly unsuited for the post, or any post. He spoke little English, which added to the prevailing linguistic

Babel, and it also became clear that he was a hardened drinker. His failures caused Fanny headaches and bouts of illness, but R.L.S. regarded his efforts with a mixture of amusement and affection. He listed Paul's attributes and failings: he was employed as "cook and steward", he was "honest, sober, industrious", he was "a glutton for work", and all in all he was "a splendid fellow". This commendation was balanced by three equal and opposite defects: "(1) no cook, (2) an inveterate bungler, with twenty thumbs, continually falling in the dishes, throwing out the dinner, preserving the garbage, (3) a drunk, well we daren't let him go to town, and he – poor, good soul – is afraid to be let go" (VII, 2266).

The staff grew rapidly, and while some remained for only a brief period, others became fixtures, as trustworthy as the faithful retainers of aristocratic estates. Ben, also known as Leni or Beni, was given the position of "boss of the outdoor boys", but he too required a high level of benevolent tolerance. "Lord love him! God made him a truckling coward . . . he cannot tell me what he wants, he dare not tell me what is wrong, he dare not transmit my orders or translate my censures," wrote R.L.S. Others were perhaps less colourful, but more dependable, as was the case with Henry Simele, a chieftain whose name was sometimes latinised to *Henricus*, occasionally with the addition of a *magnus*. His willingness to undertake any kind of work, much of which was beyond his capacities, was a hazard in itself, and provided R.L.S. with a range of anecdotes and incidents. Sosimo became R.L.S.' adoring personal valet, and Lafaele, seemingly "blackbirded" when he was young, was a "strong dull, deprecating man" whose terror of the nearby spirits was so great that he could not venture too far from the house.

There was no fixed staff roll, nor was the number of personnel established to correspond with tasks requiring to be done. In early 1892, there were "six boys in the bush under Joe Strong" and "six souls about the house" (VII, 2493). In an article written by a New Zealand journalist, W.H. Triggs, but revised and corrected by R.L.S., he agreed that he "paid lower wages than anyone in Samoa, but it is my boast that I get better served". Visitors had observed that "Vailima is the only place where you can see Samoans run."[97] In many cases, servants seem to have been hired if they could make a convincing appeal to the sympathy of either R.L.S. or Fanny. Fanny recruited a Muslim cook in Fiji, but then preferred a Samoan called Talolo, and so the unfortunate Fijian was jettisoned, but found alternative employment elsewhere. A black New Hebridean called Arrick escaped from the German plantation and presented himself at Vailima. The welts on his back from whippings were sufficient to guarantee him a welcome. Seemingly, Joe was prepared to threaten him jokingly with the whip, but Arrick dismissed the lash shown him as tame compared to the cat o' nine tails his back had known (VII, 2393). His appointment initially caused some controversy, because it provoked the anti-black feelings then deeply ingrained in Samoans, but he charmed his new colleagues and ended up being "petted and ministered to". It did not last. He was offensive to Henry, was given the chance to apologise but declined, and so was, at his own request, sent back to the German firm. Later, in 1892, the "live stock" included cart horses, riding horses, cattle, cats, and "God knows how many ducks and chickens", as well as twenty staff when dependants were taken

97 E.N. Caldwell, *Last Witness for Robert Louis Stevenson*, Norman, University of Oklahoma Press, 1960, p. 299.

into account. R.L.S. singled out for special mention Helen, the washerwoman, who was their "shame", but not for anything she had done. For R.L.S., she was a "good, healthy, comely, strapping young wench" who took a lead in hymn singing, and was to all appearances chaste, but in the eyes of Samoans she was "not of good family". She was ostracised and eventually had to go. A strange blot on the tolerance of the Samoans, and an inexplicable act by R.L.S. in not defending her from prejudice.

The family contingent increased when, in January 1891, R.L.S. set off for Sydney to greet his mother and Lloyd on their arrival from Britain. Fanny stayed on in Upolu, partly because she had been unwell and could not face another sea journey, and partly to supervise the work on the new house. Predictably, R.L.S. enjoyed the time at sea but fell ill on land. When his mother arrived, she persuaded him to stay on a little in Sydney, but Lloyd went ahead to Vailima, where he arrived in the company of a man named King, who was known to the family from the cruise of the *Janet Nicoll*. King wanted to bring his girlfriend as a companion to Mrs Stevenson, but got short shrift from Fanny. In Moors' account, King left because he found the women "too much for any man". King sought an interview with R.L.S. to complain about them, but R.L.S. sat back in his chair, and said, "Well, King, you know what women are. You understand their ways?" Moors recounts that he paused before continuing, "By Jove, no! How can you? Show me a man who does!"[98] Once again, the tone of voice is everything. By then, R.L.S. had in any case decided King was "bosh". Lloyd Osbourne wrote that R.L.S. was "emphatically what we would

98 H.J. Moors, *With Stevenson in Samoa*, op. cit., 5–2

today call a 'feminist'. Women seemed to him the victims alike of man and nature." Lloyd admitted that "little of this got into his books" (Tusitala, I, xv).

However fondly R.L.S. regarded him, Lloyd was a drain on resources and unreliable as a helpmate. He brought with him from England an ice machine and a device to distil perfume from the blossom of a fragrant tree which grew in Samoa. Neither of them ever worked. Mrs Stevenson duly arrived from Sydney with her son, bringing her own sofa. A room had been prepared for her, and she declared herself delighted. She brought with her an Australian maid, who did not adapt to the demands made by the other women in the house, and left. A few weeks later, the Strong family – Joe, Belle, and Austin – arrived. Belle was, originally at least, the most reluctant of the inhabitants. R.L.S. had taken advantage of his time in Sydney in February to have a serious tête-à-tête with her. His views on Belle and Joe underwent substantial alteration over the years. He was subsidising the Strongs and may have wished to keep them under his supervision, but the reason, as recorded by Belle, was different. "You and Lloyd are all the family I have. I want a home and a family, *my* family, around me."[99]

Although they arrived at different times, the Vailima clan-family was now complete: R.L.S. and Fanny; his mother, "Aunt Maggie"; Joe, Belle, and Austin; and Lloyd Osbourne. Austin began to take the place in R.L.S.' affections which Lloyd had occupied when a boy. He was initially given lessons in Vailima by R.L.S. and Aunt Maggie, and there is a cartoon still hanging in the house which shows a lanky R.L.S. gesticulating in an

99 Quoted in Margaret Mackay, *The Violent Friend,* London, J.M. Dent, 1968, p. 245.

effort to attract the interest of a plainly bored boy in his charge. Eventually, Austin was sent off to school in California, where he was placed under the overall care of his aunt Nelly. Lloyd was meant to go to Cambridge, but called off, in deference to the family's strained finances, he said, though more probably because he could not summon the energy and will to undertake a systematic course of study.

Everyone had a specified role at Vailima. Lloyd became general manager, subject, of course, to his mother. Joe was put in charge of the hen run, which was not as demeaning an office in the domestic economy as it might appear, and was given the role of overseer of outside labour. He was ordered to quit drinking once and for all, but this proved beyond him. R.L.S. was initially able to commend him as "most industrious, admirable", but that esteem would be quickly undermined. The chickens started dying in troubling numbers, something Fanny attributed to his having fed them too much lime too soon.

She became more and more outraged at Joe's conduct, and her own behaviour became increasingly erratic. Her state of mind was not helped when Belle began to side with R.L.S. in an attempt to maintain an often precarious peace in the household. Domestic harmony was further compromised by the "tiffs" between his mother and wife. They seemed to him "alternately in the wrong", but he admitted it was "no joke" when he had to disagree with Fanny "when her turn comes". The only consolation was that "neither of them rasp or harbour malice" (VII, 2408). Relations between Joe and Belle deteriorated, but it was R.L.S. who forced the final break. Joe was caught thieving by night from the cellar, but more serious misdeeds came to light in December 1892 when it was discovered that he had a lover in Apia. According to Fanny, his mistress was Fauuna, one of the serving maids, whose good looks had been commented on by R.L.S. Any hint of sexual impropriety or infidelity was anathema to R.L.S. He assured Belle that he would take charge of Austin and her, but that Joe had to go. The culprit returned a few days later, claiming to be filled with remorse and begging forgiveness, but his reappearance upset Fanny so much that it was responsible, she believed, for an attack of angina.[100] Joe became so completely *persona non grata* in Vailima that R.L.S. even cut his image out of photographs, adjusting what remained to ensure that the background foliage matched up and left no trace of the excision.

Belle was now closer than ever to R.L.S., eventually close enough to arouse her mother's distrust and jealousy. Meantime, she was given charge of indoor staff, and responsibility for keeping the pantry stocked – and presumably locked. Only Aunt Maggie had no assigned role, something which Fanny resented. She wore all her life the widow's cap, and she alone continued to wear shoes. Going barefoot seems to have assumed an odd symbolic importance in Vailima, especially for the women. It was not merely a habit adopted for comfort in the heat, but a facet of life to which they all drew attention, and which was noted by visitors. Trivial as it may seem, for the residents of Vailima not wearing shoes was a symbolic rejection of civilisation. When Graham Balfour arrived in Vailima in August 1892, he too was by the second day of his visit going around barefoot. R.L.S. remarked that this showed he was "the same kind of fool we are!" He had come satisfactorily through an initiation rite.

100 Stevenson and Stevenson, *Our Samoan Adventure*, op. cit., p. 208; E.N. Caldwell, *Last Witness for Robert Louis Stevenson*, op. cit., p. 186.

Fanny's supervision of the domestic domain was carried out in a spirit which would have drawn the approval of Mrs Beeton. It was a more delicate and demanding task than would be known to any contemporary American or British housewife, in part because of the servants, whose number rose and fell with desertions or expulsions, and who begged places for others in their family or objected when more prestigious roles were given to rivals; and in part because she had to take on the role of infirmarian and spiritual guide. It was she to whom the staff turned with health problems, whether physical or psychological. Working in a language and culture which were not hers, she found she had to deal with minor illnesses of the body and major ailments of the psyche. Trust in her healing powers grew as she gained the reputation for possessing semi-mystical powers sufficiently strong to ward off *aitu*. Lafaele had a poisoned toe caused, both he and the medicine man were convinced, by the malice of a devil which had entered his foot, but their fear was that it would travel up his leg and take control of his whole being. Fanny was equal to the emergency and objected "that no Samoan devil can do harm to a man that belongs to me". This reasoning was accepted by the servant and confirmed by the doctor, with Lafaele's only lingering scepticism occasioned by the fact that the devil had in all probability infiltrated his foot before he made Fanny's acquaintance. Fanny brushed aside his doubts so robustly that he was able to assure her "with great earnestness that he was not afraid of devils since [she] had promised to defend him." She added that he displayed no further evidence of fear other than "singing very loudly when he is alone".[101]

101 Stevenson and Stevenson, *Our Samoan Adventure*, op. cit., p. 119.

When irregularities occurred or discipline broke down, R.L.S. called a quasi-court presided over by him in his capacity as supreme chieftain. Evidence was heard and punishments, in the form of fines paid to a charity run by the church to which the miscreant belonged, were handed down. Talolo the cook once absconded, an absence which cost R.L.S. "about eight hours of riding and about twelve hours of sitting in Council" (VII, 2393). On one occasion when the "house boys had not been behaving well", he summoned them together and scolded them for about half an hour. His words were translated, but there is no record of what he actually said. For some misdemeanour, he cut one man's wages by half and to his surprise the man "took this smiling". For R.L.S., this was "another good sign of their really and fairly accepting me as chief" (VII, 2651).

There is no need to labour parallels with the Scottish clan system, but nor is it possible to ignore them. The ethos and culture of community, common to the clans and to Samoan *aiga*s, facilitated a deep identification with house and family. All the Stevenson family were given Samoan names, or nicknames. The most famous of them, Tusitala, the "writer of tales", was actually given by a European missionary, and the name stuck. Fanny had two – Tamaitai, a title of respect equivalent to Madam, and Aolele, which translates as "flying cloud". Belle was Teuila, a flower, so "the embellisher". To be a dependant and employee of Tusitala was a badge of honour. It endowed the individual with status. Gradually, all white servants were removed and replaced by a wholly Samoan staff, most of whom were Catholic, but all of whom, R.L.S. insisted, were proud to be in Tusitala's service.

CHAPTER 14

Fanny: The Horror of Madness

Fanny's health, like her husband's, was a recurrent cause for concern, and over the years R.L.S., recognising her need for care, was often irritated with himself for requiring attention when she was unwell. However, the actual nature of her ill health was uncertain, and here too their biographers are split in their assessments, though not according to which of the couple was the subject of the biography. Some have dismissed Fanny as a chronic hypochondriac, suffering at best from successive psychosomatic conditions or from mere attention seeking, while others believe there were real problems not of her invention. She complained of a range of ailments, from the strange condition of "inflammation of the brain" to diphtheria. Discretion among those near to her means that actual data is hard to come by, but there can be no doubt that in Samoa she underwent a period of severe mental illness, from which she did eventually make a full recovery.

Long-term problems should not be excluded. Traumas deriving from her earlier marriage to Sam Osbourne may well have undermined her. The death of her younger son, Hervey, in Paris in 1876, after she had separated from her husband, undoubtedly preyed on her mind, and may well have been responsible for her later unbalanced, neurotic behaviour. She

felt guilty at not having objected to the strange, certainly drain-
ing, and possibly damaging treatment prescribed by the doctors
over the five-month period of the boy's appalling illness, and
it would hardly be surprising if that tragedy, and the circumstances in which it occurred, changed her psychological make-
up fundamentally.

Whatever the impact of these earlier events, her decline
started within months of their arrival in Samoa. Her dismay
over R.L.S.' description of her in October 1890 as having a
"peasant soul" was undoubtedly deep, and may well have been
a contributing factor to the period of malaise she experienced.
By nature, she had little psychological resilience and failed to
develop any coping mechanisms to enable her to deal with set-
backs. In November, she had to take to bed with headaches,
which may of course have had a purely physical origin. She went
to Fiji on her own to recuperate or convalesce, but could not
settle and came back much sooner than planned. "I do not think
my wife [is] very well, but I am in hopes that she will now have
a little period of rest," he wrote in April the following year to a
young woman friend from Bournemouth days (VII, 2312). He
put that illness down to overexertion and to living in poor
accommodation over the first days on Samoa, but this in itself
was an indication that merely unusual but not disastrous events
had a hyper-debilitating impact on her. August 1892 saw the
arrival of Lady Jersey in Samoa, and almost immediately Fanny
developed a pathological dislike of her and suspicion of her
husband's evident fondness for the vivacious visitor. She was
badly affected by the fracas involving the discovery that Joe
Strong had been unfaithful to her daughter, and when after
his expulsion from the household he came back to plead for

forgiveness and readmission, the resultant squabble with him in December 1892 brought on an attack of angina.[102]

In mid February the following year, R.L.S., Fanny, and Belle went for a "month's lark" on the steamer *Mariposa*, which may have been intended to assist Fanny's recovery, but if so, it was an ill-advised effort to aid a woman who had never enjoyed time at sea. They stopped in Sydney and the two of them went together to visit Dr Fairfax Ross, whom they had previously consulted. R.L.S. was told that he could expect a normal lifespan if he were able to relax more and not overtax himself, but the doctor was less reassuring about Fanny, in whom he diagnosed both physical and mental problems. She was prone to hallucinations: R.L.S. told Baxter that in Sydney she had seen him twice, even though he was then in Edinburgh.

Fanny herself kept no diary for the first six months of 1893, while R.L.S.' correspondence suggests, unsurprisingly, that he struggled through peaks and troughs as he anxiously sought signs of Fanny's recovery from whatever disorder she was enduring. On February 21, he optimistically recorded that she "was enormously bettered by the voyage" (VIII, 2543), but by March 29 he was telling Colvin that the supposed holiday had been "amusing but tragic", and that they had "returned in disarray" (VIII, 2548). In early April, in one of his journal-letters to Colvin, he gave an account of a developing crisis. On April 5, when the fracas over "that damned Joe" was at its worst, he wrote candidly about the situation at Vailima.

> Well, there's no disguise possible: Fanny is not well, and we are miserably anxious. I may as well say now that for

102 Stevenson and Stevenson, *Our Samoan Adventure*, op. cit., p. 208.

nearly eighteenth months there has been something wrong: I could not write of it; but it was very trying and painful – and it mostly fell on me. Now we are to face the question: what next? The doctor has given her a medicine; we think it too strong, yet we dare not stop it: and she passes from death-bed scenes to states of stupor. Ross, doctor in Sydney told me to expect trouble, so I'm not surprised; and happily Lloyd and Belle and I work together very smoothly, and none of us gets excited. But it's anxious. (VIII, 2549)

One terrible night she was raving and threatening to run out of the house, and had to be held down on the bed by all three. Two days later, R.L.S. was more enthusiastic about the prescribed medicine, and hopeful that the worst was past. He was grateful that it had "quieted her at once", and made her "entirely reasonable and very nice", a bright statement that gives a glimpse of the darker reality on other days. He himself was "as tired as a man can be", and there can be no doubting the intensity of feeling behind the wish "O! if it only lets up, it will be but a pleasant memory". It is not easy to detect what could have been pleasant about the memory; the situation was grim, and in sympathy even the weather turned as bleak as it would in any Gothic novel, "grey heaven, torrents of rain, occasional thunder and lightning". The entries for the succeeding days read like a medical bulletin from a casualty ward, as Belle contracted rheumatic fever but Fanny seemed to be on the mend. However, he added the gnomic statement, "something nameless and measureless seems to draw near and strikes me cold, and yet is welcome. Anything is welcome but the one

horror of madness . . ." (VIII, 2549). These are the terrified and
terrifying words of a man staring into the mouth of the monster,
facing the point at which humanity itself fails. As the summer
wore on, he began to hope, tentatively at first but with growing
confidence, that she had made a complete recovery. Later that
year in Honolulu, where Fanny had gone to help R.L.S. – he was
visiting but had been haemorrhaging – she was herself diagnosed by Dr Trousseau as suffering from Bright's disease, in
layman's language an inflammation of the kidneys. R.L.S. was
relieved by this assessment, since he "feared much worse", and
believed that this medical judgement explained "all the symp-
toms that have perturbed and puzzled us so much" (VIII, 2645).
Looking back in June, he told Edmund Gosse, who had been
long out of touch and unaware of the traumatic times R.L.S. had
been through, that Fanny was "very much better, having been
in the early part of this year alarmingly ill" (VIII, 2587).

Such episodes stimulate the dilettante's analysis, especially
now, when the jargon of psychology is so readily to hand.
Perhaps it is simply not possible to know what causes a human
mind to lapse into such a disordered state, but this has not
inhibited enquirers from advancing the most varied diagnoses.
Terms like psychosis, hysteria, and innate emotional instability
have been bandied about, while other explanations begin with
references to the menopause and extend through neurotic
jealousy of other women like Lady Jersey and Belle, a depressive
mentality, loss of a role in R.L.S.' life, stress deriving from
the multiplicity of functions she had taken on in Valima, and
finally a clash between overweening self-love and frustration
at her inability to assert herself as artist or writer. Jenni Calder
observed that "Fanny and Louis were at the centre of a complex

web of involvements in which every difficulty and disagreement washed back over them", although as far as the staff at Vailima were concerned this was more true of Fanny than of her husband.[103] Her selflessness in looking after R.L.S. should not be neglected, even if it was conveyed in domineering language. He said, complainingly, that she wore herself out working in the fields they owned.

In examining their relationship, friends of R.L.S. gave Fanny little peace while she was alive, and critics and biographers have pursued her in the same vein beyond the grave. No doubt the main focus of sympathy, even post factum, should be the victim herself, but R.L.S. was a victim too, and this at a time when he was not a well man. He was working incessantly, producing his best work, and simultaneously striving to ensure peace in Samoa. He kept up a front of normality as visitors came and went, but Fanny's behaviour over the eighteen-month period was abnormal and disruptive, leaving him worried and baffled. He had to cope with moods, tantrums, and frenzies of fury, often directed at him but at times displaced onto Maggie or Belle. With R.L.S., Fanny "made every talk an argument", forcing him to live in isolation in his own room. Aristotle described anger as temporary hatred; Fanny's bouts of anger extended into whole periods of hatred. One of the Samoan nicknames given her by the servants was "Witch Woman of the Mountain" – not complimentary, however it may have been rendered. Moors, whose relations with Fanny were poor, was only the first to wonder if R.L.S. might have been better off not marrying her. At one point, he offered to buy the tiny Nassau

103 Jenni Calder, *R.L.S.: A Life Study*, London, Hamish Hamilton, 1987, p. 298.

Island to allow him freedom from the women in Vailima, and peace to get on with his writing.

There is no denying that Fanny inspired deep love in many who knew her. R.L.S.' letters were edited, which often means "censored", by Colvin, and sections of her diaries were scored out by unknown hands, probably Lloyd's, but possibly Belle's or her sister Nelly's, to prevent embarrassing revelations.[104] The couple's sexual life had ended some time previously. There are no grounds for believing that either was unfaithful during their married life (she had several relationships after his death). He wrote copiously to his earlier love, Frances Sitwell, but there are few letters to Fanny, and none that could be described as love letters. He did write some love poems to her, the best known entitled simply "My Wife".

> Trusty, dusky, vivid, true
> With eyes of gold and bramble-dew
> Steel-true and blade-straight
> The great artificer
> Made my mate.

> Honour, anger, valour, fire;
> A love that life could never tire,
> Death quench or evil stir,
> The mighty master
> Gave to her.

> Teacher, tender comrade, wife
> A fellow-farer true through life
> Heart-whole and soul-free

104 Subsequent editors have in many cases managed to restore the cancellations.

The august father
Gave to me. (Tusitala, XXII, 147–8)

It is a curious poem, a song of gratitude rather than of tenderness or passion, with an underlying feeling of wonder and disbelief. The qualities celebrated are toughness and strength, with the hyphenated descriptions "Steel-true and blade-straight" more appropriate in an account of a Jacobite cavalier than of a beloved wife. The poet stands in awe of his mate, as perhaps he did in life, although their relationship changed over the years in response to their circumstances. In a letter to J.M. Barrie, inviting him to Samoa, R.L.S. gave a pseudo-whimsical description of the "menagerie" he would find in Vailima, beginning with himself as "the Tame Celebrity" and including

Fanny V. de G. Stevenson
The Weird Woman
Native name, *Tamaitai*

The character sketch continued:

If you don't get on with her, it's a pity about your visit. She runs the show, infinitely little, extraordinary wig of grey curls, handsome waxen face like Napoleon's, insane black eyes, boy's hands, tiny bare feet, a cigarette, wild blue native dress usually spotted with garden mould. In company presents as the appearance of a little timid and precise old maid of the days of prunes and prisms; you look for the reticule. (But wouldn't be surprised to find a dagger in the garter, *Am.*) Hellish energy . . . Doctors everybody, will doctor you, cannot be doctored herself. The Living Partizan: A violent friend, a brimstone enemy . . . (VIII, 2550)

The comparison with Napoleon had been first made by Henry James years earlier, while the phrase "a violent friend" gave Margaret Mackay the title of her biography of Fanny. It is an arresting oxymoron. R.L.S. wrote elsewhere that marriage is a relationship which, however affectionate, is also a power struggle, but rarely is the power always on one side. At least part of the time, and not on account of her illness, R.L.S. seems to have been apprehensive of Fanny, and even at times in Samoa downright afraid of her.

It is always dangerous to probe works of fiction to extract biographical facts, but there are two stories, "The Enchantress" and "The Waif Woman", which are of interest precisely because they remained unpublished in R.L.S.' lifetime on account of objections raised by Fanny or Lloyd. "The Enchantress" does not appear in the Tusitala collected edition and only re-emerged at an auction in 1923, but "The Waif Woman" was eventually included alongside *Fables* (Tusitala, VI), though not as one of them. In both stories the male is subdued, cowed by the female, anxious to please or at least to maintain peace and harmony. The female is dominant, deceptive, wily, seductive, and willing to employ her allures as a ploy. Publication of "The Enchantress" was seemingly blocked by Lloyd, who reports it was written on board a yacht – he does not say which – when each of the passengers had to compose a story.[105] The central character is a Scotsman reduced to begging in Paris. He solicits alms from

---

105 It was eventually published in the *Daily Telegraph*, which I was able to consult in the John J. Burns Library of Boston College, in the Graham Greene archive. Greene had planned to write a biography of R.L.S. and began collecting material. He had ripped out the story but kept no note of the date of the newspaper.

an elegant, seductive lady who, after several meetings, offers him an income if he promises to marry her. The two meet as arranged in Edinburgh for the wedding ceremony, but the pledge is a ruse. She needs to be married to come into an inheritance and dismisses the man once rings have been exchanged. Was the *belle dame sans merci* too close to the bone, in some way, for Lloyd? The plot has no straightforward connection with the courtship or married life of R.L.S. and Fanny, but were there other biographical resemblances?

"The Waif Woman", an enigmatic tale, has received more attention. The story, set in Iceland, is a strange blend of saga and Edgar Allan Poe. Fanny's objection was that "it did not seem fair to take the best bit of the other man's book (i.è. the writer of the Saga)" (VII, 2496). This has not stopped people, notably Frank McLynn, from prying below the surface and detecting an unflattering depiction of Fanny in the female protagonist, Aud the Light-Minded, where the first name is presumably pronounced "odd".[106] Her husband is Finnward. The family peace is disturbed by the arrival of a trading ship carrying a woman, Thorgunna, who sits apart from the crew. She has a case of splendid gowns and cloaks and a brooch, all of which she is proud to display but which, to Aud's frustration, she declines to sell. Thorgunna comes to reside with Aud and Finnward, bringing all her goods with her, but attempts to coax her to sell the garments and the beautiful bed linen are in vain. One evening, they have company to dinner and Aud is driven to paroxysms of jealousy by Thorgunna's success with the men. She slips into Thorgunna's room at night to steal the brooch,

---

106 Frank McLynn, *Stevenson,* op. cit., p. 477.

which she thinks may be magic. She is seen by Thorgunna, who the next day summons the husband to announce that she is dying, and will leave some things to Aud and some to their daughter, but the bed linen must be burned. Finnward is minded to carry out the dying woman's instructions, but is jeered at by his wife for his willingness to destroy valuable silk. He lacks the willpower to defy his wife and do as he had promised. "Finnward's heart is heavy, and his mind divided. He feared the dead wife and the living; he feared dishonour and he feared dispeace; and his will was like a seagull in the wind."

The action unfolds in a borderland where fantasy and reality overlap, and the characters are taken from legend. The story is black and cold, and any reflections of truth are filtered through prisms. Perhaps Fanny was hypersensitive at any outline of her own character being detected, or at the portrayal of life in Vailima as being marked by "dispeace". There is no reason for saying that R.L.S. was as weak as the Finnward of the tale, even if he did have to take refuge from his wife, but their relationship was certainly often conflictual. His last words on his wife, the dedication of *Weir of Hermiston*, were more tender.

> Take thou the writing: thine it is. For who
> Burnished the sword, blew on the drowsy coal,
> Held still the target higher, chary of praise
> And prodigal of counsel – who but thou?

PART IV

The Writer at Work

CHAPTER 15

The Sense of Kinship: Scottish and Pacific Ballads

In his *Defence of Poetry*, Shelley wrote that "poetry is not like reasoning, a power to be exerted according to the determination of the will." The role and nature of the creative impulse, called by the Greeks the "muse", and by the Romantics "inspiration", has puzzled many writers, including R.L.S., who wondered about the prompts of mind and imagination which made it possible for him to write poetry. "Verse is always to me the unknowable," he told Edmund Gosse (VII, 2313). There are several passages of seemingly spontaneous verse, or doggerel, in his letters, but he admitted he could not write poetry as and when he wished. With prose it was different, even if he was subject to occasional periods of writer's block. In Samoa, he took these moments calmly, accused himself of being reduced to the idiot state, saddled his horse, and rode down to Apia to consort with beachcombers or friends, sure that the next day words would flow more easily. He had a more serious problem with *Treasure Island*, as he explained in the essay "My First Book". He had turned out fifteen chapters in "one great spurt", but with the sixteenth he "ignominiously lost hold" and had to give up since there was "not one more word in (my) bosom".

It all changed when he moved with Fanny to Davos, where the writing "flowed from me like small talk: and in a second tide of delighted industry, and again at the rate of a chapter a day, I finished *Treasure Island*".

The humours which allowed him to write poetry, as distinct from verse or dum-de-dum doggerel, were of a different order and could not be summoned up at will. His corpus of verse is substantial, but few critics view his poetic work as being of the highest order, and certainly not, as he himself conceded, equal in quality to his prose. It may be that this self-deprecating talk is an additional barrier to the full appreciation of his poetic work, causing it to be relegated in status to an instrument of value principally, or exclusively, as an aid to biography. Even his champions tend to be muted. In the introduction to her edition of his poetry, Janet Adam Smith invited critics to reconsider the work, but then undermined her own plea by admitting that "if we are looking for poetry that has mature passion and mystery, that explores sensibility, that drills down into the subconscious, we shall not come to Stevenson."[107] Edwin Morgan, Scotland's first *makar* in the modern era, accepted the challenge of reconsideration, but still concluded that it was "extremely unlikely that any real revaluation would make him more than a minor poet".[108]

These are authoritative judgements, but discussion of Stevenson's poetry as a whole is not to our purpose, which is to enquire whether the narrative pieces he wrote in the South Seas, eventually published under the simple title *Ballads*, deserve

107 Janet Adam Smith, *Robert Louis Stevenson*, London, Rupert Hart-Davis, 1950, second edition, 1971, p. vii.
108 Edwin Morgan, *Essays*, Manchester, Carcanet, 1974, p. 136.

critical attention, not only for the enlightenment they offer on his changing attitudes towards the culture of Polynesian people, but also as works of narrative verse in their own right. After receiving the proofs from Burlingame, his publisher, he admitted that the volume "had cost him more botheration and dubiety than any other I ever took in hand". Burlingame advised him to exclude some of the "verses at the end" on the grounds that "many of them are bad; many of the rest want nine years keeping, and the remainder are not relevant." He hoped that some of these works could be published elsewhere, but asked that the ballads be viewed in their own right, in the category of narrative verse.

In an extremely hostile review, first published in 1874, of a work of criticism entitled *The Ballads and Songs of Scotland*, R.L.S. scorned the author for defining the point of the ballad as "the perfect imitation of nature", and offered his own view that "the ballad as a means of expression is quite at the other end of the scale from any of the realistic arts" (Tusitala, XXVIII, 215). As a genre, the ballad enjoyed a revival in late Victorian literary circles, even if ideas of what constituted a ballad varied widely. One of those responsible for the renewal of interest was Stevenson's friend, Andrew Lang, who published the first edition of his *Ballades in Blue China* in 1851. More were later added and when the work came out in its final form as *Ballades and Rhymes*, he included an introductory discussion of the genre.[109] The old French form had been revived, he wrote, by Théodore de Banville, some of whose work Lang translated, and had been imported into modern England by Austin Dobson

109 Andrew Lang, *Ballades and Rhymes*, London, Longman, Green & Co., 1911.

and Edmund Gosse, figures well known to Stevenson. Lang also referred to an anonymous author who had "let loose upon the town a whole winged flock of *ballades* of amazing dexterity", later revealed to be W.E. Henley, another friend. Tennyson and Dante Gabriel Rossetti were other poets who composed works described as ballads, and from Samoa R.L.S. wrote to Kipling praising him on his *Barrack-Room Ballads and Other Verses*. Matthew Arnold with his *Sohrab and Rustum: An Episode*, first published in 1853, gave dignity to pseudo-epic narrative verse. Lang made a slighting reference to a "serious *ballade*" by Swinburne, who believed the genre was appropriate only for light verse. Stevenson plainly dissented from that view, and his ballads were, at least in intention, serious. He looked elsewhere and admitted that "Song of Rahéro" perhaps owed much to Longfellow's "Song of Hiawatha" (1855). A debt to Macaulay's "Lays of Ancient Rome" (1842), especially to "Horatius", is more evident.[110]

R.L.S. was open to this new wave but, as in other instances, his principal point of reference was Walter Scott. His avid curiosity regarding the folklore of the peoples he met on his travels indicated a certain similarity of purpose, noted by contemporary critics, to Scott's quest for traditional Borders ballads. The collection of material was originally part of the planned "big book", but the ballads themselves became the first instance in his writing of the identification of similar traits of mind in Scottish and Polynesian culture.

110 Roger C. Lewis, "Introduction", in *The Collected Poems of Robert Louis Stevenson*, Edinburgh, Edinburgh University Press, 2003, p. 14.

When I desired any detail of savage custom, or superstitious belief, I cast back in the story of my fathers, and
fished for what I wanted with some trait of equal barbarism: Michael Scott, Lord Derwentwater's head, the
second-sight, the Water Kelpie – each of these I have
found to be a killing bait; the black bull's head of Stirling
procured me the legend of Rahéro; and what I knew
of the Cluny Macphersons, or of the Appin Stewarts,
enabled me to learn, and helped me to understand, about
the Tevas of Tahiti. The native was no longer ashamed,
his sense of kinship grew warmer, and his lips were
opened. It is this sense of kinship that the traveller must
arouse and share. (Tusitala, XX, 13)

The "sense of kinship", the bond between Scotland and
Polynesia, meant that the ballads were not merely an excursus
into exotic realms. He hoped that the contemporary popularity
of the ballad in Britain would win him an appreciative readership. "I have a sneaking idea that the ballads are not altogether
without merit – I don't know if they're poetry, but they're good
narrative, or I'm deceived" (VI, 2243). In the event his work did
not find favour with the critics. After publication, he expressed
his gratitude to H.B. Baildon for his favourable judgement, and
reiterated his request for the application of distinct criteria
to verse of this kind.

Glad the ballads amused you. They failed to entertain a
coy public; at which I own I wondered. Not that I set much
store by my verses, which are the verses of [a] Prosator,
but I do know how to tell a yarn, and two of the yarns
were great. *Rahéro* is for its length, I think, a perfect folk

tale; savage yet fine, full of a tail foremost morality, ancient as the granite rocks; if the historian not to say the politician could get that year into his head, he would have learned some of his A.B.C. (VII, 2360)

The claims made for "Rahéro" seem extravagant, but other statements in the letter deserve examination. Stevenson was too prolific a writer of poetry to be dismissed with his own casual self-denigration as a prose stylist who, in the manner of Francis Bacon or Thomas Babington Macaulay, turned his hand occasionally to the production of polished verse. Yet he requested respect only for his ability to produce a good yarn. The two ballads he regarded as "great" are presumably "Rahéro" and "The Feast of Famine", the two Polynesian tales. Edwin Morgan did not share Stevenson's estimate even of these works, although he exempted from criticism the short poem "Christmas at Sea". Two other works based on Scottish legends, "Heather Ale: A Galloway Legend", and "Ticonderoga", the work he had read to the King of Hawaii, make up the collection.

"Heather Ale" is a jocular tale of efforts to preserve a fabled Pictish product after the defeat of the Picts. The king alone keeps the recipe for a drink "sweeter far than honey and stronger far than wine", so when a rival defeats the Picts in battle, his aim is to exterminate them as a people but continue to savour their drink. He fails to compel the defeated monarch to divulge his secret, even after killing his son, so the secrets of producing the drink vanish with the people who had devised it. The poem is an extended, droll anecdote rather than a yarn, and deals lightly with themes of war and vengeance which receive more serious treatment in the other ballads.

"Ticonderoga" was written while he was in Edinburgh after the death of his father, and appeared in December 1887. R.L.S. hesitated over including a tale set in the Highlands alongside the South Sea ballads, but its inclusion is another instance of the links he saw between the two places (VI, 2132). It is a more substantial piece than the earlier work. A member of the Clan Stewart kills a Cameron, but, fearing vengeance from the murdered man's family, goes immediately to the home of the brother of the man he has killed, where, without revealing his crime, he requests hospitality and protection. Highland traditions demand that any such request be granted, and once granted it acquires the status of a sacred oath that can never be broken. When the slain man appears to his brother in a dream, the brother is bound by the code of honour and cannot comply with the demand for vengeance. His refusal leads the ghost to utter the curse of a strange word – Ticonderoga. Like many Highlanders, the Cameron joins the British army and fights on the continent, but is then dispatched to North America to serve in the war against the rebellious American forces. The night before battle is engaged he hears the name of the place, Ticonderoga, and knows he will not survive. The murderer plays no part in the story after shackling his host. The clash is thus internal to the Clan Cameron, a conflict between the duty to avenge murdered kin and the requirement to honour a request for succour, with the second being held supreme. The two Pacific ballads deal similarly with ties of blood, the call for revenge, and the need to right wrongs done.

Local folklore yielded the subject matter for the two South Seas narrative ballads. R.L.S. gathered other information which provided plots or background material for tales he would later write, but some readers then and later wondered why he had chosen to recount these tales in verse rather than in prose. During his second visit to Hawaii, in 1893, he gave an interview to a journalist, in which he explained his thinking:

> For verse of the ballad form, such matter is best adapted by far, for here it can be used without changing to any extent the legends of the Islanders, and still bring good results. Have you read *Rahéro*? That makes my point clear. That ballad has its faults, but it is true to the legend as I heard it in Tahiti from various sources, mostly agreeing; and I believe the ballad stands for a piece of fair work. It cost me some pains. The success there, I think, lies in the fact that there is something in the ballad form – perhaps its limitations – which hides the literary defect of the subject that would be quite conspicuous in more comprehensive prose. This was my reason for using verse – I wished to reproduce the legend as nearly as possible as I found it.[111]

"The Song of Rahéro", as its subtitle – "A Legend of Tahiti" – indicates, is a traditional story from the island where Stevenson and his party arrived in September 1888. He was already unwell after the voyage and suffered a complete collapse the following month. The family retired to the quiet of the village of Tautira, where he was nursed not only by Fanny but also by Princess Moe, and where he formed a close friendship with King Ori-a-Ori, a towering, charismatic personality to whom he dedicated the poem. According to Fanny, Princess

111 Arthur Johnstone, *Stevenson and the Pacific*, op. cit., p. 103.

Moe was one of the sources of "Rahéro", although R.L.S. himself said he heard two versions of the tale and was helped by five persons, and in consequence "there seems no reason why the tale should not be true". The story was popular in the country of the eight Tevas, the clan to which Rahéro belonged, and into which R.L.S. was initiated. The similarities with the clan system of the Highlands hardly needed underlining. R.L.S. was struck by the fact that one level in the hierarchy of power was exercised in the Pacific by men who were "quasi Tacksmen in the Scottish Highlands".[112]

The ballad tells of the criminal deception perpetrated by the villainous Rahéro on the innocent and simple-minded Tàmatéa, whom he meets while Tàmatéa is on the way to pay homage to the king. The king is known as a cruel tyrant, and to appease him Tàmatéa had been dispatched by his mother with the gift of a fish. En route he is stopped by Rahéro, a man "of inherited cunning of spirit and beauty of body and face", one who is also lazy and unwilling to farm or hunt. (It is notable how frequently sloth and idleness are identified as common and wholly regrettable characteristics of Polynesian life.) In this poem, it is the anti-hero who displays these traits, and who exploits the industrious but naïve Tàmatéa. By a ruse, he manages to steal and devour the fish himself, but puts the bones back in the basket and sends the boy on his way to give his now offensive present to the king.

Tàmatéa, unaware of the deception, makes the presentation to the king, who is initially delighted by the gesture but then

112 The tacksman was a tenant who had been given by a superior landowner or chieftain control of tracts of land which were often large enough to be sublet.

outraged at what he takes as an act of effrontery. As the boy leaves the court, the king issues an edict that he must be pursued and put to death. The murder takes place as the boy has almost reached home. R.L.S. employs the epic, or mock-epic, tone with the same ease and grace as Arnold.

Night massed in the valleys; the sun on the mountain coast
Struck, end-long; and above the clouds embattled their host,
And glowed and gloomed on the heights; and the heads of
                    the palms were gems
And far to the rising eve extended the shade of their stems;
And the shadow of Tàmatéa hovered already at home.

After her son's death, Tàmatéa's mother takes on the role of protagonist and the central theme, as in "Ticonderoga", is the quest for vengeance, not justice. She travels the land to find another king who will take up her cause. She is derided in most quarters, but eventually finds a champion.

To the land of Nàmunu-ura, to Paea, at length she came,
To men who were foes of the Tevas and hated their race
    and name.
There she was well received and spoke with Hiopa the king.
And Hiopa listened and weighed and wisely considered
    the thing.

Hiopa's strategy is devious and protracted. The people in Vaiau, of whom Rahéro is one, have a reputation for gluttony, so Hiopa plans to invite them to the most sumptuous feast ever held on Tahiti. To build up the resources needed for such a grand event, he places a taboo on all pigs and forbids his people to eat fruit from the trees. The tribe, young and old, women and children as well as the warriors, are invited to the feast and arrive in their boats. They are welcomed and the grandest of meals is prepared. The pigs "screamed and were slaughtered", bananas, coconuts, bread fruit, and the taro plant collected, underground ovens prepared, *kava* made for drinking. The feast is celebrated and after indulging their gluttony the Vaiau are escorted to a newly built house to rest. The vengeful plan is now implemented. Hiopa places wood around the hut and sets it ablaze, and warriors surround the building to make sure no-one can escape the conflagration. Tàmatéa's mother, untouched by pity, exults in the death and havoc she has caused. At this point the poem conveys something of the terrifying excesses in the Greek myth of Electra and Clytemnestra, or the Hindu tale of the *Mahabharata*.

The smoke and flames arouse Rahéro, who strives unsuccessfully to awaken his wife. Leaving her, he takes hold of his son and attempts to climb up the wall of the hut, still holding the boy close to him, but as he clambers up the wood of the house, his son wriggles free and falls back into the blaze. Rahéro alone makes his escape. All other members of the tribe perish. The schemes devised by Tàmatéa's mother and Hiopa have seemingly been successful, but the obligation to take revenge in a never-ending cycle of slaughter and counter-slaughter now falls on Rahéro.

The next episodes in the plot are intriguing. Rahéro sees a fisherman on the shore and a boat on the sea. He calculates that the person in the boat is the fisherman's wife. He crawls up behind the innocent man and kills him. The man's wife approaches the shore, and in the darkness is unaware that it is Rahéro, not her husband, who boards. The two sail off and, even when recognition is made, are drawn to each other, he "comely and great of stature, a man to obey and admire", she pleasingly "broad of shoulder, ample of girdle, long in the thigh, deep of bosom" and therefore fit "to mother a war-like race". The woman may be booty, but she neither protests nor resists. The man whose crime set in motion the terrible deeds emerges as the hero, impenitent, unpunished, and free. The children he will have with this woman will continue the tribal war of vengeance.

The hostile reception of this poem in Britain baffled and dismayed R.L.S. and he made an effort to explain to his own satisfaction the failure of these works with the reading public:

> But the average man at home cannot understand an-tiquity; he is sunk over the ears in Roman civilisation; and a tale like that of *Rahéro* falls on his ears inarticulate. *The Spectator* said there was no psychology in it; that interested me much; my grandmother (as I used to call that able paper – and an able paper it is, and a fair one) cannot so much as observe the existence of savage psychology when it is placed before it. I am at bottom a psychologist and ashamed of it; the tale seized me one third because of its picturesque features, two thirds because of its astonishing psychology; and *The Spectator* says there is none. (VII, 2360)

Rome, Scotland, and the Pacific were now essential markers of R.L.S.' cultural worldview, but he detected an incompatibil-ity between them. He was by background Roman and Scottish, but his travels had equipped him with an additional intellectual slant, the culture of the Polynesian islanders. His objection to the review in the *Spectator* was that the writer was unaware of the existence of a different hierarchy of values, unknown in Europe but current in Polynesia. R.L.S. requested his readers to look beyond the barriers of what he termed Roman civilisation. Both with the Camerons in the Highlands and the Tevas in the Pacific, the tales R.L.S. told unfolded on the wrong side of Hadrian's Wall. He believed he had given his characters a psychological motivation, even if the psychology was savage. He indicated parallel tales from Highland history which had intrigued his hosts in Tahiti. These may have included the Glencoe massacre, where the Campbells were guests of the Clan MacDonald before they turned on them, as did the family of Tàmatéa.

There is in "The Song of Rahéro" no quest for justice. The author himself defined the sense of the tale as "savage yet fine, full of a tail foremost morality", which goes beyond even the morality of an eye for an eye. Rahéro, the perpetrator of the original wrong, gets off scot-free, and there is no indication in the poem that he mourns his lost wife, children, or fellows. He alone of his tribe escapes, and will suffer no retribution either for the murder of Tàmatéa or for that of the innocent fisherman. Indeed, like the chivalrous hero who has slain the dragon, he goes off into the rising sun with the fisherman's beautiful wife, the woman who will produce the future "warlike race". Chesterton quoted (his unattributed quotations are suspect) R.L.S. as saying that he wished to "fit every place with its appropriate legend", but it is also true that he was attracted by strong villains – Long John Silver, Alan Breck Stewart, the Master of Ballantrae – who each fulfil the expectations of romance by strutting off at the end into a future which promises well. As does Rahéro. The poem is close to a revenge drama, but it is not a tragedy where a balance is re-established at the end. It is a portrait of bloodshed and audacity.

There is more than a hint of cannibalism in "The Feast of Famine", an original tale in which R.L.S. "strung together some of the more striking particularities of the Marquesas". He found that "the Polynesians are subject to a disease seemingly rather of the will than of the body", and added that in "their despondency there is an element of dread". "The Feast of Famine", subtitled "Marquesan Manners", is a dark, harrowing, violent tale of love, death, and human sacrifice, with a Romeo and Juliet element to the love story. While Rua and his love Taheia are of the same clan, Rua is a "child of the dirt" and Taheia is the daughter of the chieftain. The couple are forced to meet at night in the woods, but their love story is only one element in the tale. R.L.S. was already developing the boldness he would later display in his portrayal of white beachcombers and adventurers, and honing techniques which would lead him from romance to realism.

The drumbeat metre of the first section of the ballad is hypnotic as a descriptive and narrative device, and effective in the creation of a melodramatic atmosphere of dread, despair, and helplessness. "In all the land of the tribe, was neither fish nor fruit." Faced with famine, the high priest, who has power of life and death, is required to select nine from the tribe to be slaughtered for food. The tone softens in the succeeding section dealing with the plight of the lovers.

Taheia, heavy of hair, a foolish thing have we done
To bind what gods have sundered unkindly into one,

> Why should a lowly lover have touched Taheia's skirt,
> Taheia the well descended and Rua child of the dirt?

"Heavy of hair" is a repeated description, perhaps to endow the verses with a sub-Homeric force, as Arnold had done in *Sohrab*. The rhyming couplets are sometimes forced and liable to drag as the narrative unfolds. The lovers' meeting is not merely a tryst but an opportunity for Taheia to warn Rua that he must flee, for she believes that he is one of those destined for slaughter. He withdraws to a deep ravine, defying the taboos laid on that place.

Meantime, the tribe comes together for the dire feast of human flesh.

> Dawn as yellow as sulphur leaped on the naked peak,
> And all the village was stirring, for now was the priest to
>   speak.
> Forth on this terrace he came, and sat with the chief in talk;
> His lips were blackened with fever, his cheeks were whiter
>   than chalk;
> Fever clutched at his hands, fever nodded his head,
> But, quiet and steady and cruel, his eyes shone ruby-red ...
> Braves were summoned, and drummers; messengers came
>   and went;
> Braves ran to their lodges, weapons were snatched from
>   the wall;
> The commons herded together, and fear was over them all.

This is the very style and idiom of melodrama, but it was not easy to maintain the tone of high drama or impending doom while also respecting the requirements of rhyming couplets. In spite of that, the build-up of tension is undiminished. The first eight victims are struck down, but the ninth, Rua, escapes to a clearing in the woods, from where he hears the march of the Vais, an enemy tribe. This discovery compels him to face a moral dilemma. Should he follow his duty and issue a warning to his own people and face the risk of death, or is he entitled to secure his safety by leaving them to their fate? He can no more hesitate than did Horatius when called on to defend the bridge over the Tiber as Lars Porsena's invading hordes approached the city. The ethical imperative is identical. Rua runs to the village to alert his kinsfolk, and before Taheia or the priest can call for him to be spared, he is killed by a spear, dying in the arms of his lover. His last words are a prophecy or a curse that the Vais are about to wreak havoc on the village. The ending has a mock-Homeric tone.

> And they tell that when next the sun had climbed to the
>   noonday skies
> It shone on the smoke of feasting in the country of the Vais.

"Rahéro" and "The Feast" were, R.L.S. said, "my two great adventures; either they are very good or I have made a strange error" (VI, 2138). He may well have made an error, at least in the case of the latter, which was essentially a work of Gothic horror. His letters reveal him anxiously seeking reassurance from his main correspondents, Charles Baxter and Sidney Colvin, promising to throw the poems away if they judged them not up to the mark. The *Ballads* have not fared well with critics, neither on first publication nor today. Edwin Morgan was uncompromising. "These ballads are not in fact good poems . . . and usually it's fairly clear why. He writes in a long, lolloping rhyming couplet which quickly becomes tedious in a lengthy narrative poem."[113] In the two Polynesian ballads, some verses are downright awkward on the ear or eye, and are forced or jagged. Colvin confessed he found them "unequal and uncertain both in metre and style", and his was one of the most moderate of criticisms. R.L.S. wrote in April 1890 to Edmund Gosse, in a supposedly offhand digression on the critical response in London: "By the way, my *Ballads* seem to have been dam bad; all the crickets sing so in their cricketty papers, and I have no ghost of an idea on the point myself" (VII, 2313). Gosse's overall assessment was that "the effort to become a Polynesian Walter Scott is a little too obvious, the inspiration too mechanical".

R.L.S. reworked the ballads over succeeding years, and only released them for publication when he had taken up residence in Samoa. In spite of the criticism they have attracted, they are not without merit. The nature of the action, of the social drives, the emotional urges, and the hierarchy of values were not recognisable to contemporary metropolitan critics. The psychological probe is into the deeper, darker, more primal and less restrained appetites of the human animal, akin to those which push Medea to kill her own children to avenge herself on her faithless husband Jason. The *Ballads* deal with the shamanic forces that move Hyde, totally freed from the – however inadequate – restraining conscience of Jekyll. There were laws and morals, yet as retold in these legends they were dictated not by rationalist considerations but by subterranean forces of will. What he saw of daily life and rule in the Pacific islands persuaded him of the strength and validity of the culture

113 Edwin Morgan, *Essays*, op. cit., p. 137.

dominant there. In his representation the folklore, as is the case with Western myths or folk tales, brought to the surface pre-rational energies which needed to be shackled to make communal living possible. Something of this amoral force will re-emerge in works like *The Ebb-Tide*.

CHAPTER 16

A Lot Accomplished

Towards the end of 1891, R.L.S. gave himself the opportunity to take stock, reminisce and ruminate, and even allow himself a rare moment of self-congratulation. "God bless you, what a lot I have accomplished: *Wrecker* done, *Beach of Falesá* done, half the *History*: *c'est étonnant*" (VII, 2378).

His productivity over the Samoa years was indeed astonishing in quantity and variety, even if the quality varied. He is estimated to have written some 700,000 words in the four-year period of his residence on the island. In November 1890, while Colvin was putting together an anthology of essays previously published in various periodicals, we find R.L.S. himself at work on "The Beach of Falesá". By October the following year he had completed it as well as *The Wrecker* and was unsure what to turn his hand to next. In February 1892, he was able to communicate to J.M. Barrie that "the continuation to *Kidnapped* is under way" (VII, 2389), and in November to let him know that it was completed, and that he had "another book on the stocks, *The Young Chevalier*". This last was one of R.L.S.' many unfinished projects, but we know from the sections he did write that it was to be set partly in Scotland and partly in France and would have featured Bonnie Prince Charlie. He was also at work on *Weir of Hermiston*, which too was left unfinished. The sequel to *Kidnapped* was provisionally entitled *David Balfour*, the name by which it is still known in the U.S.A., but, at the publisher's behest, it was published in Britain as *Catriona*.

It was R.L.S.' habit to work on several projects at the same time, sometimes putting one aside for a period of months before taking it up again, but often leaving it unfinished. In May 1891, he wrote to Edward L. Burlingame outlining his "prospects", which he numbered somewhat eccentrically:

3. *The South Seas*, in 2 vols, illustrated.
1. *The Wrecker*
2. "The High Woods of Ulufana", story about as long as *Jekyll*,
    not so good.
4 or 5. *The Shovels of Newton French:* a curious kind of novel
    lasting from about 1600 to 1830. I shall probably give it
    a second title, "Memoirs of a Wild Family" or such
    like, but this will jar horribly with
5 or 4. *Memoirs of a Scottish Family,* 2 vols. Being chiefly
    sketches of my grandfather and father.
6. *The Pearl Fisher*, with Lloyd. (VII, 2319)

Things were not getting any easier if in June 1893 he told Edmund Gosse, who was himself considering embarking on a novel, that he, R.L.S., had "a little lost (my) way, and stand bemused at a crossroads". He was not short of ideas, and was as prone as ever to self-criticism. "A subject? Aye, I have dozens, I have at least four novels begun, they are none good enough; and the mill waits, and I'll have to take second best" (VIII, 2585). In the early '90s, three works of fiction were written in collaboration with Lloyd Osbourne: *The Wrong Box, The Wrecker*, and

The Ebb-Tide, the last of which was initially to be entitled *The Pearl Fisher.* His own production can be divided into works with a Scottish theme, and those set in the South Seas, although the borders between the two are decidedly porous since the Scottish works contain oblique reflections on problems and subjects he was tackling in regard to Samoa, while the Samoan works draw on his meditations on Scotland's past.

The main Scottish works of fiction were *Catriona*, *St. Ives*, and *Weir of Hermiston.* Though the latter two were left unfinished at his death, substantial portions had been written, while there are only short fragments of *The Young Chevalier* and no more than a fairly full synopsis of another projected novel, *Sophia Scarlet.* What we can term the South Seas work included "The Beach of Falesá" and "Isle of Voices". The list is far from complete. He also did the work for what would be the posthumous *In the South Seas*, the family history entitled *Records of a Family of Engineers*; *Footnote to History*; several pamphlets; the polemical letters to *The Times* on conditions in Samoa; volumes of poetry; assorted memoranda on the political situation locally as well as his own massive correspondence. The sheer volume of work is certainly impressive, even if the quality is, unsurprisingly, uneven. At times he is elated, declaring *Catriona* to be his best work to date, and stating that, to his own embarrassment, he finds no greater pleasure than in re-reading his own previous work, but at others he is more doubtful about the worth of it all. In July 1894, he told Henry James that his mind was "entirely in abeyance" (VIII, 2748), which was anything but true.

As regards the trilogy of novels written jointly with Lloyd Osbourne, there is still some uncertainty over whose voice is dominant in which sections. *The Wrong Box* was undoubtedly Lloyd's idea, and the final plot follows lines traced by him, even if it was substantially rewritten by R.L.S. The story is a black farce, revealing in R.L.S. the quirky approach not merely of the fantasist, a quality he had amply displayed elsewhere, but of the humorist, the outlook familiar to Mark Twain. The core problem arises from a tontine, a financial contract whereby all the accumulated proceeds go to the last survivor. The terms of the pact mean that the desperate descendants who hope to inherit have to go to bizarre lengths to conceal the body of one of the original signatories. The work was published before R.L.S.' arrival in Samoa. The whimsical tone is rarely seen in his later work, although it is a common feature of his private correspondence.

As a novel, *The Wrecker* has drawn the disapproval of critics who were otherwise admirers. R.L.S. explained to his cousin Bob the problems of collaboration, telling him that the book "is superficially all mine, in the sense that the last copy is in my hand. Lloyd did not even put pen to paper in the Paris scenes or the Barbizon scene; it was no good; he wrote and often rewrote all the rest" (VIII, 2782). The original inspiration was given by a mysterious maritime incident reported in Hawaii while the Stevenson party was there. The seemingly suspicious cargo, the lack of a credible explanation of the shipwreck, and the implausibility of the stories recounted by the surviving members of the crew stimulated the curiosity of the two writers. Fanny reports that they sat up late on board the *Equator* discussing the enigma. Their conversation resulted in an intriguing if loosely structured novel which justifies G.K. Chesterton's description of it as having "the look of a scrap-book . . . merely the sketch-book of Loudon Dodd, the wandering art student never allowed to be fully an artist."[114] The action sprawls across continents, from bohemian Paris to bourgeois Edinburgh to Midway Island where the mysterious wreck lies. It questions, very lightly, the source of the wealth of a stolid family in Edinburgh and pokes fun at the inanity of a millionaire in the imaginary state of Muskegon. Whatever its weaknesses, it contains scenes of high drama and sketches of jeering caricature, and never lacks vitality, exuberance, elan, inventiveness, and momentum. The characters are memorable, the encounters gripping, the mystery maintained, and the descriptions of storms at sea magnificently done. By that time in his life, R.L.S. had ample experience of rough weather.

In spite of its exotic origins in the Pacific, the novel can be viewed as the most autobiographical of all R.L.S.' output, with Loudon Dodd moving in places R.L.S. had inhabited and reliving many of his experiences. Loudon may also be based on the American artist Will H. Low, to whom the book is dedicated and whom R.L.S. had known in the artists' colony in Grez. In an intriguing epilogue on the background to the book, R.L.S. playfully apologises to Low for "the prodigious quantity of theory" not in the body of the novel but in that section. Questions of literary theory were very much on his mind in the last stages of his life. He identifies three aspects of his approach to *The Wrecker* – (auto)biography, inherent in his invitation to Low "to breathe once more for a moment the airs of our youth"; the "very modern form of the police novel or mystery story"; and finally the "method of Charles Dickens in his later work". These

114 G.K. Chesterton, *Stevenson*, op. cit., p. 147.

do not correspond to the novel's three distinct sections, set in Paris, the South Seas, and England, linked only by the presence and activities of Loudon himself.

Loudon is an American whose aspiration to be an artist takes him, inevitably, to Paris. The early chapters follow his life as a bohemian *flâneur* in the French capital, with interludes in Edinburgh where his mother's family came from. Loudon's initial dependence on the generosity of his father, and his own grudging response to such beneficence, carry echoes of R.L.S.' relations with Thomas Stevenson. In Paris, he makes the acquaintance of a fellow American, Thomas Pinkerton, a naïve but open-hearted entrepreneur who offers him friendship and patronage, but Loudon's creativity is not equal to the hopes of either man. The depiction of the crudeness of outlook and the unsuccessful business endeavours of both Pinkerton and his father back home in the state of Muskegon give glimpses of an anti-Americanism which was resented in the U.S.A. when the book was published. Like R.L.S., Loudon moves to San Francisco and scratches a living in various enterprises, including organising cruise picnics under the management of Pinkerton. The lives of the two men are jolted out of their easy routine when Loudon meets the shifty crew of a ship, the *Flying Scud*, beached in the South Seas and apparently containing a valuable but probably illegal cargo. Their belief that the cargo is opium presents them with a moral dilemma, which they complaisantly resolve for themselves. At an auction, they purchase the shipwreck at a price well beyond their resources, but the fact that another bidder is prepared to match their outrageous offer convinces them there are rich pickings to be had. A voyage to Midway Island and the discovery that the ship is anything but wrecked add to the mystery. Although there are echoes of *Treasure Island*, this time there is no treasure, and the continuing search for a solution to a mystery, at whose core there lurks a strange figure who may have inherited a noble title and estate, brings Loudon to England. The suspense is maintained and the mystery resolved only in the closing page.

While providing a chronicle of adventure and a diverting tale, there are, not for the first time in R.L.S., moral issues implicit in the unfolding adventure. On the yachts in the South Seas, he had witnessed double standards and double dealing, and noted the same traits in his friend Moors in Apia. In *The Wrecker* he probes and exposes the behaviour of Western men made easily immoral when wrenched from the social and legal framework which enforces ethical standards, thus leaving them free to pursue their own interests by any means. The crime at the core of the story involves the slaughter of the actual crew of the *Flying Scud* by men from another ship who then imper-sonate them and concoct an implausible tale when they make their landing in Honolulu. This may be, as R.L.S. told Low, a crime story, but there is no detective, and no process which will bring guilty men to justice. They have no conscience, so the contrast is between those who behave openly as pirates and the seemingly respectable figures, in Edinburgh as well as San Francisco, who disregard the standards they preach. Neither Loudon, who is prepared to trade in opium, nor Pinkerton, is a positive hero. Money is king and the double standards in the city reveal them as no better than out-and-out thieves. This is a novel about Western men in the South Seas, not a novel featuring Polynesians themselves.

The third collaborative fiction, *The Ebb-Tide*, may be the

most undervalued work in the entire Stevenson canon. According to Lloyd Osbourne, it was actually written before *The Wrecker*, even if published later. It was intended to be part of a longer work, but the completed section was set aside until it was rediscovered by Graham Balfour who pronounced it excellent and worthy of being published on its own. Lloyd certainly contributed, although how much is a matter of debate. R.L.S. wrote a whimsical letter to him when he was sitting in the adjoining room, thanking him gravely for his comments and assuring him that they had all been incorporated into the final work. However, he later proposed to delete Lloyd's name from the title page, ostensibly on the grounds that he considered it "unfair on the young man to couple his name with so infamous a work". He added that he, Lloyd, had "nothing to do with the last half. The first we wrote together, the second is entirely mine" (VIII, 2624).

Whatever the motives, the description of the novel as "infamous" is not entirely ironic. Few other books by R.L.S. were the subject of such frequent discussion in his correspondence, or caused him such frustration. The many pained or jocular references to the difficulties encountered in the writing, and numerous complaints over the need for rewriting, give the reader the impression of sitting at R.L.S.' elbow as he girds himself determinedly for a job which gave him little pleasure, and with which he was never entirely satisfied. It was not the collaborative effort which caused the problems, but his doubts over the nature of the material, expressed by his recurring use of the adjective "grim". He told Henry James that "the grimness of that story is not to be depicted in words. There are only four characters to be sure, but they are such a troop of swine. If the admirers of Zola admire him for his pertinent ugliness and pessimism, I think they should admire this" (VIII, 2588). He was more concise in his choice of words to Charles Baxter, "a most grim and gloomy tale" (VIII, 2540). Even positive assessments are qualified by the same word. "If my island ain't a thing of beauty, I'll be damned. Please observe Wiseman and Wishart for the incidental grimness. Did anybody ever see such a story of four characters?" he asked rhetorically.[115]

Colvin, a serially unhelpful critic of R.L.S.' work, saw *The Ebb-Tide* as the "working out of an artistic problem of a kind". For once, his judgement was shrewd, and caused R.L.S. to retort with a robust, "Well, I should just bet it was!" (VIII, 2624). The artistic problem may have been that R.L.S. was struggling, with varying degrees of success, to orientate himself in new territory, not only geographically. He was aware that the action, characterisation, and ethics of a work like *The Ebb-Tide* would jar with his readers and challenge their expectations. Colvin suggested that the final two chapters be jettisoned as he feared they were too unforgiving, too relentless, or too dark, but he also had a problem with the central figure, Attwater, who he believed was "done from the outside". R.L.S. gave a sardonic assent, but pointed to the three different kinds of scoundrel he had created "that are gone through and lived out" (VIII, 2624).

The Ebb-Tide gives evidence of a shift of imagination to a new dimension of life. Structurally it is divided into two parts, the first section a broadly realist adventure story set in the South Seas, the second more a *conte philosophique* set on a remote, perhaps abstract, island. Many authors, from Shakespeare to

115 Wiseman and Wishart are two previous captains of the doomed vessel in the novel.

H.G. Wells, have found an island setting ideal for the creation of a closed mental and cultural world where driven men can act out idealistic or savage schemes away from social control. An island is an enclosed site, its inhabitants answerable to no community and recognising no authority but their own. R.L.S.' island is somewhere in the Pacific, but is not recorded on any map. One of the characters comes to wonder if it is a real place at all, or if they have wandered over the edge. It is a moral no-man's-land where the native people are wholly marginal and the white men have lost all psychological or moral anchors.

The trio of desperadoes who land there find it purely by chance, when lost on the seas. Davis, Huish, and Herrick are three drifters, "on the beach" in Papeete, with no future and shady backgrounds. Davis is a captain whose drunkenness caused his last ship to sink, Huish a reprobate with a criminal past, and Herrick an Oxford graduate once of great promise but who has become part of the aimless flotsam and jetsam of Pacific life. Their fortunes change when Davis is given the chance to captain to Sydney a ship whose crew has been struck down with smallpox; he hires the other two as crew. The cargo is champagne, and their plan is to hijack the ship to Peru and sell it off with the crates of wine, but champagne proves a temptation too far for such a dissolute bunch. Once away from land, they spend their time drunk, and their scheme for self-enrichment founders totally when they discover that the remaining bottles contain only water.

The tone changes, and the adventure story gives way to moral enquiry when they sight an island not identifiable from any chart, but inhabited by Attwater, a singularly enigmatic being of a type more familiar from the fiction of Joseph Conrad.

R.L.S. never before or subsequently created such a character, and it was presumably the construction of Attwater's contorted ethics that caused R.L.S. such difficulties. There were many bizarre ideas swirling about in *fin de siècle* Europe, and from a medley of them R.L.S. creates a commanding figure, a prototype of the cult leader, a sophisticated intellectual who towers above other men in physique and dominates them in personality.[116] He has the unscrupulous traits of a Nietzschean superman, with the twist that he is a fatalist and, supposedly, a believing Christian whose conversation is laced with lines from the Bible. He is even godlike: "I can do anything . . . you do not understand: what must be, must," he says. R.L.S. may have drawn on the lives and deeds of beachcombers he had encountered who, whatever nefarious crimes they may have committed, had established pseudo-Christian cults on islands in the South Seas.[117]

Attwater shows a preference for the cultured Herrick and invites him to visit before allowing the others onto the island. On landing, Herrick is confronted by a strange icon, a ship's figurehead who stares out "with what seemed irony". Looking into himself, Herrick could have found it in his heart to regret that she was "not a goddess, nor yet he a pagan, that he might have bowed down before her in that hour of difficulty". The presence and power of this symbol in the sand are an invitation to look beyond material reality and surface narrative. R.L.S. is inviting contemplation of deeper levels of life and murky areas of the psyche.

At dinner, Attwater tells how most of his followers had been wiped out by disease, but also recounts how he had driven one

116 James McCearney, *Le Pays Stevenson*, op. cit., pp. 161–3.
117 See chapter 6.

to suicide and shot another. Two opposing criminal schemes, two different stamps of the amoral mind, each calculating, unscrupulous, and callous, are formulated. Davis is convinced that Attwater has a store of valuable pearls, and, with the backing of Huish, his plan is to kill him and steal the treasure. Tormented by conscience over this scheme, Herrick contemplates suicide but lacks the determination to see it through. Attwater has his own scheme for his own world, and will kill to achieve it. The conclusion is enigmatic. Huish botches his murder attempt and is shot by Attwater. Herrick is given the opportunity to leave when another ship arrives, but Davis chooses to remain, saying he has undergone a conversion. To what? To the idiosyncratic Christianity of Attwater, but what is the sense of that change of belief? What god does Attwater, and thus Davis, worship? What is the nature of his cult? What is the basis of his power?

Death, disease, wasted lives, amoral designs, and bizarre pseudo-Christian practices feature in this strange, indecipherable, unsettling tale. The title is revealed to be metaphorical, referring not to the flow of the seas but to "the ebb tide in man's affairs". The novel may have some of the characteristics of a Stevensonian adventure story, but it is a more profound meditation on the human condition than he had attempted before. It contains questions and enigmas, with no solutions. G.K. Chesterton expressed some dissatisfaction with the depiction of Attwater, writing that he did not "object to the author creating such a loathsome person as Mr. Attwater; but I do object to his creating him and not loathing him."[118] For once,

118 G.K. Chesterton, *Stevenson*, op. cit., p. 133

Chesterton's judgement can be questioned. R.L.S. narrates. He poses the eternal *unde malum* question of the unknowable origins of evil without taking sides, though at times he leaves the impression of being simultaneously repelled and attracted. The motives and the creed of Attwater are ultimately uninterpretable and clouded in mystery, but there is no evident sympathy for him. He is left in command of his little domain, under the gaze of the curious female figurehead in the sand. Herrick gazes at the statue raised above him "with singular feelings of curiosity and romance, and suffered his mind to travel to and fro in her life history" (Tusitala, XIV, 85).

This strangely haunting novel invites unromantic analysis. Perhaps at this stage in his life, R.L.S. had renounced all effort at providing neat, rational conclusions and was more taken by the inexplicable mysteriousness of human conduct and the impulses which were already in his lifetime being identified as subconscious. He may seem to belong to a different epoch and owe allegiance to a different mode of thought, but it is worth recalling that R.L.S. was a contemporary of Pirandello, Strindberg, and Ibsen, as well as of Schopenhauer, Freud, and other writers and thinkers who probed the irrational. There is no evidence he ever read any of them, but perhaps critics spend too much time searching for influence and lose sight of possible parallelism and convergence. Irrationalism was in the air, and while R.L.S. did not adhere to irrationalism in philosophy or aesthetics, *The Ebb-Tide*, alone among his works of fiction, is imbued with a sense of the irrational.

"The High Woods of Ulufana" became "The Beach of Falesá" (1892), and appeared the same year as *The Wrecker*. "Falesá" and *The Ebb-Tide* (1894) indicate more strongly in R.L.S. a shift of perception and of aesthetics, a rethinking of his approach to the novel and a desire to overcome limitations which he found increasingly irksome. He questioned the aesthetic vision which underlay his earlier works, reflected more deeply on the novel's ability to express the fullness of human experience, and chafed against the limitations placed on a British writer by Victorian conventions and the puritan attitudes of a largely middle-class readership. R.L.S. is an unlikely rebel, and it is surprising to find Lloyd reporting that he was given to thundering against the bourgeoisie. "He thought that . . . the mass of the middle-class was hopelessly antagonistic to human advancement" (Tusitala, I, xv). A restriction which irked him greatly was the lack of freedom to discuss sexual matters. He had toyed with such notions years previously, but inconclusively. When discussing *Prince Otto* in a letter to Henley, he had blamed the reading public for preventing him from portraying female characters as he would have wished: "to be quite frank, there is a *risqué* character. The Countess von Rosen, a jolly, elderly – how shall I say – fuckstress: whom I handle so as to please this rotten public, and damn myself the while for ruining good material. I could, and if I dared, make her jump" (IV, 1095).

The plebeian language is unusual and the enigmatic verb "to jump" seems prurient, but in any case, years later, during his time in Samoa, R.L.S. sought authorisation for a new frankness in his writing. His mind was not totally made up, so that instead of greeting Hardy's *Mayor of Casterbridge* as a ground-breaking precedent in the use of the freedoms he sought, he denounced the novel. A few months before his death, he wrote a discursive letter on family history to his cousin Bob, bosom friend of his youth, for whom he never lost his feelings of intimate closeness even if he was hurt by Bob's lackadaisical unwillingness to be a regular correspondent. After discussing the origins of the Stevenson name, he turned introspective:

> If I had to begin again – I know not – *si jeunesse savait, si vieillesse pouvait* – I know not at all – I believe that I should do as I have done – except that I should try to be more chaste in early youth, and honour Sex more religiously. The damned thing of our education is that Christianity does not recognise and hallow sex. It looks askance at it, over its shoulder, oppressed as it is by hermits and Asiatic self-torturers. (VIII, 2782)

When he killed people, he said, he killed them properly, and "if his characters have to go to bed with each other, well then I want them to go" (VII, 2408). His revaluation of Zola, whose works he had earlier abominated, may be taken as a touchstone of this change of heart. He had once made his sister-in-law, Nelly, promise never to read a page of Zola, but this was not advice he himself followed, especially after Henry James encouraged him to take a fresh look at the Frenchman's later work. Zola was the leading exponent, in theory and in practice, of realism, a doctrine for which R.L.S. began in the South Seas to develop some sympathy. However realism was defined, a realist novel was not a romance. In Samoa, questions of what was acceptable became more urgent as he felt the increasing need to find a form which would allow him to delve into areas of life previously off limits. Zola went further than R.L.S. wished to go, but he began to appreciate Zola's boldness and comment on the freedoms he enjoyed. R.L.S.' new ambitions eventually led him to dismiss his own *David Balfour* as "a nice, little book, and very artistic . . . but for the top flower of a man's life, it seems to me inadequate." He appears at this time to have fallen into a mood of existential frustration over the life he had lived, reproaching himself for not having been able to "build lighthouses and write David Balfours too". In his search for "something good in art", he mentions Kipling and Zola (strange bedfellows!), but admits he could not finish reading Zola's *Débacle* (VIII, 2693). He had moments of hesitation, and complained to Gosse in relation to *The Ebb-Tide* that he had "got too realistic, and must break these trammels". He noted "with amusement" that Zola had said the same thing, and in another place agreed that *Débacle* was a "mighty big book" (VIII, 2585). These scattered thoughts cannot be assembled into one wholly coherent outlook, but should rather be viewed as a sign of discontent and of a restless, as yet unfocused, individual quest for greater liberty of expression and greater public appreciation of his right to that quest.

This new thinking coalesced around "The Beach of Falesá", which is both a moral tale and a realistic novella. He trespassed on Zola's ground by openly calling it "realist", or more specifically "the first realistic South Sea story; I mean with real South Sea characters and details of life. Everybody else who tried that got carried away with the romance . . . Now I have got the smell, and the look of the thing a great deal" (VII, 2351). "Falesá" is the darkest of all his tales. It has become customary to read it in the light of post-colonial criticism, to tut tut, even if mildly, at R.L.S.' regrettable vocabulary when referring to the native people. There are, for instance, those who find it patronising of him when he calls Samoan men "boys", or who deprecate his use of the word "nigger". Such usages were common at the

time, and critics agree that there is no trace in R.L.S. of prevailing attitudes which might betray racist superiority. His pro-
Samoan – as previously in California his pro-Chinese and
pro-American Indian – credentials are beyond dispute both in
politics and in literature.

However, although it is set in the Pacific, there might be
some value in viewing "Falesá" as part of the Scottish tradition.
The outlook, beliefs, and superstitions of the native peoples
have their equivalents in Scottish fiction. The mystical superstitions of the natives are close to the outlook inculcated into the
child Louis by Cummy, and there is even a discernible parallel
between "Thrawn Janet" and "Falesá". Evil is a frequent theme
in Scottish writing and is often given an almost physical presence. In Walter Scott and James Hogg as well as in R.L.S., it
takes the form of bogies and brownies, of witches and warlocks,
of wicked goblins and elves, of phantom creatures who snatch
babies, and spectres who haunt houses and can be glimpsed
on misty nights in woods and on remote hillsides. Burns
memorably plays with these notions in "Tam o' Shanter" when
an inebriated Tam sees visions of hell's creatures in the Kirk
Alloway, but there is no such playfulness or irony in Hogg or
Scott, or indeed in "Thrawn Janet", works which express a
folk culture and are connected to Calvinist obsessions with the
devil. In "Falesá", Stevenson twice uses the term "bogie" to
denote the devil who is believed to lie in wait for the unwary in
the island's woods. In *Virginibus Puerisque* (1881), in an intri-
guingly pre-Freudian essay on dreams, he advances the view
that creativity draws on "ancestral memory", so that when it
comes to the actual creation of plots, his "brownies" do half the
work. Interestingly, he stresses that these brownies are bereft of

all moral sense, and that the author (the ego?) has to add the moral dimension and restrain their unfettered operation.

Brownies and morals are present in "Falesá". There is a double presence of malignant spirits in the novella, firstly in the genuine beliefs of the people, and secondly in the fraudulent exploitation of these beliefs through the machines and devices deceitfully created by Case, a resident trader, and positioned to give the impression of woods haunted by the voices and faces of malign beings whose intentions are toxic. The island is not a restful place, nor an angelic land of milk and honey. It bears traces of the cloven hoof. Sinister deeds have been done, and its impact on previous white men have been dire. Case is an irredeemably malevolent character who misuses people and perpetrates criminal schemes, while his antagonist, the trader John Wiltshire, is a more ambiguous man. He has been dispatched to the island, a small and remote place, as the representative of a company which deals mainly in copra, and, as he approaches the island by boat, is told tales designed to dissuade him from landing, or at least to acquaint him with the sinister realities of life there.

The conflict occurs between the whites. The natives, notably Uma, have an ingenuousness and a goodness which is not of the Rousseauist, noble savage variety, but which springs from an untainted, uncorrupted innocence unscrupulously exploited by the whites. These are men who have shaken off all social restraints and who, displaced in the South Seas, recognise no principle. It was the depiction of their predatory sexual conduct and not anything primitive in the native islanders which shocked decent society in New York when the tale was first published. Wiltshire, a man of decent views, is told on landing that he needs a wife, and Case brings forward a woman, Uma, who appeals to him sensually and sexually. In a scene which upset the sensibilities of his publishers in both Britain and America, Wiltshire undergoes a sham marriage ceremony before a fake clergyman. The official-looking document which deceives Uma reads, "This is to certify that Uma, daughter of Fa'avao, of Falesá, Island of — is illegally married to Mr John Wiltshire for one week, and Mr John Wiltshire is at liberty to send her to hell when he pleases." In fact, in R.L.S.' original text the period of time was "one night", and Wiltshire was entitled to send her to hell "next morning", but the publishers made the change without authorisation.[119] When he saw the published text, R.L.S. gave his response in a splenetic letter to Colvin: "well, well if the dears prefer a week, I'll give them ten days, but the real document, from which I have hardly varied, ran for one night." While realising that Colvin was not responsible for the alteration, he still upbraided him for his failure to do justice to the fact that "this is a piece of realism à outrance nothing attenuated or adorned" (VII, 2408). There were other absurd instances of puritanical outrage. He complained to Barrie that his editors, those "celestial idiots", had cut out a phrase where he describes two little children as "wriggling out of their clothes and running away mother naked". The picture of naked children was too shocking for conventional tastes in Britain, where realism was not what was expected of him.

R.L.S. boasted that there was no "sugar candy epic" in "Falesá". The novella dramatises the binary clash of civilisation vs barbarism, but the barbarians are the exploitative white

119 Barry Menikoff, *Robert Louis Stevenson and "The Beach of Falesá"*, Edinburgh, Edinburgh University Press, 1984.

men who live beyond the pale. What are the ethical standards, and what the forces which make men comply with them, R.L.S. asks. What makes men behave morally? Wiltshire, who is endowed with a conscience, however fragile, feels shame over the ceremony he has participated in, and as he begins to fall in love with Uma he recognises the need to take responsibility for his own behaviour towards other human beings, of whatever race and colour. Interracial love was just about acceptable to the Anglo-Saxon public, but the account of his initially falling for the sensual allure of a woman of any colour was not. Nor was the overt polemic against the imperialist ways of the white man. Wiltshire, as R.L.S. was doing, sided with the islanders against Case, whose power was exercised partly by his hold over a corrupt priest and partly by spreading the belief that he controlled the island's devils. By revealing that the haunting noises were made by Aeolian harps, not by spirits, Wiltshire destroyed Case's standing, but he also made R.L.S.' point that evil, not just in the story, is man-made as well as existential. R.L.S. confronts both. In the armed encounter, both Wiltshire and Uma are wounded, but Case is killed.

In the closing section, Wiltshire, who by now has children with Uma, regrets his exile from England and resigns himself to never owning the country pub he had dreamed of running, but he fully accepts responsibility for his wife and "half-caste" children. He has undergone his own gauche and faltering process of conversion. R.L.S. found it possible to express in Uma the full complexity of love and sexual allure to a degree he had not managed with his white heroines. Wiltshire ended up not only in love but in awe of her. "She was a kind of countess really," he came to believe. In recognising the children as fully his, he faces the dilemma that while he will not countenance them marrying *kanakas* (blacks), where will he find whites for them? Perhaps this novella is in part an allegory of imperialism and its intrusion into other people's ways of life. Perhaps there is also a veiled rebuke to his stepson Lloyd for his conduct towards a Samoan girl whom he seduced but refused to marry. R.L.S.' presentation of the dominion of the white traders and missionaries is stark and uncompromising. Through the eyes of Wiltshire, he exposes exploitative behaviour, in the personal, public, sexual, and commercial spheres. The villains are white, their behaviour towards the islanders reprehensible and contemptible.

CHAPTER 17

A Far Cry from Samoa to Scotland?

"It might seem a far cry from Samoa to Scotland," wrote Fanny in her introduction to *Catriona*, "and yet in many ways the one recalled the other" (Tusitala, VII, xvi). The judgement that Scotland and Samoa were neighbours in R.L.S.' mind was true in a sense she did not intend. She was thinking of the waterfalls, the streams, the clouds, and the grey mist which were often found near their home on the island, but she could have added that there were parallels adumbrated in *Catriona* between the politics of contemporary Samoa and of post-Jacobite Scotland, at least as transformed by Stevenson's imagination. He was profoundly aware of the moral as well as physical disruption created in a society by war. Perhaps the novel, a sequel to *Kidnapped*, indicated a profound dissociation in Stevenson's sensibility, moved on the one hand by the consequences of the imperialist project on the island he had made his home and on the other by the outcomes of the Jacobite/Whig division in the history of Scotland. R.L.S. himself was aware of the incongruity, and told J.M. Barrie that "it is a singular thing that I should live here in the South Seas under conditions so new and so striking, and yet my imagination so continually inhabit that cold old huddle of grey hills from which we come" (VII, 412).

What is equally striking is the difference in style and

approach employed by him when treating the two cultures, histories, and lands which dominated his consciousness. He may have been searching for a new liberty to write openly about physical appetites and emotional drives, or indeed about sex, but strangely he made use of it only when writing on Polynesian subjects. In the Scottish fiction composed at the same time, he reverted to the observance of late Victorian standards, even of Victorian prudishness. It may even be that, for all his protestations, he found the climate of priggishness convenient, for he was always uneasy dealing with the psychology of desire. To adopt a distinction he made himself, if "Falesá" was a novella, *Catriona* was a romance – maybe even in the prissy meaning given to that term after his death – and a decidedly puritanical one. It sets out to deal with emotional entanglements and portray the blossoming of first love between David Balfour and Catriona Drummond, but his old, self-confessed inability to create flesh-and-blood female characters manifested itself again. Too often this inability, which he would accept, if only in a jesting style, conceals an uncomfortable truth about his unwillingness to deal with the whole emotional side of the human animal, male and, especially, female. It is perhaps no coincidence that Gauguin too revelled in a freedom to depict in Tahitian women a sensuality which he felt barred from revealing in Europeans.

Two themes are intertwined in the novel, the political-moral dilemmas facing David Balfour in Scotland following the defeat of the Jacobite insurrection and the restoration of the Whig–Hanoverian hegemony, and his developing relationship with Catriona Drummond. Many of the characters who had featured in *Kidnapped* reappear. Alan Breck Stewart is still lying low in

Scotland until David helps him make his escape to France, although he will turn up in Holland to assist David in his fumbling, maladroit efforts to court Catriona. The interim from the point where David was left at the end of *Kidnapped* may be short, but in that time he has not only come into his inheritance but has also matured intellectually and morally, causing him to display greater self-assurance. Whereas in the earlier novel he was tossed about by events and encounters, such as that with Alan Breck, or was the victim of the malice of others, notably his uncle Ebenezer, now he has developed a measure of confidence that makes him determined to help shape events and right wrongs. His moral conscience, always a strong force in this quintessentially Calvinist figure, has been sharpened. The principal injustice he feels obliged to confront is the threatened execution of James of the Glens, imprisoned and facing trial for the killing of Colin Campbell of Glenure, the estate factor who oversaw the eviction of the Clan Stewart from their hereditary lands in retaliation for their support of Bonnie Prince Charlie. In *Kidnapped*, Campbell had been in conversation with David when the fatal shot was fired, so David's presence made him a suspect, but what he had seen gave him the certainty that James Stewart was not guilty. The paradox and the clash of consciousness affecting David lies in the fact that he was a Whig and a supporter of the Hanoverian dynasty, whose main allies in Scotland were the Clan Campbell, while the Stewarts were Jacobites. By coming forward, he exposed himself to the risk of ending up in the dock and on the gallows alongside James Stewart, while if his evidence were accepted by the court, the political faction he supported would be compromised. His conscientious dilemma was whether to back justice or power, to align himself with the political cause he viewed as his own or with an individual opponent who had been falsely accused. Chesterton identified in this duality a problem that had been Scott's before it was Stevenson's, that they were intellectually Whigs but sentimentally Jacobites. To confuse matters further, in contemporary politics R.L.S. was a Tory.

The competing claims of ethics and politics, of justice and power, were very much on R.L.S.' mind at the time, both in literature and in the conduct of Samoan public affairs. In "The Feast of Famine", Rua had found himself in a predicament similar to David's when forced to choose between self-preservation and the need to serve truth. For David himself, imbued with the moral certainties of Calvinism, hesitation between justice and mere might was unthinkable. David presents himself to the Lord Advocate, Lord Prestongrange, to announce his willingness to give evidence on behalf of James Stewart. Prestongrange, a good man in the service of an ignoble cause, is one of Stevenson's more memorable and complex characters, and the scene in his house which pits the two men, one against the other, each employing eloquent rhetoric to expound and defend incompatible stances, is among the most vividly imagined in R.L.S.' oeuvre. This David come to judgment finds himself embroiled in the machinations of politics at their most Machiavellian as he listens to his adversary employ casuistry and callousness to explain that there is no hope for James Stewart, that his judicial murder is a necessary price for the maintenance of the political status quo. Prestongrange states openly that he takes his "political duty first and [his] judicial duty only second". Politics, David concludes, is a corrupt business, practised by the unscrupulous. It requires no effort to see here reflections of the situation on Samoa as R.L.S. saw it, where men in authority issued laws which made a mockery of justice and employed the tools of political power to advance their own interests. Nor is it hard to detect unstated parallels between the plight of James Stewart and Samoan leaders, either Laupepa or Mata'afa.

The deeper parallel lies in the misuse of law to exacerbate the clash between rival interests. David reflects that while the situation had the "externals of a sober process of law", it was in reality "a clan battle between savage clans", once again reflecting what he had seen between the followers of rival claimants on Samoa. In addition, the supposedly civilised Europeans there appealed to the authority of treaties and courts, while all the time seeking to further their own interests, as Lord Prestongrange was doing. For his candour and honesty, David finds himself, for the second time in his life, kidnapped, this time on the orders of the Lord Advocate, whose motivations are a complex mixture of personal affection for David and political calculation to prevent him undermining the case against James Stewart. David escapes from imprisonment on the Bass Rock, and succeeds in reaching Inverary after the hearing is completed but before judgment is delivered. The jury is packed with members of the Clan Campbell, so no Stewart has any prospect of a fair hearing from that company. The issue is decided by the faction which holds the upper hand, and it is on this point of tribal or clan rivalry that eighteenth-century Scotland and nineteenth-century Samoa most closely resembled each other. In nineteenth-century Samoa, the forces of Mata'afa and Laupepa faced each other with the same unremitting hostility as the Campbells and the Stewarts in eighteenth-century Scotland,

and each manoeuvred to use foreign powers to aid their cause. Perhaps, at least subconsciously, R.L.S. saw himself as David Balfour, the concerned, high-minded, but ultimately impotent observer, looking on with a jaundiced eye.

Although many critics have seen Catriona as Stevenson's most successful attempt to create a credible female character, it is hard now to accept that judgement. If he felt able to congratulate himself on the depiction of Uma in "Falesá", he reverted to respect for Victorian conventions when portraying Catriona. The fact that the novel is told in the first person absolves the author from the need to convey Catriona's emotions or viewpoint from within. The stream of consciousness is entirely David's, but he is prone to seeing Catriona as an enigma whose inner drives and sexuality elude him. The relationship between the two is recounted from within the frame of Victorian decorum, not in the emotionally searching, probing terms employed by, for example, Thomas Hardy. At this point in his life R.L.S. wished in the abstract to make the "rotten public" accustomed to bolder presentations, but did not take risks when portraying a Scottish maiden.

On the first meeting between the two, Catriona appears a plucky, spirited young woman, capable of shaping her own destiny, but once the adventure element of the novel is resolved and the emotional drama takes centre stage, she declines into the prim, largely passive heroine common in Victorian fiction. David first sees her among a group accompanying her father, a villain of a man imprisoned and facing charges of siding with the Prince, but prepared to perjure himself and betray his own side, even if that means sending James Stewart to the gallows. Their relationship faces difficulties in Scotland, although they have a helper in Miss Grant, the daughter of Prestongrange, who, according to Fanny's testimony, stole Stevenson's heart as he proceeded with the writing and almost forced the plot to take an unintended turn. However, owing to Miss Grant's intervention, the young couple end up on the same ship for Holland, where David is to undertake the study of law and Catriona to meet her wretched father, who has been sprung from jail in recompense for his double dealing. The father fails to honour the appointment, so David takes Catriona under his wing. He presents her to Dutch society as his sister, a ruse which the protocol of the times may have required as a defence of her honour, but which David Daiches is surely justified in suggesting gives R.L.S. a safety device to protect him from having to confront questions of sexuality.

Funds are not short to this newly enriched young man, so he has no difficulty in renting adjoining rooms in lodgings for himself and Catriona. In the Holland passages, David is an upright, unremittingly bourgeois young man with no savour of the bohemian spirit R.L.S. himself had shown in his youthful days as Velvet Jacket in Edinburgh. He is incapable of frank communication, so that his desire to preserve Catriona's honour and good name is taken by her as indifference. This situation is prolonged over time, with two separate incidents where she is driven to open aversion of David due to her misinterpretation of his behaviour, while he suffers from inner pangs which his reserve prevents him from explaining. Fortunately Alan Breck returns to rescue the situation and upbraid David for being "so mortal stupit". The reader will easily agree with that judgement, while regreting that the credible Stevensonian woman is still to emerge.

We will spend little time with the unfinished *St. Ives*, dismissed curtly by R.L.S. himself. "*St. Ives* is nothing – it is in no style, in particular, a tissue of adventures, the central character not very well done, no philosophic pith under the yarn, and in short, if people will read it, that's all I ask." This is a harsh verdict, but the implicit distinction between a novel of adventure and a novel with a philosophical underpinning gives the statement some importance. Telling a tale for its own sake was no longer sufficient. He had always shown a bent for philosophy in his essays, but now he wished to bring the essayist and the novelist together. He did not succeed with *St. Ives*, which tells the tale of a French soldier and count, imprisoned in Edinburgh castle during the Napoleonic Wars, who falls in love with the beautiful, kind-hearted Flora Gilchrist. It has the attractions of an adventure story and romance, but is also a throwback to an earlier style. In the same letter, R.L.S. compared it to his planned next novels. "I am on *Weir of Hermiston* and *Heathercat*, two Scotch stories, which will be either something different or I will have failed. *Hermiston* is a private story of two or three characters in a very grim vein" (VIII, 2744). Neither story was completed, but with *Hermiston* R.L.S. would have done himself more justice had he written "tragic" instead of "grim". It can be regarded as the third of the masterpieces of the Samoan period, and perhaps it would have been, as he himself tentatively hoped, his masterpiece *tout court*. Some are more hesitant in their judgement, but only because the book is unfinished, and R.L.S. had on other occasions shown himself incapable of bringing his fiction to a satisfactory conclusion.

Jenni Calder makes the shrewd observation that "the traditions of Border reiving and rivalry . . . in *Weir of Hermiston*, have their parallels in Pacific life," and that "the authoritarian attitudes of the novel's Lord Braxfield towards human frailty were not dissimilar to those of the imperialist powers towards the native populations."[120] Lord Hermiston was inspired by the infamous Lord Braxfield, the fearsome eighteenth-century judge who sent moderate reformers to Botany Bay for sedition, and who had intrigued and fascinated R.L.S., at least since he saw his portrait in an exhibition of works by Raeburn. He wrote a review of the exhibition in which he expressed the view that, "if he was an inhumane man (and I am afraid it is fact he was inhumane), he was also perfectly intrepid" (Tusitala, XXV, 103). Andrew Lang did him the favour of sending him a copy of that portrait, which still hangs in Vailima. There is no ambiguity between attraction and repulsion in the case of Hermiston, as there may have been with Attwater. R.L.S. was plainly repelled by Braxfield (Hermiston) all the more because of his ease of conscience.

The coarseness and brutality which Hermiston shares with Braxfield appal his son, Archie, so that once again a father–son conflict lies at the heart of a work of fiction. Archie attends the trial of the pathetic Duncan Jopp, where he is outraged by the jeering conduct of his father as he condemns the prisoner to death. After attending the execution, Archie declares his opposition to capital punishment and execrates his father in public. His later regret over this public act does not reconcile the two, and Archie finds himself dispatched from Edinburgh to the family estate in Hermiston. It is here that he meets the two Kirsties, the elder of whom had been many years in the

120 Jenni Calder, "Introduction", in Robert Louis Stevenson, *Island Landfalls*, op. cit., p. xv.

family's service and whose feelings towards Archie are reminiscent of the quasi-maternal affection shown to the boy Louis by his nurse Cummy. The other is her niece, Kirstie Elliott. Although frustratingly brief and incomplete, the narrative bursts with life and is wide enough in scope to tell of the younger Kirstie's four fearsome brothers, the Eliotts of Cauldstaneslap, each carefully delineated in their personality and pursuits. The burgeoning affection between Archie and Kirstie is narrated with a delicate insight and emotional intensity comparable to the supreme depiction of developing love in Stendhal's *Scarlet and Black*. The quarrel and estrangement between the two, caused by Archie's inept efforts to protect Kirstie from social shame, allow his duplicitous friend Frank Innes to take advantage of the situation to seduce Kirstie, and will, according to the available information about the intended future course of the plot, lead on to the tragedy, but the pages written do not go so far.

There is nothing nostalgic or romantic about the novel. Any nostalgia for an Edinburgh and Scotland R.L.S. had reconciled himself to never seeing again is limited to the dedicatory poem to Fanny.

> I saw rain falling and the rainbow drawn
> On Lammermuir. Hearkening I heard again
> In my precipitous city beaten bells
> Winnow the keen sea wind. And here afar
> Intent on my own race and place, I wrote.

Intent on his own "race and place" he may have been, but this is another meditation on Scotland in history, warts and all. However, the historical context does not overwhelm or condition the drama, as it does in *Kidnapped* and *Catriona*. Colvin was bemused by the choice of 1814 as period, and wondered why R.L.S. had not set the novel in the earlier age when Braxfield himself was active. Perhaps the novel was an act of homage to *Redgauntlet*, or in general to Scott, who is mentioned several times as "Mr Sheriff Scott". In any case the driving forces are essentially inner, not subject to the social conditions or culture of a given time, as they were in Scott's medieval novels. The novel is dark in every sense. The atmosphere of nocturnal gloom is pervasive. Archie, after excoriating his father's inhumanity, wanders around Edinburgh at night, and several of the key encounters take place after dark.

Predestination is the Scots form of Fate, and fate itself is often referred to in the novel. Archie is marked out for misfortune, but it is his own character, not some external force, which drives him on. An atmosphere of gloomy Calvinism hangs over the central clash between him and his unforgiving, unyielding, emotionally repressed father. There are two father figures, Lord Hermiston, and the kindly Lord Glenalmond who has all the benevolent virtues Archie's biological father lacks. After Archie has denounced Hermiston in public, he is told by Glenalmond that his father did care for him, and that his outward indifference was a disguise, a mask over his grim inability to show paternal, or any, feeling. Hermiston's devotion to duty is a substitute for tenderness towards any other human being. There is no psychological equivalent to the Oedipus complex to express Archie's plight, but it is his father's approval that he craves. His late mother was younger than Hermiston, and had suffered from his emotional aridity. In personality, she had been no match for his strength of character, and her unhappy life ended in early death. The sterility of this family background provides the element of ineluctable fate, which remains tragic even if it appears that R.L.S. intended to have the younger couple escape together to America. Archie's character is formed, and his choice of career in law is blocked, by the massive, inflexible, duty-obsessed, distorted, and distorting potency of his father. "It was in his horoscope to be parsimonious of pain to himself . . . to be the son of Adam Weir and Jean Rutherford."

The "philosophic pith" lies not in passages of abstract reasoning but in the book's moral seriousness, in the depth of its quests and probes into the psychological complexity of character, in its reflections on the impact of the past on the present and in the dialectic between hope and despair. R.L.S. shows a surer touch than ever in his treatment of evil. "Enter Mephistopheles" is the title of the chapter which brings Frank Innes to Hermiston after fleeing the consequences of misdeeds in Edinburgh. Innes is an ambiguous character, plainly endowed with the social skills which Archie so conspicuously lacks, but incapable of self-knowledge. He enters effortlessly into the social life of the district of Hermiston and makes friends easily, but his behaviour towards Archie is motivated by sexual jealousy and duplicity of mind. He is Iago-like in his advice to Archie to stop seeing Kirstie in private for fear of compromising her good name, and unscrupulous in taking advantage of the estrangement he creates.

R.L.S. was not satisfied with the plot of his novel, and it may be that he would have altered it, but he had every reason to be highly satisfied with the situation and, above all, with the characters he had created. Moreover he had succeeded in creating strong female characters who actively forge their own condition of life, are gifted with intellectual insight and emotional depth. This is particularly so in the case of the elder Kirstie, who is disturbed by the nature of her feelings for Archie, whom she had looked after from childhood, and who relishes their shared intimacy. Her desires, always sublimated and subtly drawn, go beyond protectiveness and fondness. "Her passion, for it was nothing less, entirely filled her. It was a rich, physical pleasure to make his bed or light his lamp when he was absent, to pull off his boots or wait on him at dinner when he returned." Such feelings change swiftly into jealous frustration as she notes his growing attachment for her niece. She chafes at the change in his habits which prevents her from enjoying the evening conversation with him as he lies in bed before sleep. The younger Kirstie is headstrong, wilful, and passionate. She will not be pacified when Archie suggests they give up their clandestine meetings until they are in a position to come out in public, and assumes that his motivation is shame at closeness with a woman of the lower orders. No previous novel was so splendid in its depiction of emotional turmoil between such masterfully drawn characters.

The novel was dictated to Belle and ended mid-sentence, after a description of a passionate quarrel between Archie and Kirsty. As he held her weeping in his arms, "there arose from before him the curtains of boyhood, and he saw for the first time the ambiguous face of woman as she is". He could not fathom her passion or his offence which seemed "unprovoked, a wilful convulsion of brute nature . . ." What fate willed that those were the last words he wrote?

PART V

Final Days

CHAPTER 18

Home is the Sailor

Even if it left him in a state of despondency, the defeat of Mata'afa did not cause R.L.S. to retire into a solitary hermitage, or sit bewailing guilt and injustice. He railed against the consuls and the authorities, campaigned on behalf of prisoners, and advocated the repeal of the Treaty of Berlin, but also continued his busy social round of balls and dinners. Guests came and went, he carried on writing and dictating to Belle, he continued riding about on Jack, and travelled around Upolu to offer support to the defeated side. He completed *The Ebb-Tide* but was laid low with a serious haemorrhage following an unwise game of tennis with Balfour. His recovery coincided with the outbreak of measles across the island, serious enough for the Samoans, who had little immunity, but potentially fatal for a man whose health was delicate. It was agreed that he had to take refuge somewhere, and in October 1893 he made a return journey to Hawaii, accompanied by Graham Balfour and his personal manservant and cook, Talolo.

Unfortunately the servant contracted measles, and it was unclear whether or not he would be allowed ashore. After negotiations, Talolo was permitted to land, but then R.L.S. had to take to his bed in Waikiki. Fanny, who had stayed behind, was summoned urgently to come and look after him, which she did.

Whatever Fanny's faults, however morose and prickly she may have been, she was always assiduous and selfless in her care of her husband. She nursed him back to health and they returned together to Samoa in November. He would not leave the island again.

R.L.S. found Hawaii in turmoil, divided between Royalists who were supporters of independence, and Annexationists of the party which had engineered a *coup d'état* to make Hawaii an American territory. The parallels with the situation in Samoa were obvious, but the futility of his situation much greater for he could do nothing other than express his backing for the Royalist faction. Arthur Johnstone recounts a curious incident during the stay. R.L.S. was fascinated by the new genre of the detective story. He corresponded with Arthur Conan Doyle and even refers to Sherlock Holmes in *The Wrecker*. While recuperating, he was contacted by a real-life predecessor of Sherlock Holmes, who had been hired to look into a criminal case. This private eye had theories of his own, but realised he was making no serious headway and wondered if the great R.L.S. could help. In Johnstone's account, R.L.S. listened to the facts of the case, fell into a lengthy silence as he considered the pros and cons, and emerged to dismiss the private eye's notions and advance his own solution. He turned out to be right.

The principal event of this visit was an address that R.L.S. delivered to the Thistle Club, a society of Scottish expats. He was invited to become Honorary Chieftain, and accepted with alacrity. There is no full account of the speech, but the topic was seemingly "the long drawn-out brawl that is Scottish history". The tone was ironic and disenchanted, as he wondered what there was to admire in the heroes of Scotland from William

Wallace to Mary, Queen of Scots, although he discussed the adventures of Bonnie Prince Charlie with greater sympathy. He told his listeners that the history of their country ended with the Young Pretender, but found some device to move on to Lord Braxfield, who was much on his mind at the time. The ending was sentimental: he said he was destined to die in the South Seas and lose his right to burial "among honest Scotch sods". The Society made him a present of a thistle badge which he wore thereafter in his lapel, and which he was buried wearing.[121]

All seemed bright in Vailima that year. The family circle was complete once again. Maggie returned from Edinburgh, bringing yet more furniture, and at Belle's insistence Austin was brought back from California and enrolled in a school in New Zealand, which meant that he would be home for the long vacation. Word arrived that Charles Baxter had negotiated the publication of the Edinburgh edition of the Complete Works. The news delighted R.L.S., not least because it would help relieve the financial situation. Baxter added that he would bring the first two volumes to Samoa in person later in the year. R.L.S. had done his best to coax his closest friends to make the journey, but while Colvin, J.M. Barrie, Conan Doyle, Henry James, and Kipling had made promising noises, only Graham Balfour had actually come. (Baxter did in fact set off, but only got as far as Johannesburg before learning of R.L.S.' death. He continued on his way and presented Fanny with the first two volumes of the edition.)

Meanwhile, a catastrophe was narrowly avoided. Laupepa came visiting, and, in accordance with the Samoan communist

121 Richard A. Biermann, *Robert Louis Stevenson in Samoa*, R.L.S. Museum, Samoa, first edition, 1939, reprint 2010, p. 167.

ways, asked R.L.S. for the present of a pistol he saw in the house. Fanny picked it up to give him a lesson in its use. She removed the cartridges, aimed it at the king, clicked the empty barrel four times, but stopped before pulling the trigger a fifth time. When she opened it, she found that there was a bullet in the fifth chamber which, had she pulled the trigger, would have blown out the king's brains. This narrowly averted tragedy might have been "on a small scale" for humankind but would have been on an unthinkably large scale for Samoa and the Stevensons, not to mention Laupepa.

Life in Vailima was complicated by the behaviour of Sosifina, one of the servants, who took to preening herself in a manner worthy of a *maîtresse-en-titre* in a French royal palace. R.L.S.' suspicions were aroused. He told Balfour that one day when he was ill and lay down on the verandah, "the miserable being stayed with me and comforted me with pillows until I really could have wept" (VIII, 2525). There was no ready explanation of why she gave herself such airs, but her presumptuous conduct agitated Fanny and distressed Belle. Finally, Lloyd was summoned and confessed he was having an affair with her. The two men had a fierce quarrel. Harry Moors suggests that the girl had fallen pregnant. R.L.S. insisted that Lloyd marry the girl, but, to his outrage, Lloyd refused. This scandalised R.L.S., whose code of sexual conduct was strict and unyielding, whatever liberty he was seeking in the realm of fiction, and irrespective of his own affairs as a young man in Edinburgh. It was not a matter of gallantry or stuffy Victorianism, but of genuine concern for the girl's well-being and future. Details are scarce, but Fanny confronted the girl, denounced her, and she disappears from the story. Margaret Mackay says she was sent back to her native village where she died shortly afterwards, allegedly of a broken heart.[122]

R.L.S. and Lloyd were reconciled, and Lloyd gives an affecting though possibly overblown account of an encounter between the two men after R.L.S. had read to the family, as was his custom, the parts of *Weir of Hermiston* he had written that day. Belle criticises Lloyd for overplaying his part in R.L.S.' life, and it may be that this incident as told glorifies Lloyd's egoistic self-image. In his introductory piece to *Weir*, Lloyd reports that, after the reading, R.L.S., flushed with author's pride, waited for the group's responses, which were fulsome. Only Lloyd failed to speak, and instead got up and went out into the night. He heard his stepfather running after him, protesting that he whose opinion mattered above all to him had no right to march off in that way, without saying a word. Lloyd justified himself by saying that he had been left speechless by the sheer perfection of what he had been listening to, that *Weir* "promised to be the greatest novel in the English language". After those words, they sat in the darkness with their arms around each other, talking deeply, "free to be ourselves, unashamed". Tantalisingly, he refuses to divulge what was said, except that it amounted to "the revelation of that tormented soul". Lloyd tells us that he had never previously "conceived the degree of his daily sufferings" (Tusitala, XVI). There we must leave it. Lloyd had no gift for insight into the minds and hearts of those around him.

R.L.S.' forty-fourth birthday was celebrated at Vailima on November 13 on a royal scale. His mother, in an awestruck account in her diary, calculated that there were one hundred guests. Maggie and Fanny began making preparations days in

122 Margaret Mackay, *The Violent Friend*, op. cit., p. 482.

advance, but "the celebration of the day itself began before 7 a.m. when Elina sent up four men to help in making the native ovens and to look after the cooking." In Samoa, cooking was always men's work. The first procession bearing gifts arrived early in the morning, and others followed until 3 p.m. The gifts, which included mats, fine *kava* bowls, fans, rings (one in silver with the name Tusitala engraved on it), quantities of wreaths, and loose flowers, were laid out in the old dining room where they "made quite a display". For the meal, a special gazebo with a roof of plaited coconut and banana leaves was erected on the lawn. Dining followed Samoan custom, so knives and forks were not permitted. Aunt Maggie apologised for not remembering all the sundries, but the list of foodstuffs she gives is formidable. "1 heifer roasted in a native oven, 20 pigs, 50 chickens, 17 pigeons, 430 taro roots, 12 large yams, 80 arrowroot puddings, 50 *palusamis*, 804 pineapples, 20 bunches of bananas." A shower of rain meant that the first dances had to take place in the large hall, but it went off in time to allow the meal to be consumed outdoors. It would seem unlikely that anyone could move after making their way through that quantity of food, but incredibly the meal was followed by Samoan dancing on the lawn. The Consul General "proposed Tusitala's health in a very beautiful way". There is a real poignancy to Aunt Maggie's final remarks in her diary that day. "Dear Lou, what cause for thankfulness it is that he has been spared to see his forty-fourth birthday in so much health and comfort."

On December 2, Thanksgiving Day, all their American friends were invited to dinner. As a special treat, they had *ice*.[123]

123 Maggie's emphasis.

"Louis gave a little thanksgiving prayer as grace." There had been "much illness and fever at Apia," but, Maggie's entry concludes, "how wonderfully free of such troubles we have been at Vailima, and how thankful we ought indeed to be for it!" No tragic dramatist could better evoke the brutal contrast between those relieved, happy words and the next entry, December 4, which begins, "How am I to tell you the terrible news that my beloved son has been called home last evening? At six o'clock he was well, hungry for dinner, and helping Fanny to make a Mayonnaise sauce; when suddenly he put both hands to his head and said, 'Oh, what a pain!' and then added, 'Do I look strange?'"[124] He did not speak again.

As is common with inexplicable disasters, in the aftermath friends recalled omens. R.L.S. had mentioned to correspondents that he did not expect to grow old, Lloyd caught him frequently looking up at the peak of Mount Vaea, and Fanny had been plagued for days with premonitions of some impending disaster. Strangely, neither she nor R.L.S. believed anything untoward would happen to them, so it was assumed that the likely victim would be Balfour, who was then at sea. Although Fanny's fears caused some gloom, life in Vailima proceeded. That day, R.L.S. continued dictating the text of *Weir of Hermiston* to Belle, but broke off mid-sentence at the point where Archie was thinking over his argument with Kirstie, attempting to identify how he had offended her. Being unable to find anything, he concluded that "it seemed unprovoked, a wilful convulsion of brute nature . . ." It was a strange point to leave off dictation, and the words about "brute nature" later acquired a resonance of their own.

124 M.I. Stevenson, *Letters from Samoa*, op. cit., pp. 309–14.

He was worried about Fanny's state of mind, and to reassure her he took out a pack of cards, although he chose to play solitaire, an odd choice of game for two people, then went to the cellar to select a bottle of burgundy. He started preparing the mayonnaise, a speciality of his, but collapsed quite suddenly, as his mother described. He had suffered all his life from some pulmonary disease, once believed to be tuberculosis, although recent studies reject this diagnosis. All the efforts and travels had been made to preserve his life from that illness, but it was a stroke which ended his life. He fell forward, was dragged to an armchair which had belonged to his grandfather, and propped up there until a bed was brought down and he was laid on it.

Every detail of the following hours has been recorded and re-recorded. The screams of the women brought Lloyd running from his cottage. He sped down to Apia to find Dr Funk. The doctor was pouring his evening cocktails, but Lloyd put him on the horse he had ridden from Vailima and took for himself a horse he found tethered along the street. He had also to carry the medical bag, since the portly doctor was unsure of his ability to ride and take the bag with him. A second doctor was summoned from the *Wallaroo*, then in harbour, and he arrived first. He had not seen R.L.S. before, and when he saw how thin the patient was, he blurted out, "how can anybody write books with arms like these". Maggie rebuked him roundly, and for the rest of his life the doctor reproached himself for his silly, inappropriate remark. It made no difference. Both doctors agreed that the case was beyond remedy. Robert Louis Stevenson died at 8.10 p.m. on December 3, 1894. Dr Funk, with Prussian precision, ordered that in the Samoan climate burial should take place by 3.00 the following afternoon.

The Rev. W.E. Clarke was among the first to arrive, and he noted that Maggie and Belle knelt at either side of the bed, but Fanny stood alone at the foot of the stairs, still, upright and rigid. The servants gathered around the body, and the Catholics among them asked permission to chant the prayers for the dead. Such permission could hardly be withheld, and Lloyd says he was awakened during the night by chanting in Latin and Samoan. He himself took charge of the practical details. R.L.S. had specified that he wished to be buried at the summit of Mount Vaea, but the mountainside was a tangle of lianas, foliage, creepers, and fallen tree trunks. Dark cloth was ordered from a store in Apia to make appropriate funeral attire, and the men who arrived from all over the island clad themselves in a *lavalava* made of this material and donned white shirts as they began the laborious work of clearing a path up the steep mountain. It must have been gruelling work in the stifling heat. Lloyd led a smaller party ahead to dig the grave. Meantime, chieftains and their followers made their way from all over the island to pay their respects, and as they gathered, keening noisily on the lawn, the body was covered with the mats which are of supreme value in Samoa. Lloyd recounts that one old chief whose forbidding appearance had initially impressed him "most unfavourably" gave a moving, impromptu elegy. "Samoa ends with you, Tusitala. When death closed the eyes of our best and dearest friend, we knew as a race that our own day was done."

The climb up the mountain with a coffin must have been an almost unbearable test of human endurance and strength. The men could only take the weight for short distances before being replaced, and at some points the coffin-bearers had to be hauled up by ropes tied round their waists and pulled by others above them. The Rev. Clarke conducted a funeral service. Later, cement blocks were put in place to create a tomb in the Samoan style. Years later, Fanny's ashes were laid beside her husband.

The tombstone carries in Samoan the Old Testament words spoken by Ruth to Naomi, "Thy people will be my people, thy God my God, where thou diest will I die." The hibiscus and the thistle are the only adornment. Engraved on the central plaque are the words of Stevenson's "Requiem":

Under the wide and starry sky
Dig the grave and let me lie:
Glad did I live and gladly die,
And I laid me down with a will.

This be the verse you 'grave for me:
Here he lies where he long'd to be;
Home is the sailor, home from sea,
And the hunter home from the hill.

The chiefs put a taboo on the use of firearms on the mountain to ensure that there would always be birdsong around Tusitala's grave. Somehow an error, keenly felt in later years by the more pedantic of intending devotees who had clambered, sweating, sick and hot up the mountain, had been permitted in the epitaph. The words given here are not exactly the words which appear on the tomb, where the seventh line reads, "Home is the sailor home from THE sea." There have even been schemes to have the engraving removed and corrected, but this has never been done. There have also been proposals from Scottish institutions to have the body brought back to Edinburgh, but these approaches have been refused by Samoa, and rightly so. Here he lies, where he chose to be.

A VISIT TO ROBERT LOUIS STEVENSON.

TO THE EDITOR OF THE TIMES.

Sir,—Having, as a traveller from West to East, lost a certain number of minutes daily for some months, and found these again accumulated and restored to me in the addition of a new day to my calendar, it happened that it was Easter Sunday in 1894 on board a little steamer bound from the Friendly Islands to Samoa on the morning before we arrived at Apia, and it was also Easter Sunday next morning when we landed. The minutes of the days lost on the journey from England had not been missed; the day gained, that second Easter Sunday, is one of the most memorable of my life, for it introduced me to Robert Louis Stevenson.

A deep blue sea, a coral shore fringed with palm trees, and, beyond it, mountains covered to the summits in tangled forest is the first impression you get of the island. Further acquaintance hardly changes it; the skies seem always blue, the seas always calm, in the forest there is always silence, in the distance a lonely sound of water breaking on the coral reef—"A land in which it seemed always afternoon." You might think that no man who had lived here for any length of time could escape its influence, that possibly a poet might write something like the "Lotus Eaters" here, probably write nothing at all, but that he could not produce work to stir the pulses of men and kindle their heroic instincts. Until you had met and spoken with Stevenson: then you realized how little dependent a man of genius is on his surroundings, how much more he has to give from within himself than to receive from without. From the road that led up through the tropical forest I passed through the gate of Vailima into the north country. I had been drifting among the islands, receiving idle impressions, desiring neither to think not to act and meeting no one who did either; and an hour after finding myself in Stevenson's company I was in a world of movement and activity, of brave effort and stimulating ideas. The silence of the forests enfolded us, the great blue ring of untroubled ocean lay beyond them, and the hush of the waters on the reef reached our ears, but now the atmosphere seemed rather that of bracing north-eastern coasts and of morning on the hills of heather.

Something, perhaps, of the welcome I received from Stevenson was due to my privilege of bearing a letter of introduction to him from the man whose work he ranked higher than that of any living author. Anyone sent to him by Mr. George Meredith would been sure of kindness, but such kindness as I received was more than vicarious; it was, as others have found it, spontaneous and complete, the outcome of a nature that neither knew half-heartedness nor understood the meaning of condescension. As I was one of the last of his British visitors and saw him some years later than most of his friends at home who keep a loving memory of his appearance in their hearts, it may be interesting to give a sketch, however rough, of the man as he impressed me. The first thing that struck me was his bearing. He was so slender that he looked taller than he really was; he was barefooted and walked with a long and curiously marked step, light but always metrical, in accord, it seemed, with some movement of his mind. It was his constant habit to pace to and fro as he conversed, and his step and speech seemed in harmony. He spoke always deliberately, if not slowly, but he never halted or hesitated; the fitting word was as ready to his tongue as to his pen—perhaps more ready, for we known the pains which he took in seeking it in his writing. He did not stoop, but in walking his body was somewhat inclined forward, and in his attitude generally there was something unusual, distinguished, almost fantastic. His bearing remains in my memory as unlike that of any other human being I ever saw, and only less noteworthy than his eyes. His face was illumined by his eyes: it was his eyes you saw first, his eyes you remembered. Regarded separately, you might notice in his jaw and chin, especially when seen in profile, contours of rude, almost aggressive strength; in the lines about his mouth an expression which suggested exceptional powers of scorn or sarcasm rather than that kindness in judgment and generous affection which were most characteristic of him in his attitude to his fellow men. But his eyes transfigured his face, and in their light its hardest lines grew attractive. You may also see them in his many photographs, wide apart, alert as at times when he was listening attentively, but not as when they brightened at a memory, not as when they flashed with indignation, nor as when the smile forerunning a humorous thought was drawing them in.

I had expected after all I had heard of his ill-health to find a pale, delicate-looking man, and his photographs had led me to picture one with long hair worn somewhat after the fashion in which popular fancy adorns a bard; but in both preconceptions I was wrong. His skin was of a ruddy tinge, his face

had a look of health, in spite of thinness, and his hair was cut short and brushed in a very ordinary fashion. Of all the photographs I have seen of him, that taken at Sydney in 1892 and reproduced as a frontispiece to the "Vailima Letters" (the Edinburgh edition reproduction is better than the etching in the first edition) is most in accord with the impression I got of him when I saw him in that last year of his life.

Of the life in Samoa there is abundant record in the "Vailima Letters," and I could add little that would be of value. There is much of interest in the island, but its chief attraction was conferred by Stevenson's presence, and what little I have to relate must be of himself. His immediate surroundings struck me as being essentially happy, affection and cheerfulness reigned in his home, the true spirit of comradeship was found there, "the true word of welcome was spoken in the door." This atmosphere of fellowship extended beyond the inner family circle; the strong clan instinct which survived in the master of the house found a response in the sentiments of the natives; his servants, all men, sixteen in number at the time of my visit, were as members of one family, jealous for its honour, as ready to fight as to cook or dig on its behalf; and his influence had gradually extended far outside the limits of his household and gave him a position something akin to that of the chief of a clan in his part of the island. Of this I heard much and saw something; for while I was staying in the house there were constant visits, sometimes from parties of natives, sometimes from chiefs of the surrounding districts, seeking his advice and ready to obey his counsel in connexion with the political troubles of which he has spoken so fully in "The Footnote to History" and the letters to *The Times*. These visitors would be received with ceremony, for he never failed to observe the traditional native customs, and, before parting, the Khava would be mixed and served with solemn rites. I believe he was proud of the position of authority he had won, without effort, by mere force of character and sympathy, and that the responsibilities which it brought upon him added much to the interest of his life in the island. At the time of my visit there was a little war going on. Tamasésé, who represented the native party hostile to the German influence, was in rebellion, and the woods about Vailima were full of native warriors. Eight of the servants were away fighting, some few heads had been taken, and the ladies (Mrs. Stevenson and Mrs. Strong) had been sent down to Apia for their better safety. Their hospitality, however, was great and their fear small, for they made the presence of a guest a sufficient reason for their return. There are no doors at Vailima, curtains only divide the lower rooms from the verandah; and before retiring on the night of my arrival I asked Stevenson whether, as the woods were full of armed men, some of them perhaps enemies of the house, it would be well to have my revolver loaded in case of surprise. He laughed at the idea and said it was an unknown thing in the annals of the island for attack to be made upon sleepers—that, indeed, the native rules of war are more like those which governed old tournaments than modern battles, each side being allowed the fullest opportunity for preparation, and a notification being sent from one side to the other before a battle naming the hour proposed for the attack.

I remember waking at 6 o'clock

next morning and finding Tusitala, as Stevenson was always called, standing at my bedside. Having congratulated me on my escape from assassination during the night, and spoken after the manner of the earlier riser on the beautiful hours of morning already wasted in bed, he conducted me across the enclosure of cleared forest west of the house and showed me the bathing place, a deep pool in the stream which flowed under Vaea Mountain. He explained to me that it was after the three streams which met hard by that the estate was named, but the word for "three waters" not being euphonious, "Vailima," which means "four waters" had been substituted, a poetic licence which he thought permissible. After my experience of the heat of the previous day the extreme cold of the water was a surprise, and at that time in the morning the air was so fresh and invigorating that it was difficult to believe that you were in the tropics; indeed, for Stevenson the cold of the stream was too severe, and he had to be content with a tub indoors. After the bathing the subsequent order of the day was as follows: —We breakfasted at seven, clothed in flannels and barefooted, for no one at Vailima wore shoes until dinner time. After breakfast I believe Stevenson was in the habit of working up to lunch time; but for the week I was with him he almost entirely abandoned work, and no one was sorry for this, for he had been working over hard, and rest and conversation with one who knew many of his old friends did him good. I was, indeed, a gainer by his abstention, for I had for long hours daily the most wonderful of comrades: his spirits never flagged, his talk was always inspiriting, his point of view always original. There was nothing of the invalid, no suggestion of failing strength about him; he had a zest for life, he "cherished it in every fibre"; there was a gift of *light* in him which seemed to radiate and make every topic he touched bright.

During these conversations he talked often of home and old friends, much of literature and of his own work, especially "Weir of Hermiston." I can see him now sitting on the side of his camp bed in the little room in which he did most of the work and reading to me the first chapters of that great book; I can hear the tone of his voice and see the changing expression of his face as he read, for he was in love with the work, happier in it, perhaps, than in anything he had ever done, and his reading showed his interest. He had no more false modesty in praising his own work when it pleased him than contempt in condemning it when he disapproved. "Now, isn't that confoundedly good?" he said to me after finishing on of the chapters in "Weir." He expressed to me, as I believe he wrote to Sir Sidney Colvin, his opinion that in this story he had touched his high-water mark; he told me something of its outline, and as in one, and that an important, point it differed from the notes furnished by Mrs. Strong, it will be heard with interest. The strongest scene in the book, he said—the strongest scene he had ever conceived or would ever write—was one in which the younger Kirstie came to her lover when he was in prison and confessed to him that she was with child by the man he had murdered. His eyes flashed with emotion as he spoke about it, and I cannot think he had abandoned this climax. It is a climax, too, which would seem to be much more in harmony with the genius and conception of the story and characters than the ending sketched in the notes, which was no

doubt an alternative with which he coquetted.

The other reading which I remember with the greatest pleasure was of poems afterwards published among the "Songs of Travel." We had had much discussion about rhythm, especially as to a tendency towards subtler and less regular rhythmical effects. He was disposed to think that in English verse the career of the regular and well-marked metres was almost complete, and that the poetry of the future would find expression in more complex harmonies. He cited the work of Mr. W. B. Yeats (whose poem "The Lake of Innesfree" was then a notable instance of the case in point) as an achievement in this direction, and he admitted that he had been attempting to tread the same path in some of his own later verse. Such were the second of the poems entitled "Youth and Love," "To the heart of youth the world is a high way side"— and that beginning "In the highlands in the country places," and perhaps also that most beautiful of all his poems, "Home no more home to me," where the music depends no less on the actual rhythm than the right emphasis and sympathetic pause. Indeed, I believe that if I had not heard him read it I should have missed much of its rhythmical beauty. His aim was towards a greater subtlety of rhythm, a very different thing from the abandonment of metrical restriction which marks so many horrible productions in *vers libre*.

In a conversation on his own writings I alluded, perhaps injudiciously, to a fear expressed by George Meredith that his banishment from the great world of men, his inability to keep in close touch with the social development of the time, might be a disadvantage to his work. He showed in reply an unexpected warmth which suggested that he really felt the burden of his exile but refused to admit it. "It is all the better for a man's work if he wants it to be good and not merely popular," he said, "to be removed from these London influences. Human nature is always the same, and you see it better when you are standing outside the crowd." Meredith thought otherwise, and defended his contention on hearing from me of Stevenson's comment. "Human nature is not always the same," he replied. "The same forces may be always at work, but they find different expression in every generation, and it is the expression that chiefly concerns the writer of fiction." It is an interesting subject for reflection, the more so that it produced such a divergence of opinion between two of the most distinguished writers of our time.

At the time of Stevenson's death I read some reports in the papers that he had grown despondent latterly about his own work, and believed that he was losing ground with his public. I believe these to have had no foundation. It struck me from all he said that he believed his best work was yet within him and that he was only beginning to get it outside him in "Weir of Hermiston." Nor was there the slightest trace of despondency in his tone either in reference to his work or his circumstances. The nearest approach to regret in anything he said about his work was a remark to the effect that he had fewer inspirations than when he was a younger man; but he suggested that he knew better how to entertain the inspirations when they came. And as to his surroundings he was undoubtedly not discontented. His banishment from his friends at home was, of course, keenly felt; but he knew that it was inevitable

and made the best of it, alluding rather to those expressions of old affection and new sympathy which every mail brought him from home than to the deprivations of his exile. The hope of seeing many of his friends as his guests at Vailima in the future was also constantly with him, and he never tired of speaking of old days and old friends; of Edinburgh, of the British Museum, of the Savile Club, of Box Hill, most frequently.

Much of our time was passed in conversation and reading, remaining indoors or on the verandah during the hotter hours of the day, and once or twice, when it grew cooler, walking or riding down to Apia. His appearance on horseback was amusing—dressed in white, with riding boots and a French peaked cap, chivalrous in his bearing, but mounted on a horse which would not have been owned by any self-respecting English costermonger, he almost suggested a South Sea Don Quixote. But in spite of appearances his horse was not an unserviceable beast, and perhaps few better could be found on the island. At dinner in the evening, when all the household was assembled, Mrs. Stevenson and Mrs. Strong, Lloyd Osborne and Count Wurmbrand, a charming and cultivated Austrian soldier acting at the time as chief cowherd on the Stevenson farm, with the addition, on one or two occasions, of M. de Lautreppe, a French naturalist on a visit to the island, a delightful companion, we were a merry and odd-looking party. The evening dress of the island is of white drill for men, and generally white of some material for ladies, but there is no very strict insistence on detail. But one rule was recognized by all of us, and that was the wearing of shoes and socks which had been dispensed with during the day. Stevenson's costumes were remarkable, and it struck me that, though quite free from vanity, he found a curious pleasure in dressing, or as children say, "in dressing up." On one evening at dinner I remember he wore an Indian costume, an embroidered thing folded and crossed upon his chest. The dinner itself was always excellent, abounding in strange dishes of the Island, chiefly vegetable, and, in spite of the absence at the war of the head cook, admirably served. And the wine was a surprise: one does not expect to find good wine in the South Sea Islands, but here was of the best. Stevenson's artistic tastes and instincts included wine, and the Burgundy laid down in the Vailima cellar was worthy of its destination. Tusitala had not only the art of conversation but the art of making others talk their and of establishing conversation but the art of making others talk their best and of establishing general conversation; and, with Mrs. Stevenson, herself one of the most brilliant of talkers, also present, the guests who did not find good cheer at table deserved to spend the rest of their lives in solitude and fasting. The music which followed dinner was perhaps the worst ever heard; it was not native music, which is beautiful, but was produced by Count Wurmbrand and myself. Every evening the Count sang the "Cruiskeen Lawn," which he had learnt in broken Irish at Vailima and sang to a tune of his own, and I played, with improprieties which were hardly noticed, so much out of tune was the piano, Scotch and Irish reels and jigs. Then arose Tusitala and, placing Teuila (Mrs. Strong) opposite to him, danced on the polished floor with a vigour seldom matched and a delight splendid to see.

It was usually between eleven and twelve o'clock before we went to bed, and as we never rose later than six in the morning the day must have been a long one, though it did not seem so at the time. My host was in the habit of conducting me to my room each night, for he was punctual in the observation of courtesies, and on our way thither we generally lingered on the verandah. Out over the great plain of the Pacific was a sky of such starlight as we do not see at home; the tropical forest all about us was profoundly silent, and from far away came the unvarying sound of the waters breaking on the coral reefs. He revelled in the beauty of the scene, but he admitted that he would gladly have exchanged it for the mist-enfolded coasts of the little islands he had left far away in the wintry seas.

My stay with him was too short: it would have been longer if I had known that I was not to see him again, and it was my own fault that it was not prolonged; but in one week he allowed me to know him intimately, and he was one of those whom to know is to love. He had the power of winning affection as well as admiration by his writings from people who had never met him, and all that personal charm which shines through his work was found in a more marked degree in himself. It is difficult to write of him critically or without enthusiasm. He seemed to me to be the most inspiring comrade that ever put hope into his fellows, the most courteous gentleman that ever conferred a favour while seeming to ask one, and the most heroic spirit that ever fought and fought to win with a good heart against desperate odds.

Your obedient servant,
S. R. LYNAGHT.
Mallow, Co. Cork.

INDEX

A

A Pattern of Islands (A. Grimble) 19, 22
Adams, Henry 225–7
Adler (German warship) 142, 145
aigas (Samoan clans) 118–19, 147, 259
aitu (spirits) 111–12, 204–6, 258
America *see* United States of America
An Object of Pity or the Man Haggard
    232
Apia, Samoa 63–4, 86, 91–2, 93–5, 96,
    97, 101, 104, 113, 114, 115, 123, 133, 137,
    139, 140, 142–6, 164, 169, 172, 173,
    176–7, 179, 180, 185, 186, 187, 189,
    191, 197, 198, 207, 232, 235–7
Arnold, Matthew 74, 276
Arrick (servant) 253
Australia 62–3, 64, 103, 116, 212–14,
    215, 254, 262

B

Baildon, H.B. 277–8
Balfour, Graham 23, 185, 189, 219, 231,
    257, 298, 327, 329
balls in Apia 185, 235–7
Barrie, J.M. 203, 267, 291, 309, 312, 329
Baxter, Charles 68–9, 119, 181, 199,
    203–4, 208, 216, 288, 299, 329
beachcombers 40, 93–4, 95, 112, 207
Becke, Lewis 140
Belloc, Hilaire 108
Bethune, Drinkwater 115
Bickford, Captain 186–7
Bierman, Karl 178–9
Bismarck, Herbert von 146
blackbirding 120–1, 252
Blacklock, William 87
Boer War 159
Boodle, Adelaide 53, 110
Booth, Bradford A. 201
Borges, J.L. 23
Bougainville, Louis-Antoine de
    36–7, 101
Bournemouth 46–7, 53, 55

Brandeis, Eugen 139–40, 141–2, 161
Braxfield, Lord 170, 183, 320, 322
British Empire 19–21, 27, 86, 138, 164
British power in Samoa 85, 86, 91, 92,
    99–100, 102–3, 104, 109, 115–16, 135,
    137, 138–9, 142–7, 164, 166–8
    see also German power in Samoa;
    Samoa, power and warfare in; Three
    Powers; United States of America
Brown, Rev. George 169
Buckland, Jack 214
Burlingame, Edward L. 40, 173, 275, 292
Burns, Robert 223, 307
Byron, Lord 24–5

C

Calder, Jenni 319–20
Calliope, H.M.S. 144–5
Calvinism 35, 73, 123–4, 222–3, 307, 315
Calvino, Italo 125
cannibalism 111, 113, 286, 287–8
capital punishment 86–7, 182–3
Casco (schooner) 43, 56–7, 59–62, 63,
    65, 67, 83
Catholicism 114, 151, 169, 172, 220–1,
    222, 335
Cedercrantz, Baron Conrad (Chief
    Justice) 26, 146, 167, 168, 177, 179–81
Chalmers, Rev. James 169
Chamberlain, Neville 25
Chesterton, G. K. 23, 34, 51, 222, 285,
    294–5, 302–3, 315
church buildings in Samoa 114
    see also missionaries, Christian;
    religion
Churchill, Lord Randolph 76
Churchward, William B. 99–100, 136,
    149–50, 157–8
Clarke, Rev. W. E. 91–3, 95, 169, 238–9,
    335, 336
Claxton, A.E. 176
clothing 91–2, 149–52, 229–30, 257, 335
coconut palms 98–9, 118, 119–20, 121–2

Coetlogon, Colonel Henry Watts 91,
    166–7
Colvin, Sidney 53, 70, 72, 75, 78, 96,
    124, 126, 127, 168, 170, 198, 201, 204,
    207–9, 227, 230, 232, 243–4, 245,
    262–3, 288, 289, 299, 309, 322, 329
Commerçon, Philibert 36–7
communism 154–8
Conan Doyle, Arthur 211, 328, 329
Congregationalist Church, Samoa 113
Congress of Berlin 145
    see also Treaty of Berlin (1889)
Cook, Captain James 36
copra trade 118, 121
Council of Apia 137, 146, 167
    see also Cedercrantz,
        Baron Conrad; von Pilsach,
        Baron Senff
Covenanters' rebellion 129
Crockett, S.R. 203
Cunningham, Alison "Cummy" 35,
    210, 222, 307, 321
Cunninghame Graham, R.B. 129–30
Curaçoa, HMS 233–4
Cusack-Smith, Sir Thomas Berry
    26, 167

D
Dalzell, Bluidy Tam 129
Damien, Father 41, 213
Dan the Convict 112
dancing 152–4, 224, 235, 236
Daplyn, A.J. 233
de Banville, Théodore 275
de Tolna, Festetics 225
decapitations 162, 186
Decline and Fall of the Roman Empire
    (E. Gibbon) 65–6
Deutsche Handels-und Plantagen-
    Gesellschaft der Südsee-Inseln zu
    Hamburg (D.H. and P.G.) 26, 116–18,
    120, 122, 137, 139–40
    see also German power in Samoa
Diderot, Denis 37
diseases, spread of Western 98
Dobson, Austin 275–6

E
Easter Island 111
Einfurer, Paul 251–2
Ellice Island 19–20, 121
Equator (schooner) 22, 47, 62, 63,
    212, 294
Eromanga Island, Vanuatu 113

F
Fakarava Island 68
Fiji 103, 182, 261
Foreign Office report on Samoa 107
Foreign Residents Society, Apia 115
France 36–7, 46, 68, 101, 102, 103,
    114, 131
Fraser, Marie 227–8
Funk, Dr Bernard 237, 334

G
Gauguin, Paul 38, 47, 125–6, 313
German power in Samoa 23, 24, 85–91,
    92, 102–4, 115–22, 128, 133, 135, 137,
    138–47, 164, 167–8, 178–9
Gibbon, Edward 65–6, 67
Gilbert Islands (Kiribati) 19–20, 22, 63
Gilfillan, Archie 21–2
Gladstone, William 160, 202
Godeffroy & Sohn 86, 115–16
gold mining in California 47–8
Gordon, General Charles 160
Gordon, Sir Arthur 182
Gosse, Edmund 24–5, 52, 203, 220,
    245, 264, 273, 276, 289, 292, 306
Grant, Ulysses S. 122–3
Greer, Germaine 50
Grey, Sir George 181–2
Grimble, Sir Arthur 19–21, 22

H
Haggard, Bazett 168, 174, 231, 232
Hammerton, Philip Gilbert 54
Hand, Captain 128
Hardy, Thomas 203, 220, 304, 317
Hawaii 22, 55, 62, 69, 82–4, 86, 139,
    209, 212, 280, 294, 327–9
Helen (washerwoman) 254
Henley, W. E. 52, 203, 250, 276, 304

Hogg, James 307
Honolulu 61, 69, 82–3, 264
Hopkins, Gerard Manley 35
hurricane in Samoa (15-16 March 1889)
    143–5
Hyde, Rev. Dr 213

I
Ide, Henry C. 168
idleness of Samoan people, perceived
    101, 124, 149–50, 157, 165–6
imperialism/colonialism 26–7, 39, 83–4,
    85–8, 102–8, 109–10, 129–30, 131–2,
    146–7, 159–60, 171, 181–2
    see also British Empire; British
        power in Samoa; German
        power in Samoa; United States
        of America
imprisonment/law enforcement 86–7,
    118, 137, 177–8, 182–3, 187, 189–91

J
Jacobite Rising (1745) 79
Jacobites 79–80, 172, 312, 313, 314–15
James, Alice 52–3
James, Henry 47, 52, 61, 70–1, 163, 203,
    226, 268, 293, 298–9, 305, 329
Janet Nicoll (trading vessel) 64, 65, 214
Jersey, Lady 230–2, 261
Johnstone, Arthur 106, 107, 328
Jolly, Roslyn 53

K
Kalakaua of Hawaii, King 83–4, 278
Katoomba, H.M.S 186, 234–5
kava (Samoan drink) 175, 186, 190,
    228–9
Khartoum, Siege of (1884-1885) 160
Kipling, Rudyard 20–1, 203, 276, 306
Knappe, Dr 87
Knox, John 223, 244

L
La Farge, John 225, 226, 227
Lackawanna, U.S.S. 138
Lafaele (servant) 247, 252, 258
Land Court, Samoa 168, 174, 178

Lang, Andrew 275–6, 320
Lapérouse, Captain 101
Laupepa (Malietoa) 26, 130, 131,
    135–7, 138, 140, 141–2, 146, 165,
    170–2, 174–6, 178, 179–80, 185–6,
    187, 188, 316–17, 329–30
lavalava 150, 151, 152, 229, 335
Leigh, Captain 231, 232
lepers on Molokai 213
letters from R.L.S. 201–4, 238
    about Belle and Joe Strong 216,
        262
    about civil warfare 187–8, 191
    about everyday life in Samoa 218,
        220, 243, 244
    about Fanny 54, 208–9, 262–3,
        264, 267
    about German plantations 119
    about Lady Jersey 232
    about missionary work 110
    about moving in to Vailima 244,
        245–6
    about Polynesian travels 61, 69,
        79, 81
    about settling in Samoa 198, 199
    about Western powers Samoa 23,
        26, 27, 85–92, 119, 124, 163, 168,
        177–8, 179–81
    about William Seed's view of
        Samoa 39–42
    about writing projects 96, 127,
        203, 211, 216–17, 244, 273,
        277–8, 288, 291, 292, 293,
        298–9, 304, 309, 312, 319
    to Adelaide Boodle 110
    to Arthur Conan Doyle 211
    to Charles Baxter 68–9, 96, 119,
        181, 199, 203–4, 208, 216, 288,
        299
    to Edmund Gosse 245, 264,
        273, 292
    to Edward L. Burlingame 40, 292
    to Elizabeth Fairchild 41–2
    to Fances Sitwell 39, 204
    to H.B. Baildon 277–8
    to Henry James 61, 70–1, 163, 203,
        226, 293, 298–9

to J.M. Barrie 267, 309, 312
to Lady Taylor 43, 198
to Philip Gilbert Hammerton 54
to Sidney Colvin 96, 124, 126, 127,
    168, 187–8, 201, 208–9, 232,
    243–4, 245–6, 262–3, 288,
    299, 309
to Sir Walter Simpson 78–9
to *The Times* 23, 26, 27, 85–92,
    177–8, 179–81, 187, 191, 293
to W.E. Henley 304
to Will H. Low 81
London Missionary Society 110–11,
    165
Low, Will H. 81, 295

M
Macaulay, Thomas Babington 276
MacGregor, Sir William 182–3
Mackay, Margaret 268, 330–1
mail services on Samoa 201–2
Mair, Lucy 104–5
Malie, Upolu 113, 133–4, 135, 172, 175
Malietoas of Samoa 86, 113, 132–5,
    141–2, 147, 170, 184
    see also Laupepa (Malietoa);
    Mata'afa Iosefo
Malua Theological College 150,
    165–6
"Manao Tupapau" (P.Gauguin) 125–6
Manono Island 142
Marie Antoinette 36
Mariposa (steamer) 262
Marquesas 39, 67, 78, 79–80, 103, 110,
    153, 165, 286
Marshall Islands 86, 141, 187
Marx, Karl 117, 157, 160
Mata'afa Iosefo 26, 78, 131, 134, 138,
    141–2, 161, 170, 172–3, 174–7, 180,
    184–7, 188–9, 231–2, 316–17, 327
Matautu (1888), Battle of 161
mats in Samoan culture 130
Mayor of Casterbridge (T. Hardy) 304
McClure, Sam 59, 69–70, 73–4
McLynn, Frank 54, 269
Mehew, Ernest 201
Meleisea, Malama 114

Melville, Herman 37, 67
missionaries, Christian 76, 83, 97–8,
    100, 104, 109, 110–11, 112–14, 134, 135,
    151–2, 162, 165, 169, 211
    see also Clarke, Rev. W.E.;
    Williams, John
The Modern Traveller (H. Belloc) 108
Moe of Tahiti, Princess 68, 280–1
Moli (Malietoa) 135
Molokai Island 213
Moors, Harry J. 63–4, 84, 92, 97, 169,
    177, 198, 199, 209, 240, 245, 248,
    254, 265–6, 297, 330
Morgan, Edwin 274, 278, 288–9
Mormons 104
"Mother Hubbard" dress style 151–2
Mount Saint Helena, Napa Valley 49
Mount Vaea, Samoa 200, 333, 335
Mulinu'u, Samoa 133, 142, 143
Murdoch, George 22
mythology/folklore, Polynesian 97,
    100, 111–13, 200, 204–7, 258, 276–7,
    279–80, 290
mythology/folklore, Scottish 205–6,
    276–7, 307

N
Nafanua (goddess) 112–13, 133
natural resources 98–9, 149–50
Nerli, Count 233
New Caledonia 103
New Guinea 182
New South Wales 103
New Zealand 103, 116, 164, 181–2, 329
Nipsic, USS 145
Norway, King of 146
Noumea Island 215

O
Olga (German warship) 145
opium 78, 165
Ori-a-Ori of Tahiti, King 280
Osbourne, Lloyd (R.L.S.' stepson) 22,
    47, 48, 57, 61, 63, 64, 65, 92, 213, 215,
    221, 224, 230, 237, 240, 254–5, 256,
    266, 268, 292–4, 298, 304, 311, 330–1,
    334, 335

Osbourne, Sam 47–9, 260
Otis, Albert H. 60, 63, 68

P
people-trafficking 120–1
plantations 119–20, 121–2, 253
Presbyterian periodical 183
Presbyterianism 22, 49–50, 113, 220
The Prince (N. Machiavelli) 183
prisons see imprisonment/law
    enforcement
Pritchard, George 115
Protestantism 110, 114, 150, 151, 165–6
    see also missionaries, Christian
Pulemelei Pyramid 111

R
Reid, Dennis 63
religion 22, 27, 76, 83, 97–8, 100, 104,
    107, 109, 110–11, 112–14, 134, 135,
    150, 151–2, 162, 165–6, 169, 172, 211,
    220–3, 335
Rhodes, Cecil 76
Ringarooma, HMS 169
Road of the Loving Heart 191–2
Roggeveen, Jacob 101
Roman Empire/civilisation 66, 77, 127,
    155, 193, 284–5
Rosebery, Lord 24, 170
Ross, Dr Fairfax 262
Rossetti, Dante Gabriel 276
Rousseau, Jean-Jacques 36, 125
Ruskin, John 76

S
Salamasina (ruler of Samoa) 133
Samoa, power and warfare in
    American power in 85, 86, 91, 92,
        102–4, 115–16, 122–3, 135, 137,
        138, 139, 142–7, 164, 167–8, 176
    British power in 85, 86, 91, 92,
        99–100, 102–3, 104, 109, 115–16,
        135, 137, 138–9, 142–7, 164,
        166–8
    Council of Apia 137, 146, 167
        (see also Cedercrantz, Baron
        Conrad (Chief Justice);

von Pilsach, Baron Senff
    (President))
    German power in 23, 24, 85–91,
        92, 102–4, 115–22, 128, 133, 135,
        137, 138–47, 164, 167–8, 178–9
    historical background of Western
        settlement 100–5
    impact of hurricane (15–16 March
        1889) 143–6
    Land Court 168, 174, 178
    power struggles/warfare 96–7, 98,
        113, 118–19, 130, 132, 135, 137–47,
        160–2, 170–3, 174–6, 178, 184–7,
        188–93, 316–17
    request to be part of British
        Empire 138, 164
    Samoan people's power structure
        113, 118–19, 130–7
    taxes/custom duties 173, 177, 178,
        179–80
    Three Powers 102, 136, 137–47,
        168, 169, 170–1, 175, 180, 187 (see
        also American power in Samoa;
        British power in Samoa;
        German power in Samoa)
    Treaty of Berlin (1889) 146–7,
        167–8
Samoa Times 180
Sanchez, Nellie Vandegrift 197, 266,
    305
Sapapalii, Samoa 109, 113
Sargent, John Singer 246
Savaii, Samoa 101, 109, 111, 113
Schmidt, Emil 168
Schwob, Marcel 216
Scotland, parallels with life in Polynesia
    79–80, 83, 118, 119, 127, 148, 172, 192,
    239, 259, 276–7, 281, 285, 293, 312–13,
    316–17
Scott, Walter 127, 199, 276, 307, 322
Seed, William 40–3, 46–7
Sewall, Harold 167
sexual allure of Pacific Islanders 37,
    40, 46–7
Shaw, George Bernard 227
Shelley, Sir Percy 210, 273
Simele, Henry 200, 252, 253

Simpson, Sir Walter 78–9
Singing, Samoan 148–9
Sitwell, Frances 39, 204
Skerryvore, Bournemouth 46, 64,
   65, 215, 241, 246
Smiles, Samuel 165–6
Smith, Janet Adam 274
Society Islands 103
Sosifina (servant) 330–1
Sosimo (valet) 239, 252
South American colonialism 129–30
South-Sea Idylls (C. W. Stoddard) 37
South Seas Islands, popular image of
   36–9, 40, 91–2
      see also Scotland, parallels with
      life in Polynesia; individual
      islands by name
Spain 129–30
The Spectator 284–5
Steinberger, Albert Barnes 112,
   122–3, 156
Stevenson, Bob (R.L.S.' cousin) 48,
   304–5
Stevenson, Fanny (R.L.S.' wife)
   burial of 336
   caring for R.L.S. 46, 54, 55, 265,
      280, 327–8
   clothing 91–2, 151
   contemporary opinion of 51–4
   death of R.L.S. 333, 335
   death of youngest son 48, 260–1
   desire to be an artist 48, 203,
      249–51
   diary/letters 58, 65, 72–3, 111,
      120–1, 172–3, 178, 185, 197–8,
      202, 231, 240, 247, 249–51,
      266, 312
   gardening and working the estate
      241–2, 247–9
   health issues 47, 55, 56, 218–19,
      257, 260–6
   initial reservations about Samoa
      197–8, 240–1
   jealousy over R.L.S. 218, 231, 238,
      257, 261
   and Mata'afa Iosefo 172–3, 175,
      184, 187

moving in to Vailima 240–2, 245
origins of 'The Bottle Imp' 209–10
people-trafficking in Pacific
   Islands 121
relationship with R.L.S. 46–57,
   70, 72–3, 265–70
religious practice 220–1
R.L.S.' 44th birthday party
   331–2
touring Pacific islands 56–7, 60,
   62, 63–5, 214, 215
Vailima staff 159, 204, 242, 247,
   251–2, 253, 258, 265, 330
Stevenson, Margaret 'Aunt Maggie'
   (R.L.S.' mother) 49–50, 55
   death of son 333, 334, 335
   diary entries/letter writing 60, 65,
      151, 153, 174, 175, 176, 202, 220,
      233–4, 240, 331–3
   move to the Pacific Islands 57–8,
      215, 329
   parties and social activities 233–4,
      331–3
   religious practice 220–1
   Samoan chiefs 174, 175, 176
   touring Pacific islands 57–8,
      60, 65
   water supply for Vailima 200, 246
   widow's clothing 229–30, 257
Stevenson, Robert Louis
   balls in Apia 235–7
   "big book" project 70–5, 78,
      79, 217
   Boer War 159
   bohemian sensibilities 43–6, 59
   Bournemouth 46–7, 55
   building and completion of the
      Road of the Loving Heart 191–3
   champions Samoan people 23,
      24–9, 39, 74, 76, 78, 82–92,
      106–7, 123–4, 127–8, 164–5,
      169–70, 178, 179–81, 190–3,
      220, 327
   Complete Works published 329
   contemporary reviews of work
      275, 277–8, 284–5, 288, 289,
      294, 302

contemporary views of move to
Samoa 23, 24–5, 26, 208
death and burial 193, 237, 329,
333–7
desire to travel 33–5
Fanny's mental health 262–5
feasts in Apia prison 190
fiction/poetry written in South
Seas 28, 34, 74, 83, 126, 173,
205, 206, 207, 208, 209–12,
213, 216–17, 239, 244, 274–90,
291–304, 306–11, 313–24
finances 46, 59, 139
first encounter with Pacific
islanders 67–8
first impression of Samoa 197
44th birthday party 331–2
freedom of expression 304–6,
313
gardening 204, 205, 206, 242–3
Hawaii 82–4, 212, 327–9
health issues 33, 34, 42, 46–7, 49,
54, 55, 64, 68, 214, 215, 217, 218,
264, 265, 280–1, 327–8
integration and Samoan language
skills 200–1
Jack, horse 219, 241
Lady Jersey visits 230–2, 261
letter writing 201–4 (see also letters
from R.L.S.)
and Malietoa Laupepa 136, 141,
165, 172, 174–6, 178, 329–30
and Mata'afa Iosefo 134, 138, 172,
174–6, 180, 186–7, 188–9, 231–2,
327
meets Rev. Clarke in Samoa 91–3,
95
meets with British colonial
governors 181–3
Monterey, California 49
origins of "The Bottle Imp"
209–10
portraits of 233, 246
relationship with Fanny 46–57,
265–70
religious practice and prayers 150,
220–3, 240

Samoan hurricane (15-16 March
1889) 143–5
Samoan warfare and politics 96–7,
98, 138, 161, 162, 170–1, 172, 173,
174–6, 184–7, 188–93 (see also
Footnote to History)
Saranac Lake, New York 55–6
settling in Samoa 197–201, 209,
214–15
sexual morals 22, 223–4, 257, 330
speech at Malua College 165–6
superstitions/folklore 204–6,
307–8
Sydney, Australia 212–14, 215, 254
and Tamasese 176
taxes 177, 178, 189–90
Thanksgiving Dinner at Vailima
332–3
Theodore Weber 116, 117, 122
threatened with expulsion from
Samoa 107, 169–70, 178
touring Pacific islands 59–71, 79,
82–3, 214–15, 280–1
travel books 34–5
trouble with Western authorities
in Samoa 107, 169–70, 177, 178–9
Tusitala nickname 259
view of capital punishment 182–3
view of missionary work 110, 169
view of Samoan people and
customs 148–9, 150, 152–6, 157,
158–60, 161, 162, 186, 214–15
view of Western powers in Samoa
77–8, 130, 138–9, 142, 164–5,
166–7, 168, 169–71, 172, 173, 178,
179–83, 220
volunteer hospital work 186
wedding and honeymoon 49
works by R.L.S.
The Amateur Emigrant 49
Ballads 83, 206, 209, 274–90
"Beach of Falesá" 28, 33, 93,
207, 208, 291, 293, 303–4,
306–7, 308–11
The Black Arrow 216, 217
"The Bottle Imp" 111–12, 176,
208, 209–12

Catriona 292, 293, 312, 313–18
A Child's Garden of Verses 33
"Christmas at Sea" 278
David Balfour 292, 305–6, 312,
    313–18
The Dynamiter 50
The Ebb-Tide (and L.
    Osbourne) 217, 290, 293,
    297–302, 306, 327
"The Enchantress" 268–9
Fables 268
Father Damien 41
"The Feast of Famine" 278,
    286–9, 315
Footnote to History 27–8, 91,
    94, 97, 123, 126–33, 135–6,
    141, 154–5, 161, 178–9, 293
*The Hair Trunk or The Ideal
    Commonwealth: An
    Extravaganza* 43–7, 101
The Hanging Judge
    (unfinished) 250
"Heather Ale: A Galloway
    Legend" 278
"The High Woods of
    Ulufana" 303–4
In the South Seas 70, 76, 293
"Isle of Voices" 293
Jekyll and Hyde 74, 93
Kidnapped 250, 291, 292,
    313–14
Master of Ballantrae 56, 222
"My Wife" 266–7
The Pearl Fisher 216–17, 293
*The Pentland Rising: A Page in
    History* 129
Prince Otto 250
*Records of a Family of
    Engineers* 127, 293
"Requiem" 336
Silverado Squatters 49–50
"Song of Rahéro" 276, 277–
    8, 280–6, 288–9
of Travel and Other Verses 34
Sophia Scarlet (unfinished)
    293
St Ives (unfinished) 293, 319

"Sunday" 221–2
"Thrawn Janet" 205, 307
"Ticonderoga" 83, 278, 279
Travels with a Donkey
    (R.L.S.) 35, 69
Treasure Island (R.L.S.) 57,
    60, 273–4
Virginibus Puerisque 307–8
"The Waif Woman" 268,
    269–70
Weir of Hermiston
    (unfinished) 239, 270, 291,
    293, 319–24, 331
"The Woodman" 205, 216–17
The Wrecker (and L.
    Osbourne) 126, 173, 213,
    214, 244, 245, 291, 292–3,
    294–7, 328
The Wrong Box (and L.
    Osbourne) 292–3, 294
Young Chevalier (unfinished)
    291–2, 293
    see also Stevenson, Fanny; Vailima
    Estate
Stevenson, Thomas (R.L.S.' father) 46,
    55, 123–4, 139, 296
Stoddard, Charles Warren 37–8
Strong, Austin (R.L.S.' stepgrandson)
    62, 82, 126, 212, 216, 218, 255–6,
    257, 329
Strong, Isabel "Belle" (R.L.S.'
    stepdaughter) 48, 62, 82, 83, 151, 175,
    185, 212, 213, 216, 218, 224, 230, 232,
    237, 245, 255, 256–7, 263, 266, 329,
    331, 333, 335
Strong, Joe 22, 62, 82, 83, 84, 92, 204–5,
    212, 213, 215–16, 218, 223–4, 253, 255,
    256–7, 261–2
Stuebel, Dr 167
Summer Cruising in the South Seas
    (C. W. Stoddard) 37
Swanston Cottage, Scotland 39
Swinburne, Algernon 276
Sydney, Australia 62–3, 64, 212–14,
    215, 254, 262

T

taboos 132, 336
Tafa'ifa title 134
Tahiti 37, 38, 68, 81, 110, 125, 126, 280–5
Talavou 136, 137, 138
Tamasese 26, 130, 131, 138, 140, 141,
    161, 170, 171–2, 176, 187
Taolo (cook) 259, 327
tattoos 150–1
taxes/custom duties 173, 177, 178,
    179–80, 184, 189–90
Taylor, Lady 43, 61, 198
Tembinoka, King 63
Tennyson, Lord Alfred 276
Thanksgiving Day celebrations 332–3
The Times 23, 26, 27, 85–92, 177–8,
    179–81, 187, 191, 293
Thistle Club, Hawaii 328–9
Three Powers 102, 136, 137–47, 168, 169,
    170–1, 175, 180, 187
    see also Samoa, power and warfare
Thurston, Sir John 24, 107, 169–70
Tonga 110
travel books 34–5, 36, 70–2
Treaty of Berlin (1889) 146–7, 167–8
Treaty of Berlin (1899) 103, 135, 187
Trenton, USS 145
Triggs, W.H. 253
Trousseau, Dr 264
Tupua title 130, 134
Turner, George 97–8, 100, 105, 156–7
Tutuila Island 153
Tylor, Edward Burnett 67

U

United States Exploring Company 115
United States of America
    American powers in Samoa 85,
        86, 91, 92, 102–4, 115–16, 122–3,
        135, 137, 138, 139, 142–7, 164,
        167–8, 176 (*see also* British
        power in Samoa; German
        power in Samoa; Three Powers)
    annexation of Hawaii 83–4, 328
Unshelm, August 116
Upolu, Samoa 62, 101, 113, 133, 137, 198

V

Vaiinu'uopo (Malietoa) 113, 134–5
Vailima Estate
    aitu 112, 204, 205–6
    entertaining visitors 173, 224–35
    livestock 248, 253–4, 256
    purchase, building and decorating
        64, 198, 199–200, 244–7
    staff 114, 151, 159, 178, 204, 229,
        239, 242, 247, 251–4, 258–9, 330
    threat of attacks against 184–5,
        198
    way of life 173, 218–20, 239–40
    see also Stevenson, Fanny;
        Stevenson, Robert Louis
Valentine (Swiss maid) 57, 62
Vandalia, U.S.S. 145
von Kotzebue, Otto 102
von Pilsach, Baron Senff von (President
    of Council of Apia) 26, 146, 167,
    177–8, 179–80, 181
von Wurmbrand, Baron 189, 190, 224

W

warfare and politics *see* Samoa, power
    and warfare in
Watson, Mackenzie 118, 135, 160–1, 162
Weber, Theodore 116–17, 119–20,
    121–2, 138
Whigs 314–15
White, Kenneth 71–2
Whitman, Walt 220
Wilde, Oscar 23
Williams, John 109, 110–11, 113, 134,
    152, 161–2
Williams, John C. 109, 114, 115

Y

Yandal, W.H. 177
Yeats, W.B. 203

Z

Zola, Émile 203, 220, 299, 305–6